ANSWERS

To Life's Enduring Questions

From Science Discoveries and Afterlife Revelations

R. Craig Hogan, PhD

Copyright © 2021 by Greater Reality Publications

You may make copies of the text I have written for any purpose that helps you or humankind develop spiritually. Don't charge money for anything in the book. Give it away freely. Please put the name of the book, copyright Greater Reality Publications, and the Web site (http://earthschoolanswers.com) on the first page of any copies you make.

Contact:

Greater Reality Publications
23 Payne Place, Normal, IL 61761
http://greaterreality.com
800 690-4232
Email: info@greaterreality.com
Order copies: Amazon.com

ISBN: 978-0-9802111-8-4

Contents

THE FOUR BOOKS XI

PREFACE XIII

1 WHY DO WE KNOW THESE EXPLANATIONS ARE TRUE? 1

PART 1: WE ARE THE UNIVERSAL INTELLIGENCE THAT WILL NEVER DIE 5

2 WHAT IS THIS WORLD WE LIVE IN MADE OF? 7
   Is the Universe Just Senseless Matter and Energy? 7
   *If There's No World of Matter and Energy Outside of Us, What Is the
      World We Live In Made Of?* 9
   *How Can We See, Hear, Smell, Taste, and Touch in a World Made of
      Consciousness?* 10
   *If Experiences Are in Our Minds, Why Does Everyone Have the Experiences
      of the Same World?* 12
   Why Do the Experiences Stay the Same? 13
   *If Everything Is in the Consciousness of Our Universal Intelligence,
      What Exists?* 15
   Is There Any Evidence We Are Creating the World Together? 16
   Don't Materialist Scientists Have Proof There Is a World Outside of Us? 17
   Don't the Laws of Physics Show There's a World Outside of Consciousness? ... 18
   *Doesn't Science Tell Us the Material World Outside of Us Gives Us Sensory
      Experiences?* 19
   How Can I Be Creating Reality When the World Seems to Be Given to Me? 21
   *Why Do We Have Different Reactions to the Same Experiences We Are
      Accessing Together?* 22
   *What Does the Fact That Consciousness Is Creating This Reality Mean for
      Our Lives?* 24

PART 2: YOU ARE NOT YOUR BRAIN, SO YOU LIVE ON AFTER YOUR BRAIN DIES 25

3 HOW CAN MY MIND LIVE WHEN MY BRAIN DIES? 27
   Aren't We Just Brains Talking to Each Other? 28
   Has Science Proved Our Minds Are in Our Brains? 29
   Do Any Scientists Suggest That Our Minds Are Not in Our Brains? 30
   Don't We Need the Brain to Store Memories? 32
   Is There Any Proof That Our Minds Can Function without Our Brains? 32
   *Is There Any Evidence That We Can Know Information without Using
      a Brain?* 45

Contents

Why Do We Know the Mind Is Not in the Brain? 50
4 IS THERE PROOF I WILL BE ALIVE AFTER MY BODY DIES? 51
Do Many People Believe Life Continues after the Body Dies? 52
Isn't It Rare for People to Communicate with Loved Ones in the Life after This Life? 52
Do the People Living in the Life after This Life Ever Tell People Things that Prove It's Them? 53
Do Physicians Working with the Dying Believe There Is a Life after This Life? .. 54
Do Any Scientists Believe the Reality of the Life after This Life When They Study the Evidence? 55
Do Psychology Professionals Become Convinced of Life after This Life from Their Experiences? 59
Do Professors of the Humanities Researching the Life after This Life Become Convinced of It? 62
Do Attorneys Who Have Studied the Life after This Life Become Convinced of Its Reality? 64
Do Clergy Become Convinced of the Nature of the Life after This Life Described by Mediums? 66
Have Any Church Bodies Studying Mediums Concluded They Speak with People in the Next Life? 67
Do Debunkers Studying Mediums Come to Believe the Life after This Life Is Real? 68
Are Accounts of the Life after This Life by Mediums the Same among the Mediums? 69
Do Any Government Bodies Treat Mediums as Though They Are Having Afterlife Communications? 69
Does Communication with the Next Life Ever Contain Information the Medium Could Not Know? 70
Do Family Members Verify that Medium Readings Are Conversations with Their Loved Ones? 71
Is There Any Evidence Mental Mediums Are Communicating with People Living in the Next Life? 75
Is There Evidence Other Types of Mediums Are Speaking to Living People Whose Bodies Are Dead? 77
What Proof Is There That Mediums Are Not Using Psychic Ability Instead of Speaking to Living People? 88
Do People Actually Materialize in Séances and Are Verified by Observers? 91
Do Individuals Whose Bodies Have Died Ever Appear and Speak at Length with People on Earth? 94
Do Mediums Receive Messages in Languages They Could Not Know During Afterlife Communications? 98

Contents

*Do Near-Death Experiences Reveal that Consciousness Survives
    Bodily Death?* 99
*Does the Way the Universe Is Set Up Provide Any Evidence It Is Being
    Created Specifically for Us?* 101
Doesn't Darwinian Evolution Prove We Evolved by Accident? 106
Then What Are We? 108

**PART 3: REASONS FOR WHAT HAPPENS TO YOU IN YOUR LIFE AND
    YOUR AFTERLIFE** 109

5 WHAT IS EARTH SCHOOL? 111
    Where Is Earth School? 112
    Who Created Earth School? 113
    How Do We Create Our Reality in Earth School? 116
    Do We Have Any Responsibility for Helping Humankind Change? ... 118
    Will Earth School End? 119
    Why Are There Beginnings and Endings? 120
    Why Are There Cruel and Violent People in Earth School? 121
    Do We Have Free Will to Choose as We Wish? 122
    Does the Person's Soul Plan the Exit Point? 123
    Does Chance Exist? 124
    Why Is There Time? 124
    Why Is There Space? 125

6 WHY IS EARTH SCHOOL SET UP AS IT IS? 127
    Why Is Earth School Set Up So People Have So Much to Be Afraid Of? 127
    Are People in Earth School Going to Be More Spiritual in the Future? 129
    What Could Earth School Eventually Become? 130
    Why Is Everything Constantly Changing in Earth School? 134
    *Are There Forces and Entities Dedicated to Promoting Humankind's
        Progress?* 135
    *Are Any of These Forces Working for Humankind's Benefit from
        Other Worlds?* 136
    Are There Forces and Entities Seeking to Retard Humankind's Progress? 139
    Are There Unseen Entities Affecting Us Individually? 140
    *Are There Such Things as Negative Thought Forms That Affect Us
        Individually?* 146

7 WHY IS THERE EVIL AND SUFFERING IN THE WORLD? 147
    Why Is There Evil in the World? 147
    Why Is There Suffering in the World? 149
    My Important Heartfelt Note to You 150
    Why Does This Life Have Mass Death Atrocities? 150
    Why Do We Have to Suffer from Having Our Loved Ones Pass Away? 152

Contents

Why Does the Body Have to Die? 153
Why Does This Life Keep Making People Suffer from Losses and Life Changes? 155
Why Does the World Have Suffering from People Harming Other People? 157
Why Does the World Have Suffering from Starvation? 158
Why Is There Suffering from Illnesses? 160
Why Do People Suffer from Mental Illness and Disabilities? 167
Why Do People Suffer from Accidents That Cause Painful Injuries or Loss of Function? 168
Why Does Life Have Suffering from Physical Pain? 169
What Makes Us Feel Suffering in This World? 170
Did We Choose to Have Events in Our Lives That Are Causing Us to Suffer? ... 170
Is There Any Way Humankind Can Bring About a World in Which There Is No Suffering? 171

8 WHY AM I HERE? 173

9 WHO AM I? 177
What Is Our Universal Intelligence? 179
What Is My Higher Self or Oversoul? 179
What Is My Soul? 182
What Is My Earth School Mind? 182

10 WHY DID MY SOUL SELECT EARTH SCHOOL FOR MY LIFE? 185
Why Did My Higher Self Decide to Enroll Me in Earth School? 186
Why Did I Choose This Time in Earth School's History? 187
Did My Soul Plan What Would Happen to Me in This Earth-School Experience? 188
How Did My Soul Plan My Life? 189
Are Any of My Planned Life Challenges More Important than Others? 190
Did My Soul Consider and Reject Any Plans for My Life? 191
How Did My Soul Plan for Me to Learn Lessons? 191
Do the Souls of the People I Live with Know about and Go Along with My Plan? 192
Does Anyone Plan a Life of Service to Humankind? 193
Does Any Soul Plan a Life Devoted to Serving the Needs of One or More Others? 193
When My Life Has Interruptions, Did My Soul Plan the Interruptions? 194
Did My Soul Plan for Me to Experience Afflictions, Accidents, and Tragedies? 194
Could My Soul Have Planned a Life with Less Structure So I Have More Freedom? 195
Does My Life Plan Include Special Opportunities to Enjoy Life? 196
Does My Life Plan Include Exit Points? 196

Contents

Could My Soul Have Planned That I Would Be Violent and Murder Someone?	197
Is Suicide in the Person's Plan?	198
How Did I Enter Earth School?	198
Did I Have Other Lives Before and Reincarnated into Earth School?	200
What Happens to an Individual Whose Potential Body Is Miscarried, Aborted, or Stillborn?	201

11 HOW CAN I HAVE A LIFE FILLED WITH LOVE, PEACE, AND JOY? ... 203

How Can I Be Happier in My Life?	204
Where Do the Feelings of Despair or Joy in My Interpretations of Experiences Come From?	204
What Are the Mistaken Ideas about Life We Have Learned During Our Childhoods?	205
Could I Make My Life Happier and More Enjoyable If I Abandoned the Mistaken Ideas?	208
Why Are People So Full of Fear Today?	209
How Can I Change the People around Me So They Make Me Happy or Stop Making Me Unhappy?	210
Why Does It Seem My Disturbing Situations Don't Change?	213
Can I Find the Security, Feeling of Belonging, and Identity I Want in Specific Things and People?	215
Why Is It Difficult to Be Open to Examining My Childhood Teaching and Accepting Alternatives?	216
Can I Find All I Need for My Life in Some Religion?	217
Can I Give Myself Some Happiness with Drugs, Alcohol, Sex, or Work?	218
Is There Some Way I Can More Quickly Make the Changes in My Life to Become What I Want to Be?	218
Does Society Have to Change for Me to Have the Maximum Love, Peace, and Joy in My Life?	219
At What Point in My Life Do I Start to Form Myself into the Person I Want to Become?	220
How Can I Change When It Seems the World Is Continually Making Things Happen to Me?	221
How Can I Change Who I Am?	222
What Are the Conditions for Developing into the Person I Enrolled in Earth School to Become?	223

12 CAN I COMMUNICATE WITH PEOPLE LIVING IN THE LIFE AFTER THIS LIFE? ... 225

Are My Loved Ones Who Have Left Earth Before Me in Good Conditions and Happy?	226
Do People Who Have Graduated from Earth School Miss Me?	227
Are My Pets in the Life after This Life?	227

Contents

Will My Loved One Come to Me When I Need Them or Want to Talk with Them? 228
Do My Loved Ones in the Life after This Life Communicate with Me? 228
Why Don't I Get Communication from My Loved One in the Next Life Now? 229
Why Can't People Living in the Next Life Just Come to Me and Communicate? 229
How Do I Know When They're with Me? 231
Why Don't I Have a Sense My Loved One Is Around Me as Much Now? 232
Are My Loved Ones Available to Communicate with Me When I Want to Reach Them? 233
Do Mental Mediums Really Communicate with People Living in the Life after This Life? 234
How Do I Pick a Qualified Medium? 235
Do Physical and Materialization Mediums Enable People to Appear in Séances? 237
Are There Methods Psychotherapists Can Use to Help Me Have an Afterlife Communication? 238
Are There Methods to Help Me Learn to Have My Own Afterlife Connections at Any Time? 245
Why Do I Have Trouble Seeing the Scenes Described in Guided Afterlife Connection Meditations? 247
When I'm Supposed to Imagine a Dialogue to Have Afterlife Communication, Why Don't I Get Words in My Mind the Way Other People Seem to Get Them? 248
Is There Any Way I Can Hear and Record Voices or See and Record Images of People in the Next Life? 249
Can I Communicate with My Loved Ones in the Next Life in Dreams? 250
Can I Get Help from My Loved Ones Living in the Next Life? 251
Can My Loved One in Spirit Predict My Future? 252
Will I Hold Them Back by Connecting? 252
What about the Teachings of My Church That It Is a Sin to Communicate with People in the Afterlife? 253
Are There Negative Beings Who Will Interfere When I'm Communicating? ... 253
Will My Deep Grief Make It More Difficult to Have an Afterlife Communication? 254
Is It Possible My Loved One Is Angry with Me and Will Be Harsh in My Connections? 255
What Are the Experiences I Might Have with Someone Living in the Life after This Life? 256
Can I Hasten along the Connections by Thinking Up Scenes in My Mind with My Loved One in Them? 258

Contents

What Is It Like to Communicate with Someone Living in the Life after This Life? 259
What Is the Procedure I Should Follow to Have an Afterlife Communication? 261

13 WHAT WILL HAPPEN WHEN MY BODY DIES? 267

What Will Happen in the Hours and Days Leading Up to the Time My Body Stops Functioning? 268
What Will Happen in the Moments of My Transition from This Life to the Next? 271
Will I Feel Pain at the Transition? 272
When Might I Experience Glimpses of the Life after This Life as I Gradually Transition? 273
Is It Possible People in the Room Could Share Mentally the Experiences as I Make the Transition? 274
Is It Possible That after the Transition I Might Appear to People Who Are a Distance Away? 275
At My Passing, Might I Feel What It Is Like to Be Out of the Body? 278
Do I Have Connections to the Body That Must Break? 279
Is It Possible I Might Have to Make the Transition Alone? 279
Are Events in a Near-Death Experience the Same as What Happens When the Person Actually Transitions? 280
How Easy Will My Transition Away from My Body Be? 280
What Will Be My Reaction to My Condition After My Transition? 281
Will I Be a Changed Person after My Transition? 281
Do People Go into "Soul Sleep" as Some Christians Believe? 282
After the Transition Will I Enter a Period of Sleep without Realizing What Happened Until I Awaken? 283
If I Go to Sleep at the Transition, Where Will I Find Myself When I Wake Up? 283
Will I Be Given Help after My Transition? 286
What Will My Experiences Be If My Body Dies Suddenly? 286
Will I Be Aware of What Happens to My Body after the Body Dies and I Go On? 288
What Will My Condition Be Immediately After My Transition? 288
Will I Have Reunions with My Loved Ones Already in the Afterlife? 289
What Happens to People Who Have No Family to Greet Them or Help Them? 289
Will I Be Required to Meet People I Do Not Want to Meet? 290
After My Transition, Can I Visit My Loved Ones Still on Earth? 291
Can I Go to My Funeral If I Want To? 291
Will My Loved Ones' Grief Hold Me on Earth? 291
Where Will I Go Upon Entering the Afterlife? 292

Contents

What Is the Second Death?	293
Will I Have a Life Review?	294
Will I Be Judged for How I Lived My Life?	295
Is There a Chance I Will Go to Hell?	295

14 What Will My Life in the Next Life Be Like? 297

What Is the World in the Life after This Life Like?	298
When I've Been in the Afterlife for a While, Will I Change?	298
Are There Diseases, Accidents, or Deformities I Might Experience in the Life after This Life?	299
Will I Be a Male or Female in the Next Life?	299
Can I See, Hear, Taste, Touch, and Smell in the Next Life as I Do on Earth?	300
Do We Remember Things in Earth School?	300
What Happens to People with Mental Conditions Such as Down Syndrome and Mental Retardation?	301
What Will Determine My Living Conditions in the Life after This Life?	301
Will I Have a Body in the Next Life?	302
Will I Be Wearing a Special Type of Clothing?	303
Who Will I Live With?	304
If I Have Had Two Spouses, Which Will I Live With?	304
Where Will I Live?	305
Can I Have Any Social Activities in the Next Life?	306
What Will My World Be Like in the Next Life?	307
Can I Have Flowers in a Garden?	307
Will I See a Sun, Moon, or Stars?	308
Will I Have Uncomfortable Cold and Hot Days?	308
Will I Attend Things in Buildings and Halls?	308
Will I Experience or Participate in Music and Art?	309
Will I Be Able to Take Walks as We Do in Earth School?	309
Will I Communicate Using My Voice or by Telepathy?	310
Are There Children in the Life after This Life?	310
Can I Relive Things That Happened During My Life?	311
Will My Desires and Expectations Change?	311
Will I Feel Any Emotions?	312
Will I Have a Job?	313
If I Am a Scientist or Engineer, Can I Continue My Work There?	314
If I Am an Artist, Dancer, Musician, or Other Master of the Arts, Will I Be Able to Inspire Performers and Artists on Earth?	315
Can I Enjoy the Recreation I Loved on Earth?	315
Are There Animals in the Life after This Life?	317
Will I Be Able to Keep Learning by Attending Classes or Schools?	317
Will I Be Able to Read Books and Go to Libraries?	318
Will I Continue to Grow in Wisdom, Love, and Compassion?	318

Contents

Is There Time in the Next Life? *319*
Is There a Government? *320*
What Religion Will I Join in the Next Life? *320*
What Are the Attitudes Toward Jesus and God among People in the Next Life? *321*
Will I Be Able to Have Sex If My Partner and I Want It? *321*
Will My Gender Identity or Sexual Orientation on Earth Have Any Effect on Me in the Next Life? *322*
How Long Can I Stay on the Next Plane of Life? *322*
What Are the Divisions, Areas, or Levels of Life? *323*

BIBLIOGRAPHY 327

ENDNOTES 345

The Four Books

This book contains easy-to-read summaries of the contents of the other three books in this series that contain detailed information, quotations, sources, and citations. This book provides the information and perspectives of the other three books without the detailed explanations, evidence, and citations. However, the contents are not based on supposition, personal opinion, or intuitions. The book is based on the 1,278 citations of researchers, knowledgeable specialists, and people living in the next life contained in the other three books.

The four books explain what we know today about the nature of reality, our purpose in this life, and what happens when we leave this life. The books contain explanations of these important truths:

1. Your Mind is not produced by or contained in your brain. Your Mind has body experiences and brain experiences, but lives perfectly well without either.

2. There is nothing but Mind and experiences. We experience the world, but the world does not exist outside of our Minds and experiences.

3. Our Minds are individual manifestations of Our Universal Intelligence that all people are part of—we are all one Mind.

4. Our one Universal Intelligence creates the world we live in based on humanity's history and our expectations for the scenery, such as mountains, oceans, a moon, and animals.

5. Because we are Our Universal Intelligence, our individual Minds continue to live after the temporary Earth School body ceases to function.

6. We have purposes for being in Earth School and can live in love, joy, and peace while we fulfill our purposes.

7. We planned our lives in Earth School and play out the plan, although our free will can adjust and deviate from the plan at will.

8. The reason for the death of the body is so we can end our Earth School experience and graduate to the next life.

This book contains summaries of the following three books.

There Is Nothing but Mind and Experiences

The first book, *There Is Nothing but Mind and Experiences*, explains that Our Universal Intelligence is the basis of reality, and we are individual manifestations of it. It explains why we know this is true and what it means for our life in Earth School.

Your Eternal Self: Science Discovers the Afterlife

The second book, *Your Eternal Self: Science Discovers the Afterlife*, was developed and updated from the book *Your Eternal Self*. This book contains the evidence that our Minds are not in our brains, our Minds don't need the brain, and we continue to live after the brain dies.

Reasons for What Happens to You in Your Life & Your Afterlife

The third book, *Reasons for What Happens to You in Your Life & Your Afterlife: From Speakers in the Afterlife*, explains what happens to us through the major stages of life: deciding to enter Earth School; planning the Earth School experience; learning to succeed in Earth School; growing in love, compassion, and understanding; graduating; and living in the life after this Earth School life.

Preface

At one time, all people knew without doubt that the earth is the center of the universe. It was obvious to anyone who gazed at the starry canopy drifting across the sky at night and witnessed the sun rising in the east and setting in the west every day. The learned scientists assured people that the earth is the center of the universe, ignoring Copernicus and Galileo when they proved the earth is just a planet in a solar system, not the center of the universe. Galileo was forced to recant his heretical views. Giordano Bruno asserted that the stars were suns with planets around them and was burned alive in 1600 for his impudence.

Today, all people know with confidence that the earth revolves around a sun that is itself revolving in the Milky Way galaxy, that is itself hurtling through a universe, that is itself expanding at 1.8 times the speed of light. Today everyone knows those facts as being self-evident, without a doubt. But it took hundreds of years of glacially slow Mind changes for all people to believe it.

You and I are experiencing a similar revolution in thought today. Most people still aren't confident they will be alive after their bodies die. They don't know what has happened to their loved ones whose bodies have died. They sob at funerals as though the person has been obliterated from life and will never be seen again. They solemnly walk across the cemetery lawn to gaze at the ground where they believe their father, mother, son, or daughter are. Their children go with them, learning from their parents that when the body dies, it's a horror to be feared, and they themselves will one day be buried in the ground or encased in a mausoleum. It's a terrible belief system that has no basis in truth, yet it holds humanity in its icy grip.

In another century or two after humankind has evolved to realize the truth about who we are, everyone will be certain, without question, that

- When the body dies, it's just our graduation from one school into the next school, and the next is filled with more love, peace, and joy than we can imagine.

- People who have graduated before us are waiting for us there, alive, happy, and available to communicate with us if we just learn to listen.

- We are all of the same spiritual essence, of one substance in the body of the Universal Intelligence.

We've been taught the falsehoods that we are separate from other people, that the purpose of life is to get as much as we can for ourselves and satisfy our needs without regard for others, that to be happy we must have certain things and gratifications in our lives, and that life and other people must do right by us for us to enjoy life. When humankind grows out of those primitive self-absorbed sentiments, all people will take for granted that our mission in life is to love abundantly, feel loved unconditionally, be happy for no reason, make other people happy, and enjoy all the wonderful experiences life has to give us.

There will be no crime because everyone will be more anxious to give than to take. There will be no anxiety because there will be nothing to fear. There will be no poverty or hunger because people will care for all other people; nations will care for other nations.

The Garden of Eden is here, now. We are living in it. We were never driven from it. We drove ourselves into the illusion that we live in an unfeeling world of senseless matter and energy in which we are helpless victims unable to find happiness because the world is so saturated with misery. You can dispel the illusion and wake up to the Garden of Eden that has always been here. You can then reside in a world of love, peace, and happiness for the remainder of your life. All you have to do is realize that what you were taught about life and reality were misconceptions perpetuated by a society that is intellectually in the technology age but spiritually in the stone age. The truth will be evident to you. Nothing else is required. It's all in your Mind.

Preface

I wrote these books to help you understand the truths that we who study consciousness and the life after this life know and that will be commonly known in the centuries ahead. When people come to accept these truths, humankind will live together in love, peace, and joy.

What you will learn in this book will give you a new perspective. The archaic perspective that the universe is made of matter and energy independent of us, that our Minds are in our brains, and that when the brain dies we die is a primitive misconception, just as the view that the earth is the center of the universe is now archaic and universally regarded as untrue. In these books, you will learn that your Mind will never cease to exist and that Our Universal Intelligence, our Minds, continually create what we experience as matter and energy, including our bodies and brains.

You will find yourself going back and forth in your perspective from the old beliefs society teaches to this new understanding. You can't help it. In these books you'll learn that the universe is created by Our Universal Intelligence, but then you'll watch videos of materialist scientists describing a universe comprising stars, galaxies, black holes, dark energy, and dark matter that they assert will eventually be destroyed by either dissipating its energy or being squeezed into a point smaller than a pinhead in a fiery crunch. You'll question the perspectives you have learned from this book. Both perspectives can't be true.

When you reexamine the evidence, you will always shift back to knowing there is only Our Universal Consciousness at the basis of reality, you are a living part of Our Universal Consciousness so you don't die when the body dies, we are all one with each other, you have unique purposes for being in Earth School, and you will graduate to go on to a glorious life in the life after this life with all your loved ones. The truth will always resurface in your Mind.

Links to Afterlife Research and Education Websites

Additional readings and links with valuable information about the subjects of the chapters are on the Web sites at www.earthschoolanswers.com and www.afterlifeinstitute.org.

1

Why Do We Know These Explanations Are True?

Today, for the first time in humankind's history, technology is allowing us to easily record and widely disseminate messages from people living in the life after this life. We have vast libraries of their descriptions of what happens before we enter Earth School, what our lives can be like if we wake up to our true nature and learn how to have a change of heart and Mind, what transpires during the transition from this life to the next, and the evidence that people live on after the body no longer functions. These communications with vast numbers of people now living in the life after this life are proof that communicators we have called "deceased" are very much alive. We have many recordings of spouses, children, and parents who left Earth School years before, speaking casually to their loved ones who are still on this side of life, as though they were sitting at the breakfast table talking about everyday events.

These many accounts of the life after this life have an extremely high level of corroboration with each other. AfterlifeData.com is the largest database of afterlife descriptions and analyses on the Internet, containing a large collection of spirit communications describing the next stage of life. The results of research comparing accounts of the nature of the afterlife in the AfterlifeData.com archives show 94.4 percent agreement on 265 specific afterlife areas. The corroborated evidence is undeniable. We have proof that we live on after our bodies cease to function. The information in this book is similarly corroborated by many reports from people living in the life after this life.

Following are some of the communications we're having commonly now that are teaching us about this life and the life after this life.

Near-death experiences: People who have near-death experiences provide corroborated descriptions of characteristics of the next stage of life viewed from their vantage point overlooking the next life from the edge of this life.

After-death communications: The detailed accounts of after-death communications agree in their descriptions of the life after this life.

Induced After-Death Communication and Repair & Reattachment Grief Therapy: From 70 to 98 percent (depending on the conditions) of patients who undergo Induced After-Death Communication (IADC™)[1] or Repair & Reattachment Grief Therapy[2] testify that they experienced an after-death communication with the person for whom they are grieving. The patients have reported to us what they were told about life and the life after this life.

Mental medium communications: Carefully controlled research has demonstrated that mental mediums communicate with people living in the life after this life. These reports provide insights into the life after this life that are consistent across time, geography, and cultures.

Direct-voice and materialization-medium communications: A number of direct-voice and materialization mediums have enabled people in the life after this life to speak to assembled groups. Direct-voice mediums and materialization mediums hold carefully controlled séances in which unmistakable voices of those in spirit are heard. The recordings of thousands of these sessions by talented mediums such as David Thompson[3] and Leslie Flint[4] are now available for anyone to listen to. The speakers have provided clear descriptions of the afterlife.

To listen to some of these recordings, link to www.earthschoolanswers.com/reunions/.

Family member communications with loved ones: Many people have taught themselves how to communicate with their husbands, wives, siblings, and children using meditation, pendulums, self-hypnosis, and other means. They have shared what they have learned in a large number of books that provide a rich source of information about the next life. Amazon lists over 10,000 books on the topic of "afterlife."

In all, we now have a vast amount of information from the citizens of the life after this life. This storehouse of knowledge has given us an understanding of pre-birth events, mental and spiritual growth during this life, what happens to someone when the body dies, what life is like on the next planes of life, and what those in the next stage of life advise for us who are still on the earth.

Recommended Sources of Evidence Proving the Reality of the Life after This Life

Evidence that proves beyond a reasonable doubt that we continue to live after the body dies includes videos, print materials, and audio clips of speakers in the life after this life; descriptions by people who have had afterlife communications; and communication by people who have learned to have their own afterlife communication experiences. The most compelling can be found at www.earthschoolanswers.com/proof/.

PART 1

WE ARE THE UNIVERSAL INTELLIGENCE THAT WILL NEVER DIE

Information in this section of the book is summarized primarily from *There Is Nothing but Mind and Experiences* published in 2020 by Greater Reality Publications. The book contains 212 citations and supporting the statements. The information that follows generalizes from the specific details in that book with fewer direct quotes and citations. You can read the sources, quotations, and more detailed information in that book.

2

What Is This World We Live in Made Of?

Is the Universe Just Senseless Matter and Energy?

Answer: The universe is not just senseless matter and energy. Our Universal Intelligence is the source of all that is. The universe is consciousness.

Because the fundamental basis of our reality is consciousness, some have suggested the universe is an illusion, but that is not true. We have real experiences—sunsets, lakes, mountains, people, the smell of a rose, a melodic birdsong, the taste of chocolate, and puppies. The world is real. But the basis of our reality is not what we have been taught it is. The basis of this reality is consciousness. There is only Mind and experiences.

In this chapter you will read a now-common interpretation among researchers of the nature of reality and the underlying basis in consciousness called idealism. It has been in some form found in the philosophies of Plato, Kant, Berkeley, Hegel, Schelling, and Schopenhauer, among others. It has been integral to Buddhism and Hinduism for millennia. Idealism is not a new philosophy, but it is gaining popularity as quantum science and other science disciplines are discovering that the most satisfying explanation for our world is that consciousness is fundamental to reality. Pioneering physicist and mathematician Sir James Jeans, who was a professor at the University of Cambridge and Princeton University, wrote his conclusions after studying the basis of reality from a physicist's perspective:

> The stream of knowledge is heading toward a non-mechanical reality; the universe begins to look more like a great thought than like a great machine. Mind no longer appears to be an accidental intruder into the realm of matter, we ought rather hail it as the creator and governor of the realm of matter.[5]

A more detailed explanation with quotations is found in *There Is Nothing but Mind and Experiences*.[6]

It may sound unusual or foreign to you to think of a world with only consciousness, with no outside reality of trees, mountains, planets, and chocolate, because we all grew up to be materialists, believing the world is matter and energy outside of us. That is not true. The basis of reality is Our Universal Intelligence, consciousness.

You may be surprised to hear the explanations that follow remove a physical world altogether. Since we know consciousness is the basis of reality, a physical reality of any kind is not necessary or possible. Your Mind can't create a stone, let alone Mt. Everest, if stones and mountains are conceived of as objects in space the way the materialists see them. Mind and what the materialists see as matter are two different substances.

A world outside of us is not necessary for us to have experiences. We have experiences in the Mind of Our Universal Intelligence and need no outside world between us and the experience. You will understand why that is true in the pages that follow.

If There's No World of Matter and Energy Outside of Us, What Is the World We Live in Made Of?

Answer: The world is experiences in the Mind, so asking what the world is made of is like asking what a thought is made of. There is nothing but Mind and experiences. We experience the world, but there is no world outside of our experiences.

Matter and energy do not create our Minds. Instead, our Minds create matter and energy. When our Minds experience a sight, sound, touch, taste, or smell, the experiences are entering our awareness from Our Universal Intelligence that we are all part of. There is no objective reality outside of our Minds that we perceive from energy entering tiny orifices in a material body.

When you look at this book, where are you having the experience of a book? Is the book somehow entering you and merging with a body or a brain? No. But you're having the experience of a book. When you look at the book, the experience of a book is entirely in your Mind. When you close your eyes and recall the image of the book, you have the sight experience of the book in your Mind. Both the sight experience you have with your eyes open and the sight experience you have with your eyes closed are sight experiences entirely in your Mind. Both are coming from Our Universal Intelligence. If you repeatedly look at the book, then close your eyes and recall the book, you will see that the experience of the book never happens outside your Mind. The experience of the book and memory of the book are both only in Our Universal Intelligence.

If you don't see a book or any other image when you close your eyes and try to imagine it, you may have aphantasia, the inability to have mental pictures. The phenomenon is very common and doesn't interfere with the person's life. Learn more about aphantasia at www.earthschoolanswers.com/aphantasia/. You may also have vaguer, blurred images. That is also a common visualizing experience. You can test your ability to visualize at the same webpage.

Your experiences in a dream are illustrations of how you can have experiences with no outside world. In a dream, you experience things that are aspects of the dream: your dream self, other characters, scenery, and events. All are arising in your Mind. You have the experiences of a vivid dream—seeing, hearing, and touching things. The events give rise to emotions because they are so real. But in the dream there are no bodies or scenery resulting in the sensed experiences you have. Your Mind is having the experiences of seeing, hearing, and touching in the dream to create the dream world in which you can experience stories, but there is no world outside of you giving rise to the experiences.

You see your friend in your dream, with her familiar face, body, and sound of her voice. Those are sensory impressions. However, she's not there. There is no face, body, or voice. You are having full experiences of specific sights and sounds, but there are no objects you are seeing and hearing, and touching.

In the same way you have dream selves, characters, and scenery that you experience with no objects in your Mind, in your daily life you experience your body, other people's bodies, scenery, and events with no objects; they are all experiences in Our Universal Intelligence, like remembering images or having a dream. There is no world separate from Our Universal Intelligence. We must abandon the concept that there is anything outside of us that we sense. There are only the senses.

That doesn't make the world we live in any less substantial. Rocks are hard, the sun is 93 million miles away, and Beethoven's Moonlight Sonata still sounds enchanting. It's all the same as it has been throughout our lives. The only difference is in realizing what all these marvelous sensual experiences are made of.

How Can We See, Hear, Smell, Taste, and Touch in a World Made of Consciousness?

Answer: Seeing, hearing, smelling, tasting, and touching all happen in the Mind, not in the body experience. The body experience is senseless. As a result, we can have sensory experiences in a waking state, in dreams, in hypnotic trance, and in memories, all with no objects. The sensory experiences are independent of anything outside of us.

We have the experiences of the five senses: sight, hearing, smelling, tasting, and touching. We also have bodily experiences, such as pain, pleasure, movement, emotion, balance, and other bodily sensations. The experiences don't give rise to the senses. The experiences **are** the senses. We smell a rose, see its red color, smell its fragrance, feel its soft petals, and are pricked by a thorn and feel pain. Each of these is an experience in the Mind. But there is no rose outside of us. There is only the set of experiences in our Mind that we identify as a rose, just as when we remember a rose we see it vividly in our Mind, feel its texture, and recall its odor; but there is no rose in our Mind, only the experience of the rose.

The experiences arise from Our Universal Intelligence in the same way that when we intend to recall the memory of a rose, a rose comes into our Awareness. "Recall," "remember," "bring to mind," "relive," "remind," and "reminisce" are all words describing the action of willing an image or thought to come into Awareness when we want it. We don't have to construct the image or put in a catalog code when we bring it to Mind. We just intend to have the rose in our Mind and it comes into Awareness from Our Universal Intelligence, with all its sight, smell, and texture details. But there is no physical rose there. We don't need a physical rose outside of us to have the experience of a rose.

Experiencing a rose in our daily life happens in the same way. We look at a table and on it see a single rose. At that moment we are having the rose experience in Awareness from Our Universal Intelligence, just as we have the rose experience come to us in our Minds when we recall the sight of a rose or dream of a rose. In all three cases there is no rose object, just the sensory experiences we identify as a rose.

If Experiences Are in Our Minds, Why Does Everyone Have the Experiences of the Same World?

Answer: We have experiences that arise in Our Universal Intelligence and are shared among everyone having the experience together. We are one Mind experiencing the one set of sensory experiences, then taking from them our individual perspectives, understanding, and memories.

You might wonder how, if there's no chair out there in the world apart from us, we can all have the experience of the same chair. The answer is that we are attuned to the same realm of experiences as everyone else now in Earth School, rather like being tuned to the same channel on a television. We spent our childhoods learning to experience this realm of experiences being experienced by others in Earth School. We learned the contents of the same dream everyone else is having with us. Our Universal Intelligence continues to have us experience the same world so our experiences are predictable, stable, and commonly held. We stay tuned to this realm of experiences. We know what this life is like and what to expect. We can then act in it to learn our life lessons, love others, and enjoy the experiences. However, there is no world outside of us that we're learning to navigate. There are only the experiences we are accessing at the same time together from Our Universal Intelligence.

To help you understand how we experience reality, imagine you share the same Mind with five other people. When you look at a sunset, all six of you are having the one sight experience of the sunset as one Mind as though you had one pair of eyes. When you hear a bird singing, all six of you are having the sound experience of the bird as if you had one pair of ears. You are one Mind. You aren't six Minds seeing six sunsets or hearing six birds. You are having one experience at the same time in your one Mind. Your bodies are separate, but your Minds are one.

Our world is just like that. When we are experiencing our day-to-day world together, our intention to act in the world brings to each of us the people, scenery, and actions Our Universal Intelligence has as the reality we are in now, just as our intention to remember an event comes to the one Mind with six individuals immediately. Because we are all one Mind in Our Universal Intelligence, we are all having the same experiences in this world. There is no objective world outside of us that we are experiencing. There are only the experiences our one Universal Intelligence is bringing into our collective Awareness.

The distinction is that each of us is an individual in our reception and interpretation of the experience. One person may notice the birds flying by while another notices the squirrels in the trees. One may be frightened at seeing a snake while another, who loves reptiles, is excited and happy at the sight of a snake. From the one experience, our individual selves take what is meaningful to us. We then also have our unique interpretations of the experiences. The memories we recall later are what each of us noticed that was meaningful to us. An experience might be made up of thousands of accessible details, but our limited Minds would only process five or ten. However, the entire set of all possible experiences is are accessible in our one Mind, Our Universal Intelligence, as one set of experiences.

Why Do the Experiences Stay the Same?

Answer: We receive the experiences we expect to receive because we all grew up with Earth School experiences. They are like memories in Our Universal Intelligence that take form as we encounter them. They are the same each time we experience them because Our Universal Intelligence provides experiences with stability and continuity that fit our expectations from past experiences.

Our Minds, which are individuated members of Our Universal Intelligence, have the same experiences because we are perpetuating them together. When we grew up, we became familiar with the experiences those around us had been experiencing in our one Mind, as though we were all in one dream. The reason the experiences are consistent and stable is that Our Universal Intelligence was providing what we expected and needed to happen based on what we experienced in life. All of us have the one common Mind that underlies reality so our understanding and expectations perpetuate this reality. We learned the experiences others before us were perpetuating, so we expect this reality to be as it is. This reality is what we experience only because everyone is receiving what we expect from Our Universal Intelligence. We are creating this reality. If everyone suddenly believed we have two moons, a second moon would appear instantly in our common experience. If we all believed elephants could fly, immediately our skies would be filled with trumpeting pachyderms. We perpetuate the world we believe to be real. You will read more about how the Mind can instantly change reality on pages 16-17.

Experiences are common to everyone who has contact with the same world in which we are having experiences. We expect this world because we grew up participating in the experiences with others who are also attuned to this world in Our Universal Intelligence. Because we are all attuned to it and expect it to be as it has been since we were children, we are creating and maintaining this reality. If we had other expectations we had all learned, we would all live in another reality together. When we graduate from Earth School, we will simply change the focus of the experiences accessible in Our Universal Intelligence. We'll change dreams. We'll share experiences in the next world of experiences given to us by Our Universal Intelligence, just as we share experiences in this world. Our life after this life will still be our one Mind in Our Universal Intelligence, just with a different attunement.

The reason for the common experiences in Earth School is that our Souls decided to attune us to this world in Our Universal Intelligence so we could learn the lessons we set out to learn, love others and grow in compassion, and enjoy the rich experiences. We must have experiences of the same people, scenery, and events so we can have experiences together. We planned the experiences before our births. We created the framework of the reality we would experience. This realm is our personal playground.

If Everything Is in the Consciousness of Our Universal Intelligence, What Exists?

Answer: It is better to say all experiences are "accessible" than they "exist." When we access sights, sounds, odors, tastes, and textures as we live our daily lives, they are provided for us in Our Universal Intelligence. Nothing exists outside of our experiences. We have sensory experiences that change from moment to moment.

When you think of a person you grew up with, immediately memories come into your Mind: that person's face, mannerisms, body structure, and personality. Where were those memories before they came into your Mind? Did they exist? No. They were simply accessible. Instead of believing there is a world of things outside of us or memories stored on a cosmic hard drive, we must conceive of them only as "accessible."

Everything in Our Universal Intelligence that is now given to us has been discovered or observed by people at some time. When they are discovered or observed, they become part of the world of experiences Our Universal Intelligence gives to us. We have found everything there because we were looking for it.

When the Hubble Telescope peered into a vast, dark area of the cosmos called the "deep field," the researchers had the sight experience of 3,000 galaxies no one had seen before. They did not become accessible until someone observed them. They never "existed" in the sense of being in a world outside of us. Now there is the potential for researchers to experience them if they look for them. The researchers didn't create them so now there are 3,000 more galaxies in the universe. They became accessible because now we know when we look at that patch of sky with powerful telescopes we will see what we expect to see. The experiences are accessible.

That doesn't diminish the fact that our experiences are real. We see, hear, feel, taste, smell, and touch real objects in a real world. We just have to think differently about where it all comes from and its underlying substance. Understanding that consciousness is the basis of reality is no stranger than believing the notions that everything in the universe is energy in some form; atoms are 99.9999999999999% empty space; only 12 fundamental atomic particles make up everything but miraculously arrange themselves into trees, mountains, and people; when someone is looking at a light beam it changes from a wave to particles; and the vacuum of empty space is saturated with a quantum foam in which virtual particles of matter and anti-matter are continually being created and destroyed. Compared to those notions, consciousness as the basis of reality is a straightforward, parsimonious concept.

Is There Any Evidence We Are Creating the World Together?

Answer: There is evidence we are creating the world together, especially in the area in which we have most control, our own bodies.

The experiences we had as we grew up in Earth School became expectations we have for the way the world must be. We all perpetuate those experiences because we are given what we intend and expect to have. We are creating this reality through our expectations for things to be as they have been in our experience and the experiences of others. The proof that we are creating reality together is in the book *There Is Nothing but Mind and Experiences*[7] and is summarized elsewhere in this book. Here are brief examples of the proof our Minds create reality.

- When people believe a medicine will cure an ailment, more often than would be expected by chance the medicine does cure them, even if they've been given a placebo that has nothing of the medicine in it. (See pages 163-165.)
- If people are hypnotized to believe something about their bodies, their bodies may change to fit their belief. In one instance a subject was told under hypnosis that he had a burn on his hand when there was no burn. Soon after he was revived a burned area appeared spontaneously on his hand with no cause. (See pages 162-163.)

- People with dissociative identity disorder (multiple personality disorder) can have dramatic body changes when they change personalities, a feat that seems physically impossible. A drunk person can instantly become sober when the personality changes. Scars, burn marks, and cysts can appear and disappear with changes to alternative personalities. (See pages 165-166.) These changes result from the changing beliefs.

- In the next realm of life, called Summerland, people have the bodies they desire to have, usually in their 20s or 30s, without intending to have them. They have them because of beliefs: they like those virile bodies, so they have them. They live in surroundings that fit their character without asking for the surroundings. People who have cold, harsh, cruel, or violent dispositions live in surroundings that are darker and unpleasant. People who have been loving, kind, and gentle in Earth School live in surroundings that are full of love, kindness, and gentleness in Summerland. The spiritual realms we enter after Earth School are created by our dispositions. Earth School is just another spiritual realm. Knowing people create their worlds without intending to do so in the next realm, we can understand why that process is occurring in Earth School. You can read about the fact that our dispositions determine our living circumstances in the next life on pages 301-302 of this book.

Don't Materialist Scientists Have Proof There Is a World Outside of Us?

Answer: No. What they conceive of as the external world is forever inaccessible to them. In their conception, we have only electrical impulses causing neurotransmitters to make neurons fire in a brain. Where the electrical impulses come from is not knowable.

Materialist scientists know they can never be sure there is a world outside of them, even though they assert it is there.[8] In the materialists' conception, the only thing that happens to us that gives us the idea there's an outside world is that molecule neurotransmitters that transmit messages between neurons cause patterns of neurons to fire when we're having experiences. The materialists tell us there is no facsimile or photo of a sunset, tree, or house in the brain; there are only neurons firing. As a result, even the materialists say we can never know there is really a world outside of us. The neurons could be firing because of a false world or a simulation world or just electromagnetic signals causing the neurons to fire and we would never know it.

As the molecular biologist and neuroscientist Francis Crick wrote, "You're nothing but a pack of neurons."[9]

Scientists have no proof of a reality outside of the neurons they say fire in the brain to give a pattern we believe represents reality. We can never access reality to be sure it is there, they believe. Materialist scientists have no proof there is a world outside of us.

Don't the Laws of Physics Show There's a World Outside of Consciousness?

Answer: The laws of physics are rule sets that give structure and predictability to our Earth School experiences. The rule sets accompany the experiences we are having in our Minds to give form to the experiential world. Neither the world nor the rule sets are in a world outside of us.

We discover consistencies about matter and energy we call laws of physics, but they are only experiences in our Minds that are expressions of Our Universal Intelligence. The Earth School environment has what Tom Campbell calls "rule sets" we must adhere to.[10] If we jump off a high cliff, we will be dashed on the rocks below. Eating high-calorie foods will result in our gaining weight. We must travel through space by our conscious effort to go from Paris to New York. We experience the arrow of time, from past to present to future. All the characteristics of Earth School are part of the environment created for us that will enable us to love, learn lessons, and have happy lives. We call these rule sets laws of physics or natural laws.

The rule set we have is unique to Earth School. Most of the rules don't apply in other realms. In the realm of life that most people enter after graduating from Earth School, which the Theosophists called "Summerland," jumping off a cliff will not result in our dashing ourselves on the rocks below. We won't need to worry about gaining weight; in fact, we won't need to eat at all. Those in Summerland perceive space as we do in Earth School, but when someone wants to visit a library a thousand miles of earth space away, that person simply intends to be there and instantly is standing before the stacks of books. Space is in our perception, not in a world outside of us.

The rule sets for Earth School give us consistency, consequences for actions, and a clear, predictable structure for daily life. We need that stability to function. Humankind then imposes other sets of rules on us that are not part of the rule set. For example, we must not take someone else's stuff against their will. We may "own" things, but the ownership is entirely by assent of those around us. We may not drive a car without a license. All of the rules society imposes add to the rules that are the rule sets for Earth School.

The laws of physics are just the structure of the Earth School experience. Experiences come to us from Our Universal Intelligence so we can participate in Earth School, love, learn, and enjoy the experiences. We can identify the consistencies in the way the world is structured; we call them laws. A stable structure avoids the uncomfortable feeling of chaos or unpredictability Earth School would have without the framework. The laws of physics give form to the Earth School experiences.

Doesn't Science Tell Us the Material World Outside of Us Gives Us Sensory Experiences?

Answer: No, even materialist science admits that the sensory experiences we have are entirely in our Mind, what they would call a pack of neurons firing. Color, texture, odor, taste, and sounds are not in even their physical world. All are created by the Mind from the experiences of bland, raw energy in the materialists' conception.

The fact that we are having sensory experiences only in the Mind is true even from a materialist's perspective. Materialists believe there is a world outside of us that exists independent of us and we have experiences by having light waves, sound vibrations, molecules with odor, or touches received by sense organs from that world of energy and matter. However, there are phenomena called qualia that are not in the world out there. They happen only in the mind.

From that materialist perspective, color is not in the energy and matter of the world they believe is outside of them. The sense of red we have when we see a rose is not in a rose even in the materialist's world. The redness is entirely in the Mind resulting from interpretations of the differing wavelengths of light entering the eye. In the materialist's conception, the energy and matter outside of people have no color, not even black and white. They state that the energy and matter also has no smell. Smell is the response, in the olfactory sensory neurons, to molecules wafting through the air that attach to olfactory cilia in the nose to trigger the neurons that give the Mind a sense of odor. Energy and matter in the materialist's outside world have no odor. There is no soft touch of a rose petal in the materialist's universe. Electrons in the rose petals and the finger repel each other so there is no actual touch, just sensations in receptors on the skin that are then translated into texture in the Mind. But there is no touch or texture in the materialist's outside world. There is no pain in the finger; only the Mind can perceive a thing such as pain. In the materialist's world, energy and matter take shape and are perceived as having a size only when the Mind gives them shape and size.

Take away the redness, the smell, the touch, the shape, and the size and what is left of the rose in the materialist's outside world? Nothing but featureless waves or fragments of energy. The rose is assembled and experienced only in the Mind, even in the materialist's conception of reality.

Science textbooks all assert that the physical properties of the materialist's matter are shape, size, taste, color, smell, and texture. They are wrong. The materialist's matter has none of these properties. These are all experiences that occur only in the Mind. The textbooks should read, "The properties the Mind gives to the flow of energy materialists call matter are shape, size, taste, color, smell, and texture."

Another way even materialists agree that reality is created in the Mind is the suggestion among neuroscientists now that what comes to the person's senses is "uncertain, indirectly related to what's out there, and ambiguous." They explain that "In order to make sense of it, the brain has to do something we call 'inference.' It has to combine this ambiguous sensory data with prior expectations or beliefs about the way the world is to then form its best guess about what caused the sensory information that it gets."[11] In so doing, the brain (in their conception) assembles and augments the sensed data to create organized perceptions. The brain adds inferences, expectations from similar memories, and imagination to fill in the large gaps from unperceived parts of the sensory experience to form a whole that is in large part an invention of the Mind, not a real world they believe is outside of us.

So even the materialists agree that what we perceive as reality is a construct of the Mind. But the materialists are incorrect in asserting that there is energy and matter outside of the Mind. There is only Mind and experiences.

How Can I Be Creating Reality When the World Seems to Be Given to Me?

Answer: It might be better to say we are given the reality we expect to have and in that way we create the reality. Our Universal Intelligence does the actual creating. We grew up in Earth School learning what to expect, and now because we expect it, the world is available to us as we expect it to be. Even though we didn't originate the world, we are continuing its creation as it is by our expectations, which are fulfilled by Our Universal Intelligence.

We are accessing experiences in a world with continuity that fits our past experiences and the past experiences of the other people in Earth School. We make changes in this world and our changes become additions to the experiences everyone is given as we all experience Earth School. We are perpetuating the world we were able to access that is accessible in Our Universal Intelligence and adding to it for others to experience. We are creating reality, but not from nothing. Humankind is perpetuating this world we are accessing because, as the totality of Minds that are members of Our Universal Intelligence, we expect the world to be as it was when we grew up in it. Whatever the world is—whether cold, harsh, and cruel or warm, loving, and gentle—we are perpetuating it and adding to it by adding either cold, harshness, and cruelty or warmth, love, and gentleness. Our Universal Intelligence gives us the experiences of the world we expect to have.

It may seem the world is being given to us without our control or influence over what comes, but actually we are in control of what comes to us and to humankind. But influencing all of humankind to change the experiences we're having is difficult. We can control our own experiences in our little sphere of influence, especially our own Minds and bodies, but all the other individuals that make up society must change their expectations for us to see monumental advancements in humankind. Part of our role as members of Our Universal Intelligence is to be instrumental in helping humankind change the experiences it is perpetuating and expecting. We can create a reality that is full of love, compassion, other-centeredness, and kindness, but we must each be a well-tuned instrument in the orchestra that creates a world of harmony and exquisite compositions.

Why Do We Have Different Reactions to the Same Experiences We Are Accessing Together?

Answer: As we grew up in our different circumstances, we learned different interpretations of life events. As adults, the interpretations that arise with the experiences result in our unique reactions that are different from other people's reactions because others grew up in different circumstances.

To the experiences we have from Our Universal Intelligence we must add something critical for our lives in Earth School: interpretations. Our interpretations are learned. We learn a coiled-up rope in the corner of our room is nonthreatening but a coiled-up snake is threatening. We respond to the coiled-up rope with calm or joy at finding the rope we thought we had lost. We respond to the coiled-up snake with fear or with joy at finding the pet snake we had lost. The interpretations are entirely in our individual Minds.

Interpretations are the second prominent property of who we are. We have experiences, and we have interpretations of the experiences. Emotions follow, but the emotions are the consequence of the person's interpretation; they are not embodied in the experiences. The interpretations are not accessible by themselves as experiences are. They are deeply embedded, fundamental properties that constitute our selves. They cannot be separated or quantified individually. They cannot be dissected. They are fundamental to our lives.

While we are accessing the same experience from Our Universal Intelligence, our interpretations are entirely individual. They are who we are. They constitute our level of spiritual maturity. One person seeing a suffering man sitting alone by a road may interpret the experience with disgust and revulsion. Another may interpret the experience with sympathy and compassion. Our level of love and compassion for people comes from our interpretations of experiences, not the experiences. That was the message of the Parable of the Good Samaritan (Luke 10:25-37). The experience was the same for the priest, the Levite, and the Samaritan who passed by. But the interpretations of the experience were profoundly different.

We learn our interpretations through the models of others who have responded to such experiences, our history with the experiences or similar experiences, and the deliberate changes we have made to have the interpretations we desire. As we go through Earth School, we grow to have interpretations with more love and compassion. We change our view of life and other people, learn lessons, and enjoy experiences by changing our interpretations about life experiences.

What Does the Fact That Consciousness Is Creating This Reality Mean for Our Lives?

Answer: We are the Universal Intelligence participating in creating the reality we live in. As a result, we can change the components of our reality that are cruel, insensitive, violent, and harmful to be caring, loving, sensitive, gentle, and nurturing. When we realize we are creating our reality, we can confidently go about changing it and us to be what we want it and us to be.

You, I, and the universe are all creations of consciousness, Our Universal Intelligence. We are manifestations of Our Universal Intelligence living our lives in the universe created by Our Universal Intelligence. Our Universal Intelligence is all there is to the universe. It will never be harmed and it will never end. Since we are manifestations of Our Universal Intelligence, we can never be harmed and we will never end. The body experience we are having is temporary and will end, just as our dream ends when we awaken. But we who are individuated manifestations of Our Universal Intelligence will simply go on to have other experiences in other realms.

We can never die.

Part 2

You Are Not Your Brain, So You Live on After Your Brain Dies

Information in this section of the book is summarized from *Your Eternal Self: Science Discovers the Afterlife*, second edition, published in 2020. The book contains 344 sources supporting the statements. The information that follows generalizes from the specific details in that book with fewer direct quotes and citations. You can read the sources, quotations, citations, and more detailed information in that book.

3

How Can My Mind Live When My Brain Dies?

Answer: There is abundant evidence from a wide range of sources that when your brain dies, your Mind will continue, alive, healthy, and joyous at your release from the burdens of a body.

It seems obvious that since we have bodies, our Minds are somehow in our brains. But that assumption is not true. Our Minds are not produced by or housed in our brains. We must learn that perspective in the same way we've learned that other seemingly obvious assumptions aren't true.

It appears the sun rises in the east, travels across the sky each day, and sets in the west. But we now know that assumption isn't true. It appears we are at the center of the universe, but we now know that also isn't true. It appears tables and chairs are made of solid stuff, but we have learned that seemingly solid objects are made of atoms that are 99.9999999999999% empty space. They're not solid at all. They're made of energy. What seems apparent isn't necessarily true.

We have been taught from childhood that our Minds are in our brains. Our language is full of references to the Mind's location in the brain and in the head: "I can't get the thought out of my brain," "I wracked my brain to figure it out." My brain doesn't work before 8 a.m." "He's all brawn and no brains." "I need to pick your brain." "I need to get my brain in gear." "She's the brains of the operation."

The location of thinking is assumed to be in the head: "He has a head for business." "I'm trying to get my head together." "You should have your head examined," "She's not right in the head." "They play head games." "Off the top of my head."

For thinking, we use words such as "brainstorming," "brain power," "brainwashed," "brainy," "no brainer," "brain drain," and "brain trust."

However, advancements in humankind's knowledge have now provided the undeniable proof that the Mind is not in the brain. The notion that the Mind is produced by the brain and is housed in the brain is as archaic as believing we are at the center of the universe. When the brain dies, we continue on with our lives.

The explanations that follow contain the evidence.

Aren't We Just Brains Talking to Each Other?

Answer: We know intuitively that we are not sacks of skin containing fats and proteins that somehow communicate with each other. We communicate with a living person who is a Mind with qualities and characteristics quite different from the body. We aren't just brains talking to each other.

Who am I talking to when I speak to you? It's certainly not your brain. That's just three pounds of fat and protein made of 85% water squeezed into the dark enclosure of your skull. Around 50,000 to 100,000 brain cells die each day, so if some of them had today's messages, no wonder you keep losing track of what your spouse tells you.

You are not your body. Your body changes constantly. The body you had at age ten when you could run like a rabbit is a different body from the one you have at age seventy when you shuffle like a turtle, and the molecules in it have all been replaced sixty times. Last year's body is different from this year's body. The body is just flesh and bone, made of the same atoms as a bowl of warm Irish stew. That's not you.

So when you talk to me, you'll insist you're not talking to any part of my body, or even the tofu-like mush inside my skull. You're talking to *me*. You know implicitly that you and I are greater than the skin and the brain. We are the Mind that is apart from flesh and bones.

Has Science Proved Our Minds Are in Our Brains?

Answer: No. Materialist scientists have no explanation for how the brain could produce a Mind, where the Mind is in the brain, or how memories are stored.

We'll start by correcting a common misconception. You most likely believe that your Mind is in the three pounds of fat and protein compressed inside your skull. That's what you were taught in school.

But the fact is that neuroscience can't explain how people have a conscious experience, where the Mind is, what memories are, or where memories are stored. That's pretty remarkable considering that the brain has been carefully mapped using CT, MRI, PET, and EEGs to find out which parts of the brain are active when a person is performing activities. In spite of all the brain mapping that's been done, they can't locate the Mind and they can't find memories.

Many neuroscientists are also saying that even if someone could locate a Mind and memories in the brain, that still wouldn't explain who has the conscious thought. Yes, there's a thought, but a thought requires someone who is thinking. Who is thinking? The brain shows activity when there's a thought, but who caused the brain to show activity? How does a human being have a conscious experience?

That's known as the "problem of consciousness" or the "hard problem," and all neuroscientists acknowledge it. They can't find a Mind or memories in the brain and they don't know how the brain creates the Mind. Here is what neuroscientists say about the brain and consciousness.

A university pathology researcher and professor: "All these experiments and descriptions of brain activation processes do not explain how neural activity is the cause for consciousness."[12]

A former editor in chief of a renowned science journal writing in *Scientific American*: "Nobody understands how decisions are made or how imagination is set free. What consciousness consists of, or how it should be defined, is equally puzzling. "[13]

An MD and consciousness researcher: "We don't know how the brain produces consciousness. "[14]

A professor of neurobiology: "Despite the awesome achievements of 20th-century neuroscience in increasing our knowledge about the workings of the human brain, little progress has been made in the scientific understanding of mental phenomena. "[15]

A director of a center for consciousness studies writing in *Scientific American*: "Consciousness, the subjective experience of an inner self, could be a phenomenon forever beyond the reach of neuroscience. Even a detailed knowledge of the brain's workings and the neural correlates of consciousness may fail to explain how or why human beings have self-aware minds. "[16]

Science doesn't know how the Mind is produced, where it's located, or how and where it stores life memories, even though the brain has been carefully studied and mapped. That has led to science's starting to look elsewhere for the Mind and memories.

Do Any Scientists Suggest That Our Minds Are Not in Our Brains?

Answer: A growing body of scientists who have carefully studied and mapped the brain have come to the conclusion that the Mind is not produced by, functioning in, or dependent on the brain.

Because scientists can't find the Mind or memories in the brain, many are beginning to suggest that the Mind isn't in the brain at all. A sampling of their statements follows.

> A physician who has studied near-death experiences: "The brain itself is made up of cells, like all the body's organs, and is not really capable of producing the subjective phenomenon of thought that people have."[17]

> A professor of engineering and applied science: "The brain is merely a transmitter and receiver of information, but not the main place for storage or processing of information (i.e., memories)."[18]

> A Freudian psychoanalyst, MD, and professor of psychiatry: "I don't think you can locate the source of consciousness. I am quite sure it is not in the brain—not inside of the skull."[19]

> One of the foremost brain researchers today: "The mind is a separate entity from the brain, and . . . mental processes cannot be reduced to neurochemical brain processes, but on the contrary direct them. . . . a mind may conceivably exist without a brain."[20]

> An educational psychologist renowned for his studies of the effect of heredity on intelligence: "The brain is not an organ that generates consciousness, but rather an instrument evolved to transmit and limit the processes of consciousness and of conscious attention so as to restrict them to those aspects of the material environment which at any moment are crucial for the terrestrial success of the individual."[21]

> A neuroscientist, physician, and brain surgeon: "The mind makes its impact on the brain but isn't in the brain."[22]

> Three authors, a professor of quantum computing and neural networks, a board-certified physician, and a quantum physicist and cosmologist, writing in the journal *Cosmology*: "Consciousness creates reality and makes it knowable . . . your consciousness is using the brain as a processing device, moving

the molecules where they are needed in order to create the sight, sound, touch, taste, and smell of the world."[23]

Neuroscientists can't tell us how we have a conscious experience, where the Mind is, or where memories are stored. Some scientists have come to the conclusion that the Mind and memories aren't in the brain at all.

That's why we know we're not speaking to the body when we speak to one another, and why we know the Mind is greater than and aside from the body.

Don't We Need the Brain to Store Memories?

Answer: No. The three to five pounds of fat and protein that is our brain does not have the capacity or ability to store a lifetime of memories.

An American computer science expert and a brain researcher working independently of one another came to the same conclusion: it is impossible for the brain to store everything you think and experience in your life. Simply watching an hour of television would already be too much for our brains.[24]

Not only does the brain not have the capacity to hold the memories, but millions of brain cells die and are replaced every second of our lives. For the memories to remain over 80 or 90 years, the brain cells would have to remain the same ones that were there when the memories were created, but that doesn't happen since they're replaced by new brain cells regularly.

We aren't using the brain to store memories.

Is There Any Proof That Our Minds Can Function without Our Brains?

Answer: We have abundant proof that our Minds function perfectly well with no reliance on or connection to the brain or the body.

We have a brain experience and a body experience, but both are only experiences in our Minds. The brain reacts somewhat in sync with our Mind, but that is only because in our Earth School story we need a location where we can assume the Mind is housed, just as we need the sun as an explanation for light and warmth, and food and water to explain how the body experience is sustained.

The Mind is not in the brain, produced by the brain, or dependent in any way on the brain. Some of the most convincing evidence is in the explanations that follow.

Terminal Lucidity Shows the Mind Is Not in the Brain

One indication that the Mind is independent of the brain is "terminal lucidity." In terminal lucidity, patients with severe psychiatric or neurological disorders who have not been lucid, perhaps for months, suddenly regain their normal conscious self just before their passing and have lucid conversations with loved ones. Their moods are elevated and they speak with vigor. In many cases the brain has deteriorated so much that such an event would be impossible if the person relied on the brain to think and communicate.

In one study in the U.K., 70 percent of nurses had observed patients with dementia and confusion become completely lucid in the hours before death.[25] In another, terminal lucidity occurred within a week of the person's passing, with 43 percent occurring on the final day of life. In an article in *The Journal of Nervous and Mental Disorders*, Greyson and Nahm describe 83 cases in which patients had brain abscesses, tumors, strokes, meningitis, Alzheimer's disease, dementia, schizophrenia, and mood disorders, all of which would preclude normal, lucid mental functioning. In spite of their conditions, the 83 patients experienced a brief, complete, lucid recovery of consciousness just before their passing.[26]

In one example, a patient had lung cancer that had spread to his brain. X-rays showed that the metastasized tumors had destroyed virtually all his brain tissue and replaced it with cancer cells. Nevertheless, one evening he woke up and said goodbye to his assembled loved ones with perfectly fluid, lucid speech, talking to them, patting them, and smiling for about five minutes. Then he went unconscious again and passed within an hour.[27]

In another case, a man had a tumor that had formed in his speech center. Over time he became bedridden, blind in one eye, incontinent, and increasingly incoherent in his speech and bizarre in his behavior. He was unable to make sense of his surroundings. When his family touched him, he slapped at their hands as though slapping at an insect. He stopped sleeping and talked deliriously through the night. After continued deterioration for several weeks, one night he suddenly appeared calm and started speaking coherently. That night he slept peacefully. The next morning he remained coherent and for the first time talked with his wife about his imminent death. Later that day he became immobile, lost his ability to communicate, and two weeks later passed away.[28]

Individuals are given the ability to bid goodbye to loved ones with perfect lucidity, even when their brains are damaged and not functioning. The reason is that their Minds are not in their brains.

Missing Large Parts of the Brain Doesn't Affect the Mind

Many people who undergo a hemispherectomy, which removes half their brain, have Minds that continue to function normally, indicating that the Mind must function outside the brain. Furthermore, after surgery patients retain their personalities and memories.[29] A study of children who undergo hemispherectomy found they often perform even better in their school work.[30]

Another phenomenon shows that a person functions normally without the use of the brain. Many instances have been recorded in which a normally functioning person was found as an adult to have virtually no brain. The brain wasn't necessary for normal functioning or memory. In one case, scans of a 44-year-old man's brain showed that a huge fluid-filled chamber called a ventricle took up most of the room in his skull, leaving little more than a thin sheet of actual brain tissue. Nevertheless, he was a married father of two children and worked as a civil servant.[31]

Among the patients with the most severe form of hydrocephalus, where 95 percent of the cranium is filled with cerebrospinal fluid, many are severely disabled, but half of them have IQs over 100.[32] One student at a university had an IQ of 126, gained a first-class honors degree in mathematics, and was socially completely normal. But he had virtually no brain. A brain scan showed he had hydrocephalus that left him with a thin layer of brain tissue with none of the important areas for speech, reasoning, judgment, memory, sight, hearing, or any other normal function.[33] To view a video of a description of the student, go to www.earthschoolanswers.com/roger/.

Another student with severe hydrocephalus graduated, passing every examination she took, had above-average intelligence, and was the only girl in the school to receive a graduate certificate in chemistry and only one of two girls to receive one in biology. The portions of her brain responsible for motor control, hearing, sight, registering sensations (hot, cold, touch), speech, understanding speech, logical thought, and rational judgment were completely missing. Yet she functioned at a higher-than-normal level in school and at work.

To view a video of an interview with her, go to www.earthschoolanswers.com/sharon/.

The fact that people function at a normal level or above with half their brains removed or with virtually no brain tissue indicates that the Mind isn't in the brain.

People Experience Sight, Hearing, Smell, Taste, and Touch Without Using the Brain

If we are outside of the body, you'd think we could learn some things about the world without using the body. In other words, if someone could prove that we can have a sight experience without using our eyes, that would mean the eyes, retina, optic nerve, and optical cortex in our brains aren't necessary for us to be able to have sight experiences.

But having sight experiences without using the eyes is very common today. Thousands of people are able to have sight experiences without using their eyes through a very common ability called "remote viewing." Remote viewers sit quietly with their eyes closed and focus on something hundreds or thousands of miles away. The person is able to have sound experiences, smell experiences, touch experiences, experiences of movement, and the emotions involved while the thing being experienced is far removed from the body.

For several decades at the end of the twentieth century, the CIA had a remote viewing program named Operation Stargate that attempted to use remote viewers to spy on the Russians. The program had remarkable results. The remote viewer spies were able to sketch areas of Russian military construction bases.

As a result, the government commissioned studies to be sure the remote viewers were legitimate—that they were able to have sensory experiences without the body or brain involved. Conducting these studies were Stanford Research Institute (SRI),[34] Science Applications International Corporation (SAIC),[35] and Princeton Engineering Anomalies Research (PEAR).[36] Other studies were performed by two highly regarded physicists,[37] a parapsychologist,[38] and a Nobel Prize-winning physicist.[39] All the studies concluded that people are able to sit quietly; focus on an object, scene, or picture that can be thousands of miles away; and accurately describe what the target is.

You can try remote viewing by taking the online test at www.greaterreality.com/rv/instruct.htm. Your Mind is not in your brain. Your brain is in your Mind.

The Mind in a Brain Would Have to Create Electricity to Make the Brain and Body Work, but It Has No Mechanism to Do So

If there were an objective world of matter and energy with bodies that must receive signals from the Mind outside of the body to access memories and perform other mental functions, the Mind would have to create electricity to generate the activities. The Mind, which is non-physical, couldn't create physical electricity to make the brain recreate a memory image. For the image to be recalled, the brain would have to generate electricity, causing millions of neurons to fire in exactly the same way they were active in the brain when photons coming to the brain through the eye created the image in the first place. But the brain has no ability to create the electricity.[40]

A Mind Influencing the Brain Would Violate the Law of Conservation of Matter and Energy

An approach to reality called the dualist approach suggests that Mind is separate from matter and influences our brains and the world of matter that is outside of us. But quantum physicist Amit Goswami explains that Mind apart from matter cannot influence matter because that would add energy from outside the system. The first law of thermodynamics, the Law of the Conservation of Energy, states that the amount of energy in the system will always be the same. If immaterial consciousness influenced matter, the action would add energy, which is not possible.[41]

The Mind could not be outside of the brain linking to the brain that contains the thinking, feeling, and sensing centers. That would violate the Law of the Conservation of Energy. The sensory experiences come with no contact with a physical brain.

Biophysicists Can Detect No Electrical Activity in Neurons Going from the Sense Organs to the Brain

Attempts to measure electricity along the sensory neurons when a person is apparently sensing something have failed to find traces of it. The laws of thermodynamics dictate that electrical impulses must produce heat. Yet attempts to detect the heat from electricity when impulses are traveling along nerves to produce sensory experiences have found no heat, indicating that no electricity is traveling over the neural fibers connecting sensory organs to the brain.[42] The researchers have no explanation for how the brain could be having sensory experiences. The reason is that the brain is not having the experiences. The Mind is having the experiences. The brain is just part of the scenery of the realm we are living in, so it lights up when the Mind is having an experience but is not necessary for the Mind to have the experiences.

A Unified Visual Image in Our Mind Can't Be Accounted for Using Brain Neurons

Studies of the brain fail to show how the light waves entering the eye can come together in the brain to form a complete image. The materialist states that when we have vision experiences, light enters the eye and turns into nerve impulses in the retina that travel along the optic nerve to the brain. When they arrive at the brain, they are fragmented and sent to different areas of the brain. Science can find no location in the brain that is able to bring the visual experience together into one sight experience. The author of one study wrote that there was only one explanation: there must be a conscious Mind outside the brain that influences it and uses it to make patterns.[43]

People Rendered Temporarily Blind Are Able to Locate Things on a Computer Screen

Blindsight is the ability to have sight experiences without use of the eyes. In studies when people were made blind temporarily, they were still able to locate things on a computer screen. The sensory organs and brain are not necessary to have the experience of sight.[44]

Blind People Perform Actions and Describe Colors That Show They Are Having the Experience of Sight

David Linden, professor of neuroscience at Johns Hopkins University, found that if the visual cortex is damaged, people assert that they cannot see anything, but when asked to pick up an object in an unknown location within reach, many can do so on the first try. They also can judge an emotional expression on a face, especially anger, more often than chance would predict they could.[45]

Research has also shown that patients with lesions in their primary visual cortex, rendering them blind, are able to perceive colors and motion.[46]

The reason people who have no functioning vision centers in the brain can still show signs of sight experiences is that the Mind is not in the brain. The Mind has experiences of sight without using the brain.

The sight experiences then register in the brain as part of the story in Earth School.

"Echolocation" Experiments Show Blind People Can Have Sight Experiences without Using Eyes or the Brain

Another phenomenon called "echolocation" also shows that blind people can have visual experiences of objects in their environment even when they can't use their optical organs. In echolocation, the blind person makes sounds by tapping, clicking, or speaking, and while doing so, is able to walk or even ride a bicycle through an environment filled with obstacles. The assumption has been that the blind person hears the echoes of the sounds reflected back from objects in the environment and can interpret the sounds to identify the objects. But that is not possible.

A boy who had lost his sight to cancer as a toddler had two artificial eyes made of plastic. But he walked without a cane or seeing-eye dog, played video games, and identified objects he passed by name: "That's a fire hydrant" or "That's a trash can." In a pillow fight, he was able to throw a pillow to hit a target person even when the person was moving and silent.[47] Making clicking sounds could not result in the level of visual ability the boy showed. He was receiving the visual experiences from his Mind outside of the brain. You can watch a video about the boy at www.earthschoolanswers.com/ben/.

A second blind person who believes he is using echolocation had lost his sight when his optic nerves deteriorated as a child. He now is completely blind but is able to identify objects in his surroundings with an accuracy far beyond the capability of using clicks in a sonar-like fashion. He can ride a bike while avoiding obstacles, distinguish a bush from a tree, and tell a footpath's direction. The way he describes it, he is actually imaging the world around him.[48] A neuroscientist has determined that he can tell if an object is moved only a few inches, something he could not do using echolocation.[49]

You can see a video about the man's ability at www.earthschoolanswers.com/brian/.

Scientists studying echolocation have found that the visual cortex in the Minds of the blind people becomes active, even though no images reach it from the optic nerve. The brain lights up in response to what the Mind is seeing, but the sight does not originate in sensory organs or the brain.

Blind People, Whose Brains Cannot Process Sight Images, Are Able to See During Near-Death and Out-of-Body Experiences

Blind people, including those blind from birth, have clear sight experiences during near-death experiences (NDEs) and out-of-the-body experiences (OBEs), suggesting that their Minds must be independent of their bodies, which are unable see. Psychologists studying the responses of blind people during NDEs discovered that 80 percent of the blind people in the study reported visual experiences correctly, some in detail. For example, they correctly reported actual colors and their surroundings.[50]

In one example provided by Dr. Larry Dossey, former chief of staff of Medical City Dallas Hospital, a blind woman was able to see clearly during her NDE. She lay comatose during her cardiac arrest, but after she was revived she described accurately the conversation of the surgeons and nurses, the operating room layout, the scribbles on the surgery schedule board in the hall outside, the color of the sheets covering the operating table, the hairstyle of the head scrub nurse, the names of the surgeons in the doctors' lounge down the corridor who were waiting for her case to be concluded, and even the unmatched socks her anesthesiologist was wearing.

What made Sarah's vision even more remarkable was that she had been blind since birth. Her Mind was having experiences, including sight experiences, when her body was unable to see because she was both unconscious and blind since birth.[51]

Her sight when the brain was not conscious and her brain did not have the capability of sight demonstrates that her Mind was not in her brain.

Other Near-Death Experiencers See, Hear, and Remember When the Brain Is Not Functioning

During NDEs, many people see and hear what is going on as physicians and nurses work frantically to revive them and they are unconscious. They recount statements made by those in the room, describe people and instruments, and even see and hear what is going on in other rooms of the same building. They then remember all the details and recount them to the astonishment of physicians, nurses, and family members.

During the NDE, no sensory experiences and no memory production would be possible if the Mind were located in the brain. During these times, people whose brain activity is being monitored show absolutely no life in the brain. When someone faints, the person falls and doesn't know what happened because the brain isn't working. The memory systems are especially sensitive to unconsciousness. People remember nothing when they are revived from fainting. Yet in an NDE people have clear, lucid experiences they remember in detail. Science cannot explain it using the materialistic paradigm.[52]

Michael Sabom, MD, a cardiologist in Atlanta, Georgia, studied NDEs to see whether people really were seeing and hearing while their brains were completely non-functioning. He asked patients who had NDEs to describe in as much detail as they could what went on during their resuscitations. To see whether someone could simply guess the details of what was happening in the trauma scene or recall the procedure from some chance reading about it in the past, he asked other patients who had cardiac arrest but no NDE to describe the events involving their resuscitation during their cardiac arrests.

Virtually all of the patients who said they did not have an NDE made at least one major error in their account. All of the patients who had near-death OBEs described the resuscitation successfully in specific facts or in the general procedure. Six of those who had NDEs accurately described in great detail specific facts they could not have learned while lying unconscious that were peculiar to the situation, not simply general information about resuscitation.[53]

These Individual Near-Death Experiences Show the Mind Has Sight Experiences Although the Brain Is Not Involved

A number of verified NDEs on record provide unusually convincing evidence that the brain is not involved in the NDE.

A woman having an NDE felt herself floating upward, out of the hospital. As she rose she saw, on a third-story window ledge of the hospital, "a man's dark blue tennis shoe, well-worn, scuffed on the left side where the little toe would go. The shoelace was caught under the heel." Health care workers investigated and found the tennis shoe precisely where the woman had described it. The shoe was dark blue, had a well-worn scuff on the left side where the little toe would go, and had a shoelace caught under the heel.[54]

In another, similar incident, after an unconscious patient was revived she described floating above the hospital, where she saw a red tennis shoe on the roof. A janitor investigated and found a red tennis shoe, just as the patient described.[55]

While having an NDE outside his body during triple by-pass surgery, a man clearly saw his surgeon flapping his arms with his hands in his armpits. When the patient came back to his body after surgery, he described what he had seen while anesthetized and his eyes were closed. His surgeon confirmed that he was keeping his hands sterile by holding his arms at his chest and gesturing with his elbows to instruct staff about preparation for the operation.[56]

In another documented case, a nurse had removed the dentures of an unconscious heart-attack victim and put them into the drawer of the table in the operating room called a "crash cart." A week after the incident, as the nurse was distributing medications, she came to the heart-attack victim's room and he exclaimed excitedly, "'Oh, that nurse knows where my dentures are. . . . Yes, you were there when I was brought into hospital and you took my dentures out of my mouth and put them onto that cart; it had all these bottles on it and there was this sliding drawer underneath and there you put my teeth."[57] The man was also able to describe correctly details about the small room in which he had been resuscitated and the appearance of those present. His brain was not functioning, but his Mind outside of the brain had clear sensory functions.

People Commonly Describe the Mind Functioning Away from the Body During Out-of-Body Experiences

In out-of-body experiences (OBEs), people describe being conscious outside of their bodies and having normal sensory experiences such as traveling to locations, listening to conversations, and seeing distant people while the body is motionless.

In May 1980, Dr. Glen Gabbard of the Menninger Foundation, Dr. Stewart Twemlow of the Topeka VA Medical Center, and Dr. Fowler Jones of the University of Kansas Medical Center presented the findings of studies of OBEs to the American Psychiatric Association's annual meeting in San Francisco. They concluded that experiencers can sometimes be detected at distant locations during their OBE travels using animal, human, and sometimes physical detectors at the location the OBE experiencer has travelled to. Some OBE experiencers make surprisingly correct observations at distant locations while traveling out of the body.[58]

In one instance reported by Dr. Melvin Morse, associate professor of pediatrics at the University of Washington, a woman was undergoing a heart transplant when, at exactly 2:15 a.m., her new heart stopped beating. It took the frantic transplant team three hours to revive her. At that moment her son-in-law was awakened to see his mother-in-law at the foot of his bed. She told him not to worry, that she was going to be alright. She asked him to tell her daughter (his wife). He wrote down the message and the time of day and then fell asleep. Later at the hospital, the woman regained consciousness. Her first words were "Did you get the message?" She was able to confirm that she left her body during her NDE and was able to travel to her son-in-law to communicate the message to him.[59]

In a study of a woman who was able to have an OBE at will, Charles Tart, MD, instructor in psychiatry at the School of Medicine of the University of Virginia and professor of psychology at the University of California at Davis, set up a test to see whether she could have an

OBE while asleep in which she floated out of her body and could read five numbers on a paper placed high enough in a room that she would be unable to see the paper by physically going to the location and trying to look at it. He set up a bed and electroencephalograph (EEG) to measure her brain activity while she was asleep. Electrodes were placed on her head with very little slack between the electrodes and the equipment. She could turn over in bed but not raise her head or move from the bed. If she had removed the electrodes to stand up, that would have been recorded on the equipment, so she was effectively confined to the bed.

On the evening of the study, he placed a small piece of paper with five randomly selected numbers on it, facing upward, on a shelf about 5.5 feet high on the wall of the experiment room. The woman was confined to the bed because of the short cables to the EEG. She was to sleep that evening and, if she awoke after having had an OBE, she was to notify Tart and tell him what she saw.

At 6:04 the next morning she awoke and called out to the researcher that the target number was 25132. That was, in fact, the number written on the small piece of paper.[60]

In another study of OBEs, Karlis Osis and Boneita Perskari studied whether an adept experiencer was able to travel to a distant location he knew nothing about and describe the environment. The traveler did not know that a psychic was at the location, and the psychic was not told when the traveler would "arrive." After the OBE, the traveler was able to describe the unique environment of the location. The psychic said she sensed the traveler at the location at the time he said he was there, and she described his shirt with rolled-up sleeves and corduroy pants. He was in fact wearing a shirt with rolled-up sleeves and corduroy pants as he lay asleep having his OBE experience, and the time recorded by the psychic was the time when the OBE occurred.[61]

In all of these instances, people's Minds were functioning perfectly away from their body and brain.

Is There Any Evidence We Can Know Information without Using a Brain?

Answer: There is a large amount of evidence from studies and from common knowledge that people can know information not accessible to their brains or bodies. The evidence is presented in the pages that follow.

People Know Information without Having Contact with the Source of the Information

A large number of studies have demonstrated that people can know information without having contact with what they have learned about. From the 1880s to the 1940s, there were 142 published articles describing 3.6 million individual trials with 4,600 people attempting to identify the number and suit of a playing card face down in front of them. In addition, ESP tests performed on the radio added 70,000 participants to the database. The studies were performed at over two dozen universities around the world by hundreds of respected professors.[62] Participants were, on average, able to identify the cards at rates higher than chance. They knew information they could not have received unless their Minds were able to obtain it without using the body. The studies demonstrate that the Mind is able to acquire knowledge without using the body's sensory organs, so the brain is not involved.

Psychics Know Information Their Brains and Bodies Haven't Experienced or Sensed

Records of psychic investigations have shown that psychics know information they are not getting from their body's senses. They describe in great detail information about people's lives, dead and alive.

In one example, a psychic detective had been brought in on a case because two men had apparently drowned in a fast-moving stream, but their bodies could not be found. He said that in his Mind's eye he saw a red flower floating down the stream where the body of the larger of the two men would be found, but it was late winter, so that didn't seem possible. He sat before a map and pinpointed a pool of water where he said the larger man's body would be found.

The detectives went to the pool of water and found the larger man's body. They also found red flowers floating down the stream. With no knowledge of the psychic's words, friends of the deceased had dropped flowers as a memorial into the water where the man most likely fell in. The flowers had floated downstream to where the body was found.[63]

In another example a psychic was brought in on the case of a murdered police officer. He told detectives that it was a robbery gone bad, five individuals were involved, the murdered officer knew the killer through his drug-unit police work, he saw in his Mind's eye a basketball hoop near the body, and he felt the killer had the tip of his trigger finger missing. The police confirmed that the murder took place on a basketball court.

As a result of these statements, detectives pulled photos of suspects known to the drug unit the murdered officer had worked in, narrowing them down to 35 or 40 suspects. They asked the psychic if men in any of the photographs seemed to be among the murderers. He picked five of the photos and the detectives interrogated all five men. Three were eventually found guilty of the murder. The convicted shooter was missing the tip of his trigger finger.[64]

Psychic activity such as that reported in these documented cases happens commonly today. The psychics are using their Minds to learn information they could not know if their Minds had been confined to brains inside a skull.

People React to Pictures Seconds Before Seeing Them and Before a Computer Has Selected Them at Random

People's Minds know information before the sensed data are available to the brain. Dr. Dean Radin, senior scientist at the Institute of Noetic Sciences, performed carefully controlled studies in which people seated before a computer monitor were shown calm pictures (pastoral scenes and neutral household objects) and emotional pictures (erotic and violent scenes). The pictures were selected at random by a computer and shown in random order. Their skin conductance levels (SCL) were measured continually during the entire test. The skin conductance test is like a lie detector that shows whether the person feels stress. As we might expect, people showed stress at seeing the emotional pictures and calm when shown the calm pictures.

But remarkably, the tests consistently showed that some people reacted to the pictures with the appropriately matched calm or stress as early as six seconds before the pictures were shown, even though the computer hadn't selected them at random yet. The people weren't using sensory organs to learn about the pictures, and the information wasn't available to the brain because the events had not happened when the Mind knew what would happen.[65]

What this means is that the person's Mind must have already been having sight experiences and reacting to them before the information even existed in the physical realm for the eyes to see.

People Can Successfully Predict Targets to Be Shown a Few Seconds and Up to a Year before the Targets Are Shown

Other evidence demonstrates that the Mind knows things before a brain is involved. Dr. Charles Honorton, who was the director of the Division of Parapsychology and Psychophysics at Maimonides Medical Center in New York, examined all the tests performed from 1935 to 1987 to see whether people could predict a target about to be shown from several possible targets. He studied reports of 309 experiments in 113 articles published from 1935 to 1987, done by 62 different investigators. Combined, they totaled 2 million individual trials with over 50,000 subjects. The time intervals between the guesses and the random selections of targets ranged from milliseconds to a year. The results were that the subjects were able to predict which target would be selected more often than would occur by chance guessing, with the odds against it being by chance at ten trillion trillion to one.[66]

Other studies followed. They found that gamblers began reacting subconsciously shortly before they won or lost and people terrified of animals reacted moments before they were shown the creatures. The odds against all of these trials being wrong is millions to one.[67] The Mind outside of the body knows information before the information is available for any of the body's senses to receive it.

People Successfully Anticipate Someone's Call or Visit

This ability of the Mind to know things before the brain could even have access to the information is common in people's everyday lives. We've all had the experience of thinking of someone and a few minutes later that person calls or knocks on the door. It could be someone we haven't seen for days or weeks.

To find out whether that really is a premonition, Rupert Sheldrake, a British biologist, performed experiments in which he gave subjects a list of four people and had the subjects sit quietly beside the phone. They were then asked to select which of the four people they believed was about to call. Then one person among the four was selected at random by rolling a die, so no one would know who was going to call.

Sheldrake studied a number of people using this setup. We would expect that the subjects would guess correctly 25 percent of the time just by chance (one out of four). Sheldrake, however, had results of 45 percent correct, showing that people often did know before a person called who was going to call.[68]

That knowledge apparently was coming from a source outside of the person, another indication that the Mind is not confined to the brain.

People React to a Touch About to Happen before It Happens to the Body

Benjamin Libet, PhD, a neurobiologist at the University of California Medical Center, measured how quickly the brain registered stimulation, such as a touch on the arm, using electrodes to measure when the brain responded. The surprising result was that test subjects stated that they were aware of the sensation a few thousandths of a second following the stimulation, but the subjects' brains didn't register the touch until after that. In other words, it seems that the subjects' Minds knew about the stimulation before the brain did.[69]

People Prepare to Act Before the Deciding Part of the Brain Begins to Show Activity

A similar finding resulted from other studies by Dr. Libet. He conducted experiments in 1985 that showed the motor area of the brain prepares to act a measurable length of time before a person uses the part of the brain that decides to act. He asked test subjects to decide to lift either the right finger or the whole right hand. The subjects were connected to brain-wave-measuring machines (EEGs) to see when the decision-making part of the brain was working and when the motor or muscle part of the brain was working. The times on the EEG recordings were carefully monitored. The results were that the part of the brain that governs movement was getting ready to raise the finger or hand before the decision was even made in the brain, on average by a half second.[70] The Mind had made the decision before it told the brain.

Studies Showed People Are Able to Predict the Future

A meta-analysis of precognition experiments conducted at Stanford Research Institute from 1973 to 1988 was conducted by Edwin May, PhD, a researcher in low-energy, experimental nuclear physics, and his colleagues. The analysis was based on 154 experiments with more than 26,000 separate trials conducted over 16 years. They concluded that the studies showed that people were able to predict the future, with the statistical results of this analysis showing odds against chance of more than a billion billion to one.[71]

These studies and the conclusions of researchers who have reviewed them indicate that the Mind must obtain information from some source outside the body and brain that it knows and remembers.

Why Do We Know the Mind Is Not in the Brain?

Answer: The evidence from a broad range of disciplines demonstrates that the Mind is not produced by the brain, housed in the brain, or dependent upon the brain.

Neuroscientists can't locate your Mind or your memories in the brain, so many are now suggesting that the Mind is not in the brain. The data seem to support that because the brain doesn't have the capacity to hold all the memories, and missing large parts of the brain doesn't affect memory or thinking. At the same time many people, including me and units of the CIA, can see objects and scenes thousands of miles away without using our eyes. Blind people see clearly in near-death experiences and have the remarkable ability to locate objects and even ride bicycles without using physical eyes. People having near-death experiences when the brain is completely nonfunctioning, as shown on brain-monitoring equipment, can see, hear, and know more clearly than when they are fully awake, and the experiences are stored in memory while the brain shows no functioning. Out-of-body experiences demonstrate that people lying in bed at one location can see scenes far away without using their closed eyes. People's Minds react to pictures before a computer has even chosen them, showing the brain couldn't be involved, and we commonly know someone is going to call or visit with no sensory organs sending information to the brain to tell us.

The Mind has sensory experiences and learns information without using the body or brain.

4

Is There Proof I Will Be Alive after My Body Dies?

Answer: Yes. There is a great body of research, testimonies by everyday people, reports by highly educated professionals, studies of mediums, and other evidence showing that we survive the death of the body. Not believing the proof requires that a person actively ignore or deny the existence of verified evidence.

You know you are your Mind that goes through the day having experiences. The physical world is the scenery for the plays you create, given to us by Our Universal Intelligence. But you are not the scenery. Your Mind isn't in a brain. No neuroscientist can locate a Mind in a brain; the brain couldn't hold all of your life memories, stimulating the brain doesn't result in a single Mind function; and people have sensory experiences without using the brain at all. You aren't in a brain. Your Mind is outside of the brain.

That leads to a remarkable conclusion. When the body stops functioning, your Mind must still be there. Your Mind simply continues as it was when it was using the body, just as when you take off your overcoat and leave it in the closet, you walk into the living room and hug your loved ones without a thought for where your coat is. We know that's true from all the evidence we've accumulated over the last two centuries. The Mind is your real self, and your Mind continues living after the body dies.

You are an eternal being having physical experiences because you have attuned to Earth School with the rest of us attuned to the same experiences.

Do Many People Believe Life Continues after the Body Dies?

Answer: Yes. The evidence is so compelling and is becoming so widely known that growing numbers of people today know the reality that we transition to the next stage of life and do not die.

The widespread accessibility to information today has resulted in a sharing of knowledge unprecedented in humankind's history. As people compare their experiences, they are realizing that what they individually always felt to be true is shared by most other people. In a 1970 poll, 77 percent of Americans said they knew the reality of the life after this life. But in a 2000 poll, 82 percent of Americans said they knew its reality. In 1970 19 percent of Jews said they knew the life after this life is real. But 56 percent said they were convinced of it in 1998.[72] Humankind is growing out of the superstitions of both religion and science about the life after this life by learning new perspectives and truths as people compare what they know to be true.

Isn't It Rare for People to Communicate with Loved Ones in the Life after This Life?

Answer: No. Communication with people living in the life after this life is very common.

A broad range of studies of communication with people living in the life after this life have shown that such communication is common. In one study, 50% of widowers reported visions of departed spouses while in the waking state.[73] In another study, 70% to 80% of widows and widowers had such visions.[74] A study of adults in Los Angeles found that 55% of blacks, 54% of Mexican-Americans, 38% of Anglo-Americans, and 29% of Japanese-Americans reported afterlife communications with loved ones.[75]

The number of people who have had such experiences with loved ones in the life after this life is increasing, in part because of the openness to the phenomenon today. Communication with loved ones now living in the life after this life is a common, everyday occurrence. More people are also having the experiences because we are learning new, successful ways of communicating and more people are learning they have the ability to help people have afterlife communication.

Do the People Living in the Life after This Life Ever Tell People Things that Prove It's Them?

Answer: Yes. The people living in the life after this life are anxious to prove to loved ones that they are alive and well, so they willingly provide evidence that it is they who are speaking. Mediums also are anxious to give people confidence and verification, so they ask for and receive validations.

It is common for people communicating with someone living in the life after this life to receive messages about things they could not have known if the messages had not come from the person living in the next life.

In one example, a patient of Dr. Allan Botkin, formerly a psychotherapist with a large Chicago area VA hospital, with whom I co-authored the book, *Induced After-Death Communication: A New Therapy for Grief and Trauma,*[76] told Dr. Botkin that he had had a dream about his ex-wife in which she wanted to tell him something of great concern to her. She said he needed to start playing a more important role in rearing their children and even offered very specific suggestions about each child. He said his experience was much clearer than a dream. The next morning he learned that his ex-wife had been killed in a car accident during the night. She later appeared to him five times in dreams, each time offering further advice about their children.[77]

In another case, someone's life was saved by the appearance of an apparition. One evening in her apartment building a woman saw a young man in the hallway. He did not speak but led her downstairs into the apartment of a young widow she barely knew. She found the young woman collapsed on a bed after slashing her wrists. After she recovered, the young woman showed the woman a photograph of her late husband. The woman recognized it immediately as the young man who had led her downstairs and into the apartment.[78]

In both accounts, a person in the life after this life had contact with someone living on earth in ways that demonstrated they had survived bodily death.

Do Physicians Working with the Dying Believe There Is a Life after This Life?

Answer: Yes. The studies conducted to discover physicians' convictions about the life after this life demonstrate that most are convinced of its reality.

Physicians work with dying patients regularly. We would expect them to know something about death and the life after this life from their experiences. In fact, a 2005 survey of physicians found that 76 percent believe in God and 59 percent believe in some sort of life after this life.[79] Those beliefs are in the face of strong sanctions within the scientific community against speaking of belief in God or the life after this life, a result of the materialistic ignorance from the seventeenth through twentieth centuries that is now falling away.

Do Any Scientists Believe the Reality of the Life after This Life When They Study the Evidence?

Answer: Some people think scientists don't believe in an afterlife. That is not true. A great number of hard-nosed, skeptical scientists who have taken the time to study the life after this life and mediums seriously have become convinced of the reality of the survival of consciousness and the life after this life from their encounters, often after they began their research with the goal of debunking mediums.

A list of some of the scientists follows. There are, of course, many other scientists who have come to the same conclusion — this is just a small sampling of some of the most prominent. Most came to the study of mediums and the life after this life as skeptics. That makes the testimonies of their conclusions after extensive research especially credible.

Ron D. Pearson – British scientist, university lecturer, and engineer in thermodynamics and fluid mechanics. Dr. Pearson wrote *Survival Physics*, in which he asserts that "survival of death is a natural fact of physics and efforts to discredit evidence of survival after death are in error."[80]

Jan Vandersande – Physicist, holder of three patents on thermoelectric materials, consultant to NASA, manager at the Jet Propulsion Laboratory, professor at Cornell University, and president and CEO of Mountain Province Diamonds. After investigating materializations of those appearing from the life after this life for over eight years, he became convinced that the materializations are people from the life after this life and that the life after this life is a reality.[81]

Thomas Alva Edison – Inventor of the phonograph and electric light bulb. Edison was a Spiritualist and experimented with mechanical means of contacting the dead.[82]

Sir Joseph John Thompson – Discoverer of the electron, professor of experimental physics at Cambridge, and winner of the 1906

Nobel Prize in physics. Thompson asserted that people continue to live after the body dies.[83]

Abdus Salam – Nobel Laureate and director of the International Centre for Theoretical Physics. Salam studied the results of investigations of the evidence of the life after this life, concluding the life after this life is a reality.[84]

Sam Nicholls – Researcher into subatomic phenomena. Nicholls believes that people in the life after this life are composed of slightly different atomic components and that they exist in and share the same space with people on the Earth plane.[85]

Augustus De Morgan – Considered one of the most brilliant mathematicians of the 19th Century. De Morgan wrote about his first-hand experiences with mediums and that he was satisfied that the physical mediumship phenomena he witnessed was real.[86]

Robert Hare – Emeritus professor of chemistry at the University of Pennsylvania and world-renowned inventor. Hare set out to prove that the messages from the dead were either hallucinations or unconscious muscular actions on the part of those present. After extensive, critical study, he concluded the communications with his parents, sister, brother, and dearest friends were real.[87]

James J. Mapes – A professor of chemistry and natural philosophy at the National Academy of Design in New York and later at the American Institute. Mapes investigated many mediums in an effort to debunk them. He changed his views and both his wife and daughter became mediums. He concluded his study by writing, that "spirits can and do communicate with mortals, and in all cases evince a desire to elevate and advance those they commune with."[88]

Allan Kardec – Professor of chemistry, physics, comparative anatomy, and astronomy. After thoroughly studying many mediums, Kardec concluded, "that communication could be received through speech, hearing, sight, touch, etc., and even through direct writing of the spirits themselves – that is to say without the help of the medium's hand or of the pencil."[89]

Alfred Russel Wallace – Co-originator with Charles Darwin of the natural selection theory of evolution, and a naturalist who provided Darwin with his parallel theory, including the "survival of the fittest," before Darwin went public with their two theories. Wallace was a hard-core materialist until he began investigating mediums. He soon became one of the greatest proponents of the life after this life.[90]

Sir William Crookes – Physicist and chemist who discovered the element thallium, pioneer in radioactivity, and inventor of the radiometer, the spinthariscope, and a high-vacuum tube that contributed to the discovery of the x-ray. Crookes set out to "drive the worthless residuum of spiritualism" into the "unknown limbo of magic and necromancy." However, after thorough investigations of mediums, he wrote that the phenomena in séances "point to the existence of another order of human life continuous with this and demonstrate the possibility in certain circumstances of communication between this world and the next."[91]

Sir William Barrett – Professor of physics at the Royal College of Science in Dublin for 37 years, discovering a silicon-iron alloy important to the development of the telephone and in the construction of transformers. Barrett was knighted in 1912 for his contributions to science. His study of the life after this life led him to conclude, "I am personally convinced that the evidence we have published decidedly demonstrates (1) the existence of a spiritual world, (2) survival after death, and (3) of occasional communication from those who have passed over."[92]

Sir Oliver Lodge – Professor of physics at University College in Liverpool, principal at the University of Birmingham, and pioneer in electricity, the radio, and the spark plug. Lodge was knighted in 1902 for his contributions to science. After studying extensively the séances of Leonora Piper and Gladys Osborne Leonard, he concluded, "People [in the life after this life] still continue to take an interest in what is going on, that they know far more about things on this earth than we do, and are able from time to time to communicate with us. . . . I do not say it is easy, but it is possible, and I have conversed with my friends just as I can converse with anyone in this audience now."[93]

Camille Flammarion – World-renowned astronomer, founder of the French Astronomical Society, known for his study of Mars, and pioneer in the use of balloons to study the stars. Flammarion investigated psychic phenomena, including mediumship, for more than

50 years and concluded, "I do not hesitate to affirm my conviction, based on personal examination of the subject, that any man who declares the phenomena to be impossible is one who speaks without knowing what he is talking about."[94]

Charles Richet – Professor of physiology at the University of Paris Medical School, world authority on nutrition in health and disease, and winner of the Nobel Prize in 1913 for his work on allergic reactions. While convinced of the reality of mediumship, Richet remained publicly agnostic toward the afterlife. According to Sir Oliver Lodge, his good friend, Richet accepted it before his death. He wrote, "It seems to me the facts are undeniable. I am convinced that I have been present at realities [medium sessions]."[95]

Robert Crookall – Lectured at Aberdeen University before joining the staff of the British Geological Survey and specializing in coal-forming plants. Crookall's research into the life after this life was so compelling to him that he resigned from his geology work in 1952 to devote the rest of his life to psychical research. He wrote, "There is no longer a 'deadlock' or 'stalemate' on the question of survival. On the contrary, survival is as well established as the theory of evolution."[96]

Raynor C. Johnson – Physicist; Oxford scholar with a doctorate from the University of London; lecturer in physics at King's College, University of London; and master of Queen's College at the University of Melbourne. Johnson studied survival in depth to judge whether it was true. He concluded that "if survival of death is not rigorously proven, it is nevertheless established as of that high order or probability which, for practical purposes, can be taken as the same thing."[97]

John Logie Baird – Inventor of the television and infra-red camera. Baird stated that he had contacted the deceased Thomas A. Edison through a medium. He confirmed the contact: "I have witnessed some very startling phenomena under circumstances which make trickery out of the question."[98]

George Meek – Scientist, inventor, designer, and manufacturer of devices for air conditioning and wastewater treatment. Meek referred to himself as a "natural skeptic" who felt that talk of a life after this life just didn't make sense. To study the concept he traveled the world interviewing top medical doctors, psychiatrists, physicists, biochemists, psychics, healers, parapsychologists, hypnotherapists, ministers, priests, and rabbis. He concluded that people are immortal and wrote his findings in his book *After We Die, What Then?*[99]

Archie Roy – Professor Emeritus of Astronomy at the University of Glasgow; Fellow of the Royal Society of Edinburgh, the Royal Astronomical Society, and the British Interplanetary Society; and head of the Advanced Scientific Institutes for NATO. After extensive study of psychic and medium activity, he wrote, "I am convinced now of the reality of such [psychic] phenomena.[100]

A. P. Hale – Physicist and electronics engineer. Hale conducted careful tests of electronic recordings of voices coming from the life after this life. He concluded, "In view of the tests carried out in a screened laboratory at my firm, I cannot explain what happened in normal physical terms."[101]

Sir Robert Mayer – Businessman and patron of music. After studying electronic recordings of voices coming from the life after this life, Mayer concluded, "If the experts are baffled, I consider this is a good enough reason for presenting the Voice Phenomena to the general public."[102]

Do Psychology Professionals Become Convinced of Life after This Life from Their Experiences?

Answer: Yes. Psychologists and psychotherapists have studied the reports of communicating with people in the life after this life using their knowledge of the workings of the human Mind. As a result of their thorough studies of mediums and their own experiences of patient after-death communication, they come to agree that the Mind survives the death of the body.

Dr. William James – One of America's foremost psychologists; wrote widely in psychology, philosophy, and religion while teaching at Harvard for 35 years; his *Principles of Psychology* (1890) became the seminal work in his field; also wrote the classic *Varieties of Religious Experience*. After investigating life after this life by sitting with medium

Leonora Piper, James concluded, "One who takes part in a good sitting has usually a far livelier sense, both of the reality and of the importance of the communication, than one who merely reads the records."[103]

Dr. Allan Botkin – Clinical psychologist who discovered induced after-death communication (IADC) in 1995, now used by hundreds of psychotherapists. From the book Botkin and I co-authored: "I cannot imagine that if the afterlife is a reality, IADCs, ADCs, and NDEs are hallucinatory aberrations produced by our brains that lead us into misunderstanding."[104]

Dr. Cesare Lombroso – Professor of psychology at the University of Turin, Inspector of Asylums for the Insane in Italy, and pioneering criminologist known worldwide for his book *The Criminal Man*.[105] He began investigating psychic phenomena in 1891 and as a result of his study concluded, "There can be no doubt that genuine psychical phenomena are produced by intelligences totally independent of the psychic and the parties present at the sittings."[106]

Dr. Bruce Greyson – Professor of psychiatry at the University of Connecticut, Chester F. Carlson Professor Emeritus of Psychiatry and Neurobehavioral Sciences at the University of Virginia, and near-death experience researcher for over 25 years. Greyson has written countless articles on the subject for the *Journal of Scientific Exploration, Journal of the American Medical Association, American Journal of Psychiatry*, and other leading science and medical publications. He concluded that "the survival hypothesis is the most parsimonious explanation for the growing database of near-death experiences."[107]

Dr. Julian Ochorowicz – Professor of psychology and philosophy at the University of Warsaw. Ochorowicz helped establish the Polish Psychological Institute in Warsaw and served as director for the International Institute of Psychology in Paris.[108]

Baron (Dr.) Albert Von Schrenck-Notzing – A forensic psychiatrist and member of the German aristocracy. Schrenck-Notzing collaborated with Richet, Lombroso, Lodge, and others in many investigations for over 30 years.[109]

Dr. Carl A. Wickland – Member of the Chicago Medical Society and American Association for the Advancement of Science, and director of the National Psychological Institute of Los Angeles, specializing in schizophrenia, paranoia, depression, addiction, manic-depression, criminal behavior, and phobias of all kinds. Wickland's direct experiences led him to conclude that spirits on the next planes of life communicate with and affect people on the Earth plane.[110]

Dr. Gardner Murphy – Hodgson Memorial Fund research grant recipient at Harvard, president of the American Society for Psychical Research for 20 years, assistant psychology professor at Columbia University, and chairman of the Psychology Department at City College of New York. After studying medium session records, Murphy wrote, "It is the autonomy, the purposiveness, the cogency, above all the individuality, of the [séance] sources of the messages, that cannot be by-passed. . . . The case looks like communication with the deceased."[111]

Dr. Gary Schwartz – PhD from Harvard University, professor of psychology and psychiatry at Yale University, and director of the Laboratory for Advances in Consciousness and Health at the University of Arizona. Schwartz conducted extensive research with mediums, detailed in his book *The Afterlife Experiments*.[112] He concluded, "I can no longer ignore the data [on research into the survival of consciousness] and dismiss the words [coming through mediums]. They are as real as the sun, the trees, and our television sets, which seem to pull pictures out of the air."[113]

Dr. Jon Klimo – Psychology professor for over 30 years, most recently at the American School of Professional Psychology, Argosy University. Klimo has done extensive research, writing, teaching, and presentations in psychology, parapsychology, consciousness studies, new paradigm thought, metaphysics, and the transpersonal domain. He concluded, "I personally choose to believe that we do meaningfully survive death and can communicate back through mediums and channels."[114]

Dr. David Fontana – Professor of transpersonal psychology in Great Britain, past president of the Society for Psychical Research, and Fellow of the British Psychological Society. Dr. Fontana has done extensive survival research and is the author of many books, including *Is There an Afterlife?*[115] He wrote, "If your answer [to questions of our existence] is that you are more than a biological accident whose ultimately meaningless life is bounded by the cradle and the grave, then I have to say I agree with you."[116]

Dr. Brendan Rooney – Director of the Institute of Psychology in Dublin. After investigating electronic voice recordings of the deceased speaking to the living, Rooney concluded, "I have apparently succeeded in reproducing the phenomena. Voices have appeared on a tape which did not come from any known source."[117]

Carl G. Jung – Eminent psychoanalyst, contemporary of Freud, and father of Jungian psychology. Jung wrote after his own NDE, "What happens after death is so unspeakably glorious, that our imagination and feelings do not suffice to form even an approximate conception of it."[118]

A Large Contingent of Well-Known Scientists – One hundred well-known scientists, all profoundly skeptical and some openly hostile, declared themselves, without exception, completely convinced after having worked under the direction of Dr. Schrenck-Notzing with his medium Willy Schneider.[119]

Do Professors of the Humanities Researching the Life after This Life Become Convinced of It?

Answer: Yes. Professors of the humanities are astute critics of the content of writing in a variety of contexts. After they study mediums, they agree that the reports of mediums' communication with people in the next life are valid.

The same conclusion the physicians and scientists willing to study the life after this life and mediums come to has been voiced by professors of the humanities. A small number of the many who changed their views after examining the evidence follows.

Frederic W. H. Myers (1843-1901) – English poet, critic, and essayist; fellow, classical lecturer, and school inspector at Trinity College, Cambridge; and co-founder of the Society for Psychical Research, London. After studying mediums and the life after this life, Myers concluded, "messages of the departing and the departed, have, to my Mind actually proved: a) In the first place, they prove survival pure and simple; the persistence of the spirit's life as a structural law of the universe; the inalienable heritage of each several soul."[120]

Dr. Richard Hodgson (1855-1905) –MA and LLD from the University of Melbourne, poetry and philosophy instructor at University Extension, and instructor of the philosophy of Herbert Spenser at Cambridge. Hodgson and William James decided to witness a number of séances to, as he wrote, "discover fraud and trickery." After hundreds of sittings with medium Leonora Piper over 18 years, he concluded, "The truth has been given to me in such a way as to remove from me the possibility of a doubt [of the continuance of life after death]."[121]

Dr. James H. Hyslop (1854-1920) –PhD from Johns Hopkins University; LLD from University of Wooster; philosophy teacher at Lake Forest University, Smith College, and Bucknell University; professor at Columbia University. Hyslop wrote three textbooks: *Elements of Logic* (1892), *Elements of Ethics* (1895), and *Problems of Philosophy* (1905). His research brought him to conclude, "Personally, I regard the fact of survival after death as scientifically proved."[122]

Dr. Hamlin Garland –Pulitzer Prize-winning author of 52 books. Garland was intimately involved with major literary, social, and artistic movements in American culture. His experiences in séances convinced him of the survival of consciousness.[123]

Maurice Maeterlinck –Nobel Laureate in literature; poet, author, and playwright; and psychic researcher. Based on his research he concluded that there is no "trickery" in afterlife communication in séances. The experiences are genuine.[124]

Dr. William R. Newbold – Professor of philosophy at the University of Pennsylvania, where he was a member of the advisory council of the American Society for Psychical Research. Newbold had numerous sittings with medium Leonora Piper. He concluded that the evidence in medium experiences of "the essential independence of the Mind and the body, of the existence of a supersensible world, and of the possibility of occasional communication between that world and this . . . [is] evidence that is worthy of consideration for all these points."[125]

Dr. C. J. Ducasse – Chairman of the Department of Philosophy at Brown University. A French-born American philosopher, Ducasse came to the United States as a teenager. He had many sittings with mediums and lectured extensively on psychical research. He concluded,

> The belief in life after death, which so many persons have found no particular difficulty in accepting as an article in religious faith, may well be capable of empirical proof. That the occurrence of paranormal phenomena does appear to have such implications is, I submit, sufficient reason to give them far more attention and study than they have commonly received in the past.[126]

Dr. Hornell Hart – Professor of Sociology at Duke University and author of several important books on social and psychological problems. Hart reviewed the literature on the life after this life and concluded, "Human personality does survive bodily death."[127]

Colin Brookes-Smith – British engineer Brookes-Smith joined a group to study the life after this life and psychic phenomena. As a result of his experiences, he stated in the *Journal of the Society for Psychical Research* that survival should be regarded as a sufficiently well-established fact to be beyond denial by any reasonable person. He described it as "a momentous scientific conclusion of prime importance to mankind."[128]

Arthur Balfour – British Prime Minister from 1902-1905, Secretary of State, and author of *A Defense of Philosophic Doubt*.[129] Balfour studied the life after this life and mediums and felt sufficiently convinced to write elaborately about them in the *Proceedings of the Society for Psychical Research*.

Do Attorneys Who Have Studied the Life after This Life Become Convinced of Its Reality?

Answer: Yes. Attorneys are trained in analyzing testimonies and data from witnesses. When they carefully analyze the activities of mediums, they certify that mediums are communicating with people living in the life after this life.

Attorneys who review the evidence for the life after this life are convinced of its reality.

Edward C. Randall – Prominent Buffalo, New York, trial lawyer; and member of the board of directors of a number of large corporations. Randall had more than 700 sittings with direct-voice medium Emily S. French over 22 years. He wrote, "Hundreds, yea thousands [of spirits], have come and talked with me, and to many whom I have invited to participate in the work – thousands of different voices with different tones, different thoughts, different personalities, no two alike; and at times in different languages."[130]

Victor James Zammit – Retired lawyer of the Supreme Court of New South Wales and the High Court of Australia. Zammit's extensive education includes a BA in psychology, a graduate degree in education, an MA in legal history, a Bachelor of Laws, and a PhD in law. After examining the evidence for the life after this life, he wrote, "After many years of serious investigation, I have come to the irretrievable conclusion that there is a great body of evidence which, taken as a whole, absolutely and unqualifiedly proves the case for the afterlife."[131]

John Worth Edmonds – Circuit judge, state Supreme Court judge, member of the New York assembly, and colonel in the militia. Confused about death and the life after this life, and with no confidence in either the church or mediums, Edmonds launched an investigation into the activities of mediums. He visited a variety of mediums and evaluated their sessions using various devices. As a result of his investigation, he wrote that "the phenomena were not produced by any person in the rooms."[132]

William Dean Shuart – Surrogate judge of Monroe County, New York. Shuart attended the same circles as Edward C. Randall did, conducted a variety of "exacting experiments," and became equally convinced of their reality and validity.[133]

Aubrey Rose, OBE, CBE –British human rights lawyer. After empirically investigating transmissions made by one of his colleagues through direct voice medium Leslie Flint, Rose stated that without doubt the voice he heard in a session came from the life after this life and was that of Judge Lord Birkett, who had crossed over some time before.[134]

Do Clergy Become Convinced of the Nature of the Life after This Life Described by Mediums?

Answer: Yes. When clergy study the reports about mediums and observe mediums communicating with people in the next life, they agree that the mediums are communicating with people whose bodies have died.

Members of the clergy have an especially difficult time in voicing their convictions about the life after this life described by mediums because of the narrow views of most religions. But those who do study the imminent life after this life become convinced of its reality as the mediums describe it, not as religion teaches it.

Isaac K. Funk –Lutheran minister, co-founder of Funk and Wagnalls, and editor-in-chief of the *Standard Dictionary of the English Language*. After his studies, Funk wrote, "I have the absolute assurance that when the something we call death comes, it will only mean a new and larger and more complete life."[135]

Charles Drayton Thomas – Graduate of Richmond Theological College and Methodist minister. Thomas served on the Council of the Society for Psychical Research in London for 19 years. Beginning in 1917, he had more than 500 sittings with Gladys Osborne Leonard, probably England's most famous medium. He concluded that there should be "a general acceptance of this evidence for survival."[136]

Pere Francois Brune – Catholic priest, member of the Catholic Institute in Paris and Biblical Institute in Rome, theologian, and professor in a number of leading seminaries. Brune wrote that the Catholic Church's attitude about communication from the life after this life is changing: "I believe that, as several of these messages assure us, we in fact are never alone. Some deceased, once they have arrived in the

Beyond, appear to have the wish of continuing their life through us, and come to sponge on us."[137]

In another statement Brune wrote about the changing position of the church on the life after this life:

> We do not have to do an official change of the Church's position. But it is in fact an evolution that without any doubt is due to the realization that the phenomena exist, and that they — how complex they ever may be — indeed correspond very often to an authentic communication with our dead.[138]

Dr. Peter Bander – Senior lecturer in religious and moral education at the Cambridge Institute of Education. Bander is a psychologist and Christian theologian. He began his investigation of the life after this life stating clearly that it was impossible for people who are dead to communicate with the living, that it was not only far-fetched but outrageous to even think about. However, after participating in a study of electronic voice production (EVP), he concluded: "I noticed the peculiar rhythm mentioned by Raudive and his colleagues. . . . I heard a voice. . . . I believed this to have been the voice of my mother who had died three years earlier."[139]

Have Any Church Bodies Studying Mediums Concluded They Speak with People in the Next Life?

Answer: Yes. An official church body studied mediumship for two years and concluded that mediums do speak with people whose bodies have died.

A committee of the Church of England studied mediumship records for two years, analyzing a great volume of the evidence on mediumship to investigate Spiritualism because it was so popular in England at the time. Its investigations included clergy sitting with some of the leading mediums in England. At the end of their thorough investigation, seven of the ten members of the Committee — against enormous pressure — came to this conclusion: "The hypothesis that they (spirit communications) proceed in some cases from discarnate spirits is the true one."[140]

Do Debunkers Studying Mediums Come to Believe the Life after This Life Is Real?

Answer: Yes, well-educated, highly regarded scholars determined to debunk mediums assert after their efforts that the mediums are communicating with people whose bodies have died.

Dr. Hereward Carrington – American psychic investigator and author. After moving to the U.S. from Great Britain in 1899, Carrington served as assistant to Dr. James H. Hyslop at the Society for Psychical Research. His first of many books on psychical phenomena was published in 1907 and explained the fraudulent practices of physical mediums. However, Carrington came away from his investigation of Eusapia Palladino convinced of the reality of some of the phenomena. He wrote,

> I myself have observed materializations under perfect conditions of control and have had the temporary hand melt within my own, as I held it firmly grasped. This hand was a perfectly formed physiological structure, warm, lifelike, and having all the attributes of the human hand – yet both the medium's hands were securely held by two controllers, and visible in the red light. Let me repeat, this hand was not pulled away, but somehow melted in my grasp as I held it.[141]

Dr. Harry Price – British psychic researcher and author. A debunker of fraudulent mediums, Price came to believe in genuine psychic phenomena and founded the National Laboratory of Psychical Research, later the University of London Council for Psychical Research. About his research he wrote, "And if I were not convinced of these [medium phenomena], I would not waste another moment of my time or penny of my money in further research."[142]

Are Accounts of the Life after This Life by Mediums the Same among the Mediums?

Answer: Yes. There is remarkable agreement in messages given by people in the life after this life through mediums. This could only be true if the mediums were all describing the same realm that exists. By contrast, accounts given by individuals and religions vary greatly in their descriptions of the life after this life, validating the authenticity of like-minded reports through mediums.

Dr. Robert Crookall, principal geologist with the British Geological Survey, resigned from his geology work in 1952 to devote his life to psychical research. Over nine years he collected and analyzed medium communications from every country he could, including Brazil, England, South Africa, Tibet, Europe, India, Australia, and the Hawaiian Islands. He found that in all countries, among all cultures, people described the same characteristic accounts of out-of-body experiences, near-death experiences, and communications with people in the next life through mediums. He concluded that his findings were strong evidence for the existence of the life after this life because an intellectually consistent set of statements came from many independent sources.[143]

Do Any Government Bodies Treat Mediums as Though They Are Having Afterlife Communications?

Answer: The fact that mediums receive information from those who have survived bodily death was acknowledged by British government officials startled by the truth of the information.

Helen Duncan was a Scottish medium in the twentieth century who gave hundreds of séances, with those attending describing them with superlatives such as "astonishing." In January 1944, while World War II was raging, Helen Duncan held a séance at 3:30 one afternoon in

Edinburgh. Brigadier Firebrace, who was Chief of Security in Scotland, happened to attend. During the séance Duncan, in a mediumistic trance, reported that the British ship HMS Hood had been sunk that day in the North Atlantic. No one could have known that at the time. Immediate announcements of calamities in televised newscasts didn't exist and there was great secrecy about military movements and events during wartime.

The astonishing revelation worried the British Admiralty. They could find no explanation for it. Then six months later, at another séance, a young man materialized saying he had been severely burned and died in the sinking of another British warship, the HMS Barham. The British Admiralty admitted that, in fact, the HMS Barham had been sunk but that they had kept it secret because they feared that its loss would have had a serious impact on public morale.

After the two uncanny revelations of information she couldn't have known, the alarmed British Admiralty had Duncan arrested and charged with witchcraft under a law dating to 1735. She was imprisoned for nine months.

The alarm of the British Admiralty, their acknowledgement that she couldn't have gotten her information from any earthly source since there was no way it could have been communicated that quickly or within that level of secrecy, and the fact that they had to convict her using a 1735 law against witchcraft demonstrated that they knew she had received the communication from the deceased who had been on the ships that had sunk. They had to silence her until the war was over. The British government, in fact, provided official acknowledgement that Helen Duncan was communicating with the spirits of people who had passed away.[144]

Does Communication with the Next Life Ever Contain Information the Medium Could Not Know?

Answer: Yes. It is common for medium readings to include information unknown to the observers or the person being read. The information is later verified, showing that the medium is receiving information about people living in the life after this life; it is not coming from reading living people's Minds.

In one account, an extended chess game was played by a living grand master (Viktor Korchnoi) and a deceased chess master (Maroczy) through medium Robert Rollans. At one point a researcher asked Maroczy, through Rollans, about a detail that would verify that it really was the deceased chess master coming through. The researcher had found an article stating that Maroczy in 1930 had played a match against a player called Romi. So he asked Maroczy whether he had defeated an Italian named Romi in a match. Maroczy replied that he didn't recognize that name, but he did defeat a man named Romih, spelled with an "h" on the end of the name. The researcher delved further and found an actual program from the match. The name was in fact Romih, not Romi.[145] The revelation demonstrated that Maroczy was alive and mentally capable although his body was dead.

Do Family Members Verify that Medium Readings Are Conversations with Their Loved Ones?

Answer: Yes. In the great number of séances on record in which a living person and a deceased loved one have a dialogue through a verified medium, the living person is always adamant that the person with whom they communicated was the loved one living in the life after this life. They have fluent dialogues about intimate affairs known only to the two people.

Thousands of such recordings are from Leslie Flint sessions. Leslie Flint would sit in a darkened room with the person on this side of life and the voice of the loved one living in the life after this life would come through in the room. Four examples will serve as illustrations. The family members could not be mistaken that they were having conversations with their loved ones in spirit. The content, intimate details, voice, and idiosyncrasies

A young man named David Cattanach, who died at age 18, made many visits to the Leslie Flint séances over a period of 10 years, speaking with his mother at several of them. Gordon Smith, who knew the mother personally, wrote this about her and the séances:

> I know her personally and she is someone I would describe as very astute, someone who would not easily be fooled, especially when it came to her son, and she had no doubts that she was hearing his voice.[146]

Listen to this recording of David Cattanach speaking in a Leslie Flint direct-voice session at www.afterlifeinstitute.org/cattanach/.

Mrs. Cattanach: Is Bob working with you?

David: Yes. We're very close because we house together.

Mrs. Cattanach: Oh, that's lovely.

David: We do a great deal of work together as a matter of fact.

Mrs. Cattanach: And Darling, is Tom with you still?

David: Yes, yes.

Mrs. Cattanach: Good.

David: I say, can you hear me?

Mrs. Cattanach: Yes, very well, Dear.

A man named Michael Fearon, killed during World War II, was also a frequent visitor to the Leslie Flint séances, at which he often spoke with his mother. The British Broadcasting Corporation arranged a broadcast during which they played a tape of a séance in which Mrs. Fearon was speaking to her son. After the tape played the moderator asked her, "Mrs. Fearon, as Mike's mother, what makes you so sure that it's your son's voice that you hear?" She answered, "Well, Mike was twenty-seven when he died and I'd been with him all that time . . . and I ought to know at the end of that, oughtn't I?"[147]

You can listen to a recording of Michael Fearon speaking to his mother at www.afterlifeinstitute.org/fearon/. A transcript of the conversation follows:

Michael: Satisfactory. I mean, I love coming to talk to you; it's a wonderful opportunity and it means so much to me, as indeed it does to everybody who has the opportunity to come through and speak to those who they love on earth.

Mrs. Fearon: I know, speaking to those . . .

Michael: It would make such a vast difference to people if they understood this and realize that death isn't what they think it is. It isn't the severing of the contact between us.

Mrs. Fearon: There is no death.

Michael: It's only an illusion. Man has created death in his own mind . .

In another example of family members conversing casually with loved ones on the other side of the veil, between 1970 and 1984, retired doctor of chemistry, Dr. Dinshaw R. Nanji of Birmingham University, visited London twice a year from his home in Gothenburg, Sweden, for private sittings with Leslie Flint in which he had casual conversations with his wife in spirit, Annie, who passed away in 1966.

Dr. Nanji would sit in a darkened room with Leslie Flint. After a short time his wife Annie would begin speaking through an ectoplasm voice box that form spontaneously on Flint's shoulder. Almost every sitting was a success. Many recordings of Dr. Nanji speaking with Annie are available today. The fact that Dr. Nanji was able to communicate with his wife living in the life after this life is the most compelling evidence that we live on after leaving the Earth plane.

A sample conversation follows. You can listen to the recording of this conversation at www.afterlifeinstitute.org/cemetery/. Eighteen other recordings of Dr. Nanji speaking with his wife are at this link: www.afterlifeinstitute.org/nanji.

Annie: Why do you still go to the cemetery?

Dr. Nanji: Well darling, how can I pass your birthday without my…

Annie: I appreciate it, but I'm not there! I'm not there!

Dr. Nanji: No, no, I know that!

Annie: And, uh, I see you go there and it makes you depressed.

Dr. Nanji: Yeah I – no, no, I am not depressed darling.

Annie: No?

Dr. Nanji: No, no, no. I am not depressed.

Annie: And the flowers.

Dr. Nanji: But the fact that I have cleaned it up and…and I put the bushes round…

Annie: I know. I see you. I watch you do it and I think…

Dr. Nanji: Yes. I was there, I was there a week ago.

Annie: The only time I am ever in the cemetery is when you go there.

Douglas and Eira Conacher were another example of a spouse communicating with her loved one in the life after this life. The Conachers were a devoted married couple with a publishing business in Central London. They were conventional in every way but one: they were determined that whoever died first would try to contact the other from the afterlife.

Douglas, 20 years older than Eira, died first on June 6, 1958. A few months later, Douglas contracted Eira through the medium Leslie Flint. They carried on regular conversations and authored two books together with both their names on the cover. It's quite obvious from the intimate conversations that Eira Conacher, living on the Earth plane, was having normal conversations with her husband Douglas, living in the life after this life.

You can listen to part of a recording made in 1965, seven years after Douglas passed. Flint and Eira were the only ones in the room. In the recording, Eira speaks first. The recording with some additional dialogue is at www.afterlifeinstitute.org/conachers/. A transcript of the conversation follows.

Eira: Was that your light I saw last night?

Douglas: Yes. You know, I'm wondering if you do see as much as I hope you do. I try to attract your attention in various ways and I felt sure... in fact, the other evening, I felt sure you realized I was there. You do sense my presence even though you don't see me.

Eira: Yes.

Douglas: You know, sometimes during your sleep you come here... and we're together.

Eira: Yes.

Douglas: We're together a great deal, you know.

Eira: Really? I wish I could remember. I have occasionally remembered.

There are thousands of the recordings of Leslie Flint sessions. Spouses talk to one another across the veil. Parents talk to children. Children talk to their parents and siblings. The extended, regular conversations could not be fabricated. Family members know when they are speaking with their loved ones. The Leslie Flint recordings are among the most compelling forms of evidence that we continue to live in the life after this life when we no longer are using the Earth body.

Is There Any Evidence Mental Mediums Are Communicating with People Living in the Next Life?

Answer: Yes. Carefully controlled experiments by researchers in university and institute settings have shown that mental mediums are receiving messages from people living in the next life whose bodies have died.

In an effort to run a controlled experiment to determine whether mediums do receive accurate information from the deceased, Gary Schwartz, Linda Russek, and Christopher Barentsen conducted a study for the Human Energy Systems Laboratory at the University of Arizona testing three talented mediums: Laurie Campbell, John Edward, and Suzane Northrop.

The study revealed that the mediums identified details about the deceased loved ones at a rate much higher than chance, leading the researchers to conclude that "The findings appear to confirm the hypothesis that information and energy, and potentially consciousness itself, can continue after physical death."[148]

A Second Study Also Concluded that Mediums Are Able to Identify Details about People Alive in the Next Life

Gary Schwartz performed a second study with three other researchers from the University of Arizona Human Energy Systems Laboratory for a video-recorded HBO documentary on the life after this life. The study used five well-known mediums: George Anderson, John Edward, Anne Gehman, Suzane Northrop, and Laurie Campbell.

The result was that the mediums' average accuracy score was 83 percent for one subject and 77 percent for a second subject. To test whether guessing could achieve the same results by chance, 68 control people were asked to guess details about the deceased loved ones of the two subjects. Their scores averaged 36 percent hits by chance. In other words, the accuracy of the mediums' details was far beyond chance guesses.[149]

The Miraval Silent Sitter Experiment Showed the Same Ability to Communicate with People Alive in Spirit

The Miraval silent-sitter experiment involved mediums Suzane Northrop, John Edward, Anne Gehman, and Laurie Campbell and ten subjects. The study consisted of two parts for each reading with each subject. The first was a "silent" part in which the medium described details about the deceased without receiving any responses from the subject. In the second part, the medium was able to receive "yes" and "no" answers from the subject.

In this study, the mediums' accuracy score was 77 percent during the silent period and 85 percent during the "yes" and "no" questioning period, showing again that the mediums were far more accurate than would be expected by chance (based on the 36 percent accuracy rating in the previous study's control group).[150]

More Stringent Studies at the University of Arizona Showed Mediums Are Communicating with People in the Next Life

Gary Schwartz, PhD, and Julie Beischel, PhD, of the University of Arizona, performed another study under even more stringent, triple-blind conditions with more mediums. In this study, the subjects weren't present for the reading. Another person sat in as a "proxy sitter." The readings were conducted by phone to eliminate even the presence of the proxy sitter with the medium. Eight mediums were involved to increase the validity of the data.

The result was that the average summary rating for the readings actually intended for the subject was 3.56 on the 6-point scale. The average summary ratings for the readings not intended for the person (that were actually readings for someone else) was 1.94. For three of the best-performing mediums, the summary scores were in the range of 5.0 to 5.5 out of 6, meaning they were dramatically accurate.[151]

A list of recommended, legitimate mediums, some of whom do phone readings, is at www.afterlifeinstitute.org/connect-loved-one-spirit/.

Is There Evidence Other Types of Mediums Are Speaking to Living People Whose Bodies Are Dead?

Answer: Yes. There is a large body of evidence from activities of many mediums other than mental mediums demonstrating that they are also receiving messages from individuals alive in the next life whose bodies have died.

Since the nineteenth century, when mediums could hold séances without fear of retribution, many capable mediums have held thousands of séances. The most talented attracted the most attention, of course, and as a result were the most tested by skeptics and debunkers. That offers us a vast storehouse of records of rigorous, repeated testing and testimonies by credible witnesses, many of whom were avowed skeptics before the testing.

Following are brief summaries of a small number of mediums' accomplishments and results of their testing by credible witnesses, including government officials, scientists, and royalty. Enough is included, with citations, to demonstrate that they communicated with people whose bodies were dead who are living on the next plane of life and that rigorous, repeated testing found no fraud or deception in their activities. The people they were communicating with are alive, just not using bodies on the earth plane.

Gladys Osborne Leonard

For over forty years, Gladys Osborne Leonard's mediumship was studied exhaustively by members of the Society for Psychical Research. The tests always confirmed that her communication was with the deceased. In none of the many tests was there a hint of fraud.

The Rev. Charles Drayton Thomas, a Wesleyan minister and member of the British Society for Psychical Research (SPR), sat with her over 100 times to test her abilities. Thomas's own father came through and offered to assist in the tests. Thomas had an extensive library. The deceased father told the son, through Mrs. Leonard, to go to the lowest shelf in his library and take the sixth book from the left. On page 149, three-quarters of the way down, he would find a word conveying the meaning of falling back or stumbling. Thomas located the book, found page 149, and looked at the words: ". . . to whom a crucified Messiah was an insuperable stumbling-block."

Over a period of 18 months' experimentation, the deceased father was able to pick up more and more words and numbers even more accurately, both in his own library and in a friend's library. The words and numbers were all verified.

They decided to try having Thomas's deceased father provide information from newspapers and magazines not yet printed. On January 16, 1920, Thomas was told to examine the *Daily Telegraph* the following day and to notice near the top of the second column of the first page the name of the place he was born, Victoria Terrace on Victoria Street in Taunton. When Thomas checked the paper the following day, he found the word "Victoria" exactly where his father said it would be.

Mrs. Leonard was able to satisfy every test she was subjected to, and the researchers were convinced she was indeed speaking with the living individuals who were simply not using a body anymore.[152] The tests demonstrated that people whose bodies have died are living on in the next life.

Leonora Piper

Leonora Piper was a nineteenth century medium who was also tested repeatedly by a wide range of skeptical observers. The Society for Psychical Research conducted several thousand sittings over two decades with carefully controlled environments to preclude fraud. The sittings were remarkably accurate, and those who knew the deceased acknowledged that the contacts were with their loved ones, based on the unmistakable content and detail.

Piper was studied repeatedly by Richard Hodgson, one of the leading members of the Society for Psychical Research. He started out as a skeptic determined to expose Piper as a fraud. In the end, he had no doubts that she was speaking to people whose bodies had died who are living in the next life. His report is 300 pages long, with detailed descriptions of the controls he used to prevent fraud. Leonora Piper was never caught in trickery and her achievements were described as "baffling."[153]

One of the many case studies of Piper's remarkable mediumship follows. It was experienced and recorded by Hodgson.[154]

George Pelham, a lawyer and acquaintance of Hodgson, died in an accidental fall at age 32. Pelham had followed Hodgson's work with Piper and was skeptical about life after this life, calling it inconceivable. But he told Hodgson that if he died, he would try to contact Hodgson. Five weeks after his death, Piper sat in a séance with Hodgson and John Hart, a close friend of Pelham. She announced that George Pelham was there to speak.

The spirit of George Pelham provided a long list of details about himself, his early life, his friends, and his family that could be researched and verified to prove he was indeed George Pelham, still alive in the life after this life. For example, when Pelham's body had died, his father had sent his friend John Hart (who was sitting in this séance), some shirt studs of Pelham's to keep as a memento. Hart happened to be wearing the studs that evening and Pelham, through the medium, identified the studs Hart was wearing as formerly his. He also told Hart how his mother had chosen the studs and how Pelham's father delivered them to Hart.[155]

In another sitting, Pelham told Hodgson he had seen his (Pelham's) father take a photograph of the deceased Pelham to an artist to have it copied. After the séance, Hodgson contacted Pelham's mother to see whether that had been true. She said that, in fact, Pelham's father had taken a photograph to an artist to be copied.[156]

In another sitting with family members who verified that the communication was with their loved one living in the life after this life, Mrs. Piper was asked by the Reverend and Mrs. S. W. Sutton if she could communicate with their recently deceased little girl. She did establish contact and the little girl communicated things verifying that it was she who was speaking.

- She confirmed that she used to bite buttons.
- She identified her Uncle Frank and a friend who had died with a tumor and referred to her brother by his pet name.

- She referred to her sore throat and paralyzed tongue and that her head used to get hot before her death.
- She referred to her doll Dinah, her sister Maggie, and her little toy horse.
- She named the two songs she had sung immediately before she died. The Suttons had no doubt that they had made contact with their little girl and were especially happy when she reassured them: "I am happy . . . cry for me no more."[157]

Rudi Schneider

Eugene Osty, MD, was the director of the Metaphysic Institute in Paris. Intent on understanding the remarkable abilities of a young medium, Rudi Schneider, he set up controlled conditions and was able to produce genuine physical phenomena without fraud. During Schneider's séances, people on the next plane of life would move objects placed on tables while the room was dark. Osty tested Schneider by placing objects on a table to have Rudi Schneider's spirits move them and by setting up a sophisticated arrangement of infra-red rays and cameras to "catch" any human that touched objects during the séance. In the sittings with the arrangement, objects were moved on numerous occasions, flashes were set off, and the plates developed. They showed only the table top. Something had nevertheless been moving about over the table because the beam of infra-red rays had been interfered with and the objects had been displaced.[158]

Osty also set up controlled conditions to identify the presence of the person in spirit. To do this the experimenter devised an apparatus, a galvanometer, by means of which it would be possible to register the oscillation or the vibration rate of the intelligence once the experiment commenced. As soon as the experiment commenced, the person in spirit began to move things around indicating that the person was present. Then the galvanometer began to register the "pulsation" of the invisible intelligence. As Carrington states: "It was somewhat like taking the pulse of an invisible being standing before them in space!"[159]

Eileen Garrett

Eileen Garrett was a medium who held séances in the early twentieth century. One séance was interrupted by a man who identified himself as Flight Lieutenant H. C. Irwin of the Airship R101. Those at the séance later learned that Airship R101 had crashed three days before, but the government had not revealed it to anyone. The airman was very much alive after his body died in the crash.

During the séance, Irwin described the airship's destruction in great detail. The account was presented to the Air Ministry Intelligence, who were startled and impressed at the accuracy and the details they had not known that were revealed in the séance. They were sufficiently convinced of the authenticity of the source that Major Oliver Villiers, of the Air Ministry Intelligence, arranged seven additional séances with Garrett to hear the deceased Irwin describe more details about the crash. The major learned about technical subjects Garrett could not have understood, using technical vocabulary such as "useful lift of the airship," "gross lift," "disposable lift," "fuel injection," "cruising speed," "cruising altitude," "trim," "volume of structure," and other jargon.

Irwin also described top-secret information about a classified experiment the ministry had been engaged in. They had been attempting to use a mixture of hydrogen and oil in airships, but the information was strictly protected. The ministry officials agreed that the information that came from Irwin through Garrett was completely accurate, even to the town the airship passed over before it crashed and the locations of hidden diaries crew members had kept that revealed their fears about the secret project.[160]

The case demonstrates that the airman survived bodily death. He retained his technical knowledge and communicated with no diminishing of his memory, intelligence, or ability to articulate technical explanations.

Shirley Bray

Direct-voice mediums have voices come from the air around them at various places in the room, which must be darkened. Skeptics devised tests to ensure that the voices did not come from the medium.

Such tests were used to authenticate the voices recorded during séances with Australian medium Shirley Bray. The voices of three people living in the life after this life who regularly manifested through her were recorded on tape. These tapes were put through the high-tech voice-recognition machine the British police used to analyze the voices of serial killers. The voice machine measured variables such as pace, rhythm, breathing patterns, and accents and showed that the three voices from Shirley Bray were unique individuals. The researchers stated unequivocally that it was not possible for one person to produce three voices on the tape because the voice pattern-vibration for an individual is just like a fingerprint: different from person to person.[161]

This finding provides evidence that the medium was in contact with people who had survived bodily death and were able to communicate clearly.

Elwood Babbitt

Another ingenious test of medium authenticity was devised by a history professor named Charles H. Hapgood. He tested medium Elwood Babbitt using an electroencephalograph (EEG) to measure changes in brain-wave patterns when Babbitt was "taken over" by deceased people during trances. Hapgood measured the brain wave patterns when Babbit was out of trance and during the trances. If the EEG patterns were the same in both instances, it would indicate that Babbitt could be consciously creating the voices. Hapgood took EEGs of Babbitt while three different entities were in control. The EEGs were found to be completely different from each other and from Babbitt's EEG. An EEG expert, Dr. Bridge, noted that the EEGs were characteristic of people of different physical ages and could not belong to one person.[162]

These findings are additional evidence that the people whose bodies had died were communicating.

Daniel Dunglas Home

D. D. Home (pronounced "hume") was a well-known medium of the mid-nineteenth century. His mediumship demonstrates the reality of communicating with those on the next plane of life because the feats were attested to by well-known people who experienced them. In 1855 his mediumship was witnessed in France by Prince Murat, Napoleon III, and Empress Eugenie. Home held a séance with Napoleon and the Empress. After the séances Napoleon said, "There is a difference between believing a thing and having proof of it, and I am certain of what I have seen."[163] During the séances,

- Napoleon's and the Empress's unspoken thoughts were replied to.
- The Empress was touched by a materialized hand she recognized as that of her late father because of a defect in one of the fingers.
- The room was shaken.
- Heavy tables were lifted or adhered to the floor by an alteration of their weight.
- A phantom hand appeared above the table, lifted a pencil, and wrote the single word "Napoleon" in the handwriting of the deceased Napoleon I.[164]

As a result of the hundreds of carefully controlled examinations researchers conducted without finding a hint of deception, even skeptics unsympathetic to mediumship were forced to acknowledge that nothing fraudulent could ever be found in Home's medium sessions.[165] His mediumship provided further evidence of the survival of consciousness.

Leslie Flint

Leslie Flint conducted séances in which thousands of people spoke to deceased loved ones and the deceased responded in normal conversations. The people whose loved ones came through all expressed with certainty that the voices were their loved ones' and that they had had conversations with the real, living person, although they had been dead, at times for decades.

Flint had the remarkable ability of having people from the next plane of life speak audibly using a voice box they created in the air from a substance that came from the medium's body (ectoplasm). They did not use their own voice boxes because their voice boxes were moldering away in the ground somewhere or reduced to ashes in a funeral urn. Nevertheless the voices were clear and authenticated by people who knew the speakers, especially their immediate families who carried on conversations with the deceased during the séances.

Flint was described as the most tested medium in all of history. In one instance, to ensure he hadn't been doing the speaking, "He held a certain amount of pink water in his mouth. Then his mouth was sealed by an adhesive strip. After the séance, he returned the entire amount of water—quite a difficult achievement!"[166]

The creativity of his testers was remarkable: "He was bound to a chair, his mouth sealed with tape. At other experiments he wore a throat microphone to detect possible vibrations in his vocal organs. He was observed through an infra-red viewer." At no time did sound come from his mouth. In no tests by qualified, skeptical scientists was anything found to be fake or deceptive.[167]

You can read about the verification of Flint's mediumship at www.afterlifeinstitute.org/validity. You can hear some of the audio recordings of people in the life after this life speaking during Leslie Flint séances at http://earthschoolanswers.com/lf/. The audio recordings are compelling evidence that the people whose bodies died are alive and well in the life after this life.

David Thompson

David Thompson conducted séances in Australia and around the world in which, with careful, rigid controls, a variety of people experienced voices of the deceased and materializations of those in spirit. One of those is Victor J. Zammit, lawyer and author of *A Lawyer Presents the Case for the Afterlife*.[168]

Montague Keen was head of the Parliamentary and Legal Department of the National Farmers Union of England and Wales, journalist, magazine editor, and secretary of the Society for Psychical

Research Survival Research Committee. Keen investigated David Thompson's physical medium abilities on October 25, 2003, using tight controls that prevented the medium from uttering a sound or moving. In spite of the strict controls, the medium was transported, with the chair to which he was strapped, to a different part of the room, the medium's cardigan was reversed on his body while the straps binding him were intact, and four distinctive voices were heard. These were Keen's conclusions:

> The voices themselves could not have come from the gagged medium. The only other "regulars" on whom suspicion might rest were Bianca, his wife, Paul the leader who was seated next to me, and whose voice and location would have clearly identified him, and DF, the host, who was seated at the opposite end of the room from the medium. Any of these possibilities would have easily and immediately detectable by those present, as well as likely to be defeated by listening to the tape recording.[169]

You can hear a recording of Montague Keen speaking, after his body had died, at a David Thompson séance at www.afterlifeinstitute.org/monty.

You can hear an audio recording of a man in the life after this life speaking during a David Thompson séance at www.earthschoolanswers.com/dt/. The encounter between a woman sitting in the séance and her love whose body had died provides further proof that people survive bodily death.

Warren Caylor

Physical Medium Warren Caylor's mediumship was studied by researcher Eckhard Kruse of the Baden-Wuerttemberg Cooperative State University, Mannheim, Germany. The séance room had four microphones spaced apart so, if voices were recorded during a séance, the position of the voices in the room could be calculated. In several séances over one year with the medium, audio was recorded when entities spoke in the room. One of the results was that four entities were recorded: Yellow Feather, Luther, Winston, and Tommy. Each spoke from a different position in the room. No voices came from the cabinet where the medium was sitting. The researchers concluded no one in the room could have produced the voices because of their various locations and the voices had distinctively different characteristics when the audio was analyzed.[170]

The Scole Experiments

For six years a group in Norfolk, England, conducted experiments of contact with the life after this life. The following professionals participated in the experiments: David Fontana, Arthur Ellison, Montague Keen, Dr. Hans Schaer, Dr. Ernst Senkowski, Piers Eggett, Keith McQuin Roberts, Dr. Rupert Sheldrake, and Professor Ivor Grattan-Guiness. A group of NASA scientists participated, as well as professionals from the Institute of Noetic Sciences.

The experiments resulted in communication with a variety of deceased people, revelations of information that nobody but the deceased could know about, appearance of objects that came from nowhere, voices of the deceased heard by all experimenters in attendance, and materialization of people whose bodies had died. Rolls of film were placed in locked boxes by experimenters and images appeared on them. Video cameras recorded the appearance of deceased people.

A scientific report titled "The Scole Report" was produced by the Society for Psychical Research based on the experiments. They concluded that "None of our critics has been able to point to a single example of fraud or deception."[171]

A stage magician, James Webster, was brought in to see if any magic tricks could produce the phenomena. Webster had more than fifty years' experience in psychic research, applying his knowledge of magic tricks to such phenomena. On three occasions he attended sittings with the Scole group and published this conclusion in an English newspaper in June 2001: "I discovered no signs of trickery, and in my opinion such conjuring tricks were not possible, for the type of phenomena witnessed, under the conditions applied."[172]

What Proof Is There That Mediums Are Not Using Psychic Ability Instead of Speaking to Living People?

Answer: People who have spoken to individuals whose bodies have died carry on dialogues through mediums, learn information they did not know was true that is verified, receive information through several mediums that make sense only when taken together, and receive messages for them even when someone else sits with the medium during the reading. The information could not have come to the medium psychically.

Mediums and psychics receive information in different ways. Mediums converse with people who are personalities, alive and fully functioning. They carry on dialogues. Mediums are clearly not doing psychic readings, which are very different. Psychics receive information from a vast cosmic storehouse of information about life and people. All psychics say they're receiving psychic information, not communications from the deceased, and all mediums say they're getting information from living people on the other side, not simply psychic information.

You would expect that some psychics would feel confusion or doubt about the source of their information, and some mediums would similarly express doubt about whether they are communicating with real people alive in the life after this life. But neither the psychics nor the mediums have any doubt about their different sources of information.

Most importantly, relatives of the deceased attest to the fact that they have been speaking with their deceased loved ones. The following statement was made by Professor James Hyslop, Columbia University, after speaking with his deceased relatives through medium Leonora Piper:

> I have been talking with my (dead) father, my brother, my uncles. . . . Whatever supernormal powers we may be pleased to attribute to (the medium) Mrs. Piper's secondary personalities, it would be difficult to make me believe that these secondary

personalities could have thus completely reconstituted the mental personality of my dead relatives.[173]

Cross Correspondences

More objective proof that the mediums are speaking to living people in the life after this life comes from research called "cross correspondence." In cross correspondence, a series of messages is given by someone in the life after this life to different mediums in various parts of the world. Individually, the messages are not meaningful, but together they have a clear message. That means a single medium couldn't be receiving psychic information. Instead, the person living in the life after this life has carefully planned to give the messages to a number of mediums.

The Myers Cross-Correspondence is the best-known example of such a study.[174] Frederick W. H. Myers was a Cambridge classics scholar and writer in the nineteenth century who was one of the founders of the Society for Psychical Research. He originated the concept of cross correspondence.

After Myers transitioned from earth in 1901, over a dozen mediums in different countries began receiving incomplete scripts through automatic writing that were all signed by Myers. The scripts were all about obscure classical subjects that would have been known to Myers, a classics scholar. When all the scripts were assembled like piecing together a jig-saw puzzle, they formed a complete message. Myers, living in the life after this life and communicating through the mediums, had planned and executed the writings so they proved no single medium was receiving psychic knowledge rather than communication from a deceased person.

Later, two other leaders of the Society for Psychical Research transitioned into spirit: Henry Sidgwick and Edmund Gurney. Soon after each of their transitions, fragments of messages came to mediums around the world from them; the Myers "study" was replicated successfully. Over the next 30 years more than 3,000 such scripts were transmitted to mediums around the world, some as long as 40 typed pages. They now fill 24 volumes of 12,000 pages. As investigators involved in the research transitioned, they joined the study on the other side by communicating incomplete messages through a number of mediums around the world that formed complete wholes when brought together.[175]

Hundreds of other accounts of such cross correspondence are recorded in the *Proceedings of the Society for Psychical Research*.

Proxy Sittings

Other evidence that the contact in medium readings and séances is with the actual, living person on the next plane of life comes from "proxy sittings." In a proxy sitting, someone comes to the medium reading or séance to have a reading for someone else. The proxy sitter knows only the name of the person in spirit and the name of the individual wanting to have contact with the person. That decreases the likelihood that the medium is simply doing a psychic reading of the person without really receiving communication from the loved one speaking from the next plane of life.

The Reverend Charles Drayton Thomas, a Methodist minister, repeatedly acted as a proxy sitter investigating the mediumship of Gladys Osborne Leonard for the Society for Psychical Research. For example, from 1936 to 1937 Thomas went to four sittings with Leonard as a representative for a woman about whom he knew only her name, Emma Lewis, and that she wanted to contact her father, Frederick William Macaulay. With those two pieces of information, Leonard provided seventy items of information, which Thomas recorded and conveyed to Emma Lewis. She confirmed, beyond a doubt, that they came from her father because of the unique content only he would have known.[176]

In another example, Professor Eric R. Dodds, a Regius Professor of Greek at Oxford University and president of the Society for Psychical Research, supervised a series of proxy sittings with medium Nea Walker. He concluded, "The hypothesis of fraud, rational inference from disclosed facts, telepathy from the actual sitter, and co-incidence cannot either singly or in combination account for the results obtained."[177]

Do People Actually Materialize in Séances and Are Verified by Observers?

Answer: Yes. We have many accounts of materializations of people whose bodies have died, including photographs and audio recordings, demonstrating that the people are alive, have materialized, and have spoken to, touched, and even kissed sitters who knew the people well.

Perhaps the most remarkable evidence of the continuation of life after the body dies is the materializations that have been observed and verified by a large number of professionals, royalty, scientists, and others whose testimony is above question. These are not "ghosts" or "apparitions." They are the full appearances of people who carry on conversations and have been touched and hugged by loved ones sitting in the séances.

Carlos Mirabelli

One of the most compelling materialization mediums was Carlos Mirabelli in Brazil. He was able to have full materializations of people in broad daylight. He also performed other remarkable feats.

At a séance conducted in the morning in full daylight in the laboratory of the investigating committee in front of many people of note, including ten men holding the degree of Doctor of Science, a little girl materialized beside the medium. Dr. Ganymede de Souza, who was present, confirmed that the child was his daughter who had died a few months before and that she was wearing the dress in which she had been buried. Another observer, Colonel Octavio Viana, took the child in his arms, felt her pulse, and asked her several questions, which she answered with understanding. Photographs of the apparition were taken and appended to the investigating committee's report. After this the child floated around in the air and disappeared, after having been visible in daylight for thirty-six minutes.

In a second materialization, the form of Bishop Jose de Camargo Barros, who had recently lost his life in a shipwreck, appeared in full uniform with the insignias of his office. He conversed with those present and allowed them to examine his heart, gums, abdomen, and fingers before disappearing.

At a third séance, conducted at Santos at 3:30 p.m. before sixty witnesses who attested their signatures to the report of what happened, the deceased Dr. Bezerra de Meneses, an eminent hospital physician, materialized. He spoke to all of the assembled witnesses to assure them that it was he. His voice carried all over the room by megaphone and several photographs were taken of him. For fifteen minutes, two doctors who had known him examined him and announced that he was an anatomically normal human being. He shook hands with the spectators. Finally he rose into the air and began to dematerialize, with his feet vanishing first, followed by his legs and abdomen, chest, arms, and last of all head. The photographs accompanying the report show Mirabelli and the apparition on the same photographic plate.[178]

Helen Duncan

Helen Duncan is one of the best-known materialization mediums of all time. She reunited thousands of people with their deceased loved ones. These are some of the accounts verified by witnesses and the families of the people in spirit from testimonies at her trial for witchcraft.[179] They demonstrate that people live on with full mental faculties and the ability to communicate, although their bodies have died.

> Nurse Jane Rust testified on oath at the Old Bailey [courthouse], among other things, that she, through Helen Duncan, actually met a loved one again—her husband who materialized from the afterlife and kissed her. "'I have never been more certain of anything in my life before," she said. She stated that she had been enquiring for 25 years as a skeptic but it was only when she met Helen Duncan that she was able to actually meet her loved ones including her mother who had passed on.
>
> A high ranking Air Force officer, Wing Commander George Mackie, stated on oath that through Helen Duncan's

materialization gifts he actually met his "dead" mother and father and a brother.

James Duncan (no relation), a jeweler, testified that both he and his daughter had seen his wife materialize on eight different occasions, in good light. Duncan had seen her close up at a range of 18 inches and they had talked of domestic matters including a proposed emigration to Canada that they had previously kept secret. He had, he said, not a shadow of a doubt that the voice was that of his wife. He also claimed to have seen materializations of his father, who was about his own height and bearded, and his mother.

Mary Blackwell, President of the Pathfinder Spiritualist Society of Baker Street London, testified that she had attended more than 100 materialization séances with Helen Duncan at each of which between 15 and 16 different entities from the afterlife had materialized. She testified that she had witnessed the spirit forms conversing with their relatives in French, German, Dutch, Welsh, Scottish and Arabic. She claimed that she had witnessed the manifestation of ten of her own close relatives including her husband, her mother and her father, all of whom she had seen up close and touched.

Links to full transcripts of twenty-two witnesses are at www.afterlifeinstitute.org/witnesses.

David Thompson

David Thompson is now conducting séances with direct voices and materializations of those in spirit in the presence of a variety of people with careful, rigid controls, including inspections by more than one sitter before the seances begin of the gag across the medium's mouth and zip ties binding the medium's body to the chair.

In one recorded séance with David Thompson, a man named Nick materialized and spoke to Sarah, his beloved companion, who was among the sitters. You can listen to this reunion between Sarah and Nick at http://www.afterlifeinstitute.org/sarah-nick/.

Do Individuals Whose Bodies Have Died Ever Appear and Speak at Length with People on Earth?

Answer: Yes. There are many examples of people whose bodies have died spontaneously appearing and conversing with people they knew on earth. Three such examples follow.

Elisabeth Kübler-Ross

Dr. Elisabeth Kübler-Ross was an internationally renowned physician, author, speaker, and expert on death and dying. She was listed as one of the 100 most important thinkers of the century by *Time* magazine in 1999 and received 20 honorary degrees for her achievements. She published 20 books on death and dying. *On Death and Dying*[180] was named one of the 100 most influential books of the century. She was included in the International Biographical Centre's list of the foremost women of the twentieth century.

In her renowned book *On Life After Death*[181] Dr. Kübler-Ross described her visitation in a physical form by someone who had passed away two years earlier:

> I was at a crossroad. I felt I needed to give up my work with dying patients. That day, I was determined to give notice and leave the hospital and the University of Chicago. It wasn't an easy decision because I really loved my patients.
>
> I walked out of my last seminar on death and dying towards the elevator. At that moment, a woman walked towards me. She had an incredible smile on her face, like she knew every thought I had.
>
> She said, "Dr. Ross, I'm only going to take two minutes of your time. If you don't mind, I'll walk you down to your office." It was the longest walk I have ever taken in my life. One part of me knew this was Mrs. Schwartz, a patient of mine who had died and been buried almost a year ago. But I'm a scientist, and I don't believe in ghosts and spooks!

I did the most incredible reality testing I've ever done. I tried to touch her because she looked kind of transparent in a waxy way. Not that you could see furniture behind her, but not quite real either. I know I touched her, and she had feeling to her.

We came to my office, and she opened the door. We went inside, and she said, "I had to come back for two reasons. Number one, I wanted to thank you and Reverend Smith once more for what you have done for me. But the real reason why I had to come back is to tell you not to give up your work on death and dying. Not yet."

I realized consciously that maybe indeed this was Mrs. Schwartz. But I thought nobody would ever believe me if I told this to anybody. They really would think I had flipped!

So my scientist in me very shrewdly looked at her and said, "You know, Reverend Smith would be thrilled if he would have a note from you. Would you terribly mind?" You understand that the scientist in me needed proof. I needed a sheet of paper with anything written in her handwriting, and hopefully, her signature.

This woman knew my thoughts and knew I had no intention to ever give her note to Reverend Smith. However, she took a piece of paper and wrote a message and signed it with her full name. Then, with the biggest smile of love and compassion and understanding, she said to me, "Are you satisfied now?"

Once more, she said, "You cannot give up your work on death and dying. Not yet. The time is not right. We will help you. You will know when the time is right. Do you promise?" The last thing I said to her was "I promise." And with that; she walked out.

No sooner was the door closed, I had to go and see if she was real. I opened the door, and there was not a soul in that long hallway!

Dr. Kübler-Ross's experience is compelling evidence that Mrs. Schwartz lived on after her body died and was aware of current events occurring in Dr. Kübler-Ross's life.

Raymond Moody

Raymond Moody, MD, PhD, professor of psychology, and chair in Consciousness Studies at the University of Nevada, taught courses in perception and consciousness. Dr. Moody had an experience in which his deceased grandmother materialized, had a lengthy conversation with him, and calmly left. This is his account of what happened:

> It is very difficult to put this experience into language; I am at a loss to explain some of it in words. Yet, I have no doubt whatsoever that I was in the presence of my deceased grandmother for an extended period and did in fact converse with her at length. At first, as I said, I did not recognize this person, though she immediately seemed somehow familiar. She looked somewhat as she had while alive on the earth, but appeared younger than she had been even when I was born. When I recognized her as my grandmother and confronted her with this fact, she immediately acknowledged it and began to use the nickname she alone had used for me when I was a child. She talked with me about events only my grandmother and I knew. She imparted to me certain very personal information about my early life that has been quite important and revealing.[182]

Dr. Moody's experience is another demonstration that people survive bodily death with their senses and mental faculties fully intact.

J. B. Phillips

J. B. Phillips was an English Bible scholar, translator, author, and ordained Anglican priest. He created the *Phillips Translation of the New Testament.* Phillips was an esteemed scholar with no history of hallucinations or mental illness. In these two incidents, the renowned author C. S. Lewis appeared to him before Phillips was aware Lewis had transitioned.

J. B. Phillips was suffering from a life-threatening depression. He refused to leave his room, would not eat, and would not exercise. He had begun to doubt God's love for him. This is his account of what happened from his book, *Ring of Truth*.

> Many of us who believe in what is technically known as the Communion of Saints, must have experienced the sense of nearness, for a fairly short time, of those whom we love soon after they have died. This has certainly happened to me several times. But the late C. S. Lewis, whom I did not know very well and had only seen in the flesh once, but with whom I had corresponded a fair amount, gave me an unusual experience. A few days after his death, while I was watching television, he "appeared" sitting in a chair within a few feet of me, and spoke a few words which were particularly relevant to the difficult circumstances through which I was passing. He was ruddier in complexion than ever, grinning all over his face and, as the old fashioned saying has it, positively glowing with health. The interesting thing to me was that I had not been thinking about him at all. I was neither alarmed nor surprised nor, to satisfy the Bishop of Woolwich, did I look up to see the hole in the ceiling that he might have made on arrival! He was just *there* —"large as life and twice as natural"! A week later, this time when I was in bed reading before going to sleep, he appeared again, even more rosily radiant than before, and repeated to me the same message, which was very important to me at the time. I was a little puzzled by this, and I mentioned it to a certain saintly Bishop who was then living in retirement here in Dorset. His reply was, "My dear J...., this sort of thing is happening all the time."[183]

Another source explains Phillips's reference to the "few words which were particularly relevant to the different circumstances through which I was passing."

> In this vision, Lewis spoke only one sentence to Phillips: "J.B., it's not as hard as you think." One solitary sentence, the meaning of which is debated! But what is not debated is the effect of that sentence. It snapped Phillips out of his depression, and set him again following God. After Lewis spoke that cryptic sentence, he disappeared.
>
> Phillips came out of his chambers only to find that Lewis had died moments before the appearance, miles away. He pondered this in his heart, with wonder, and never returned to his depression.[184]

Philips attested to the materialization of C. S. Lewis, but the most convincing evidence that C. S. Lewis had survived the death of his body and spoke to Philips was the fact that it "snapped Phillips out of his depression and set him again following God."

Do Mediums Receive Messages in Languages They Could Not Know During Afterlife Communications?

Answer: Yes. Mediums speak and understand messages in languages not known to them, demonstrating that they are in contact with native speakers of other languages whose bodies have died.

Dr. Neville Whymant, a British professor of linguistics, was a specialist in languages who knew 30 languages. He attended a séance at the home of William Cannon, a New York City lawyer and judge, performed by medium George Valiantine. In the séance, a man came through speaking ancient Chinese. Whymant knew modern Chinese and knew the literature of ancient China, so he was able to interpret it as perfect ancient Chinese. He learned that the speaker was Confucius, whose writings Whymant knew well. He asked the speaker, in Chinese, about poems people had puzzled over for centuries that Confucius had written. Before Whymant could finish the poems, the spirit spoke the remaining words. Confucius then explained the errors in copying that had occurred after his death, solving the puzzles.[185]

Confucius had survived the death of his body in the fifth century BCE and continues to live nearly 2,500 years later.

In 1931 a young English girl named Rosemary began to speak in an ancient Egyptian dialect under the influence of the personality of Telika-Ventiu, who had lived in approximately 1400 BCE. In front of Egyptologist Howard Hume, she wrote 66 accurate phrases in the lost language of hieroglyphs and spoke in a tongue unheard outside academic circles for thousands of years that was verified by Hume. The accounts are in the files of the Society for Psychical Research.[186]

In this case also, the ancient Egyptian demonstrated that he survived his bodily death 3,400 years ago and continues to live in the life after this life.

Pearl Curran, a housewife from Saint Louis who was barely literate, began to write in astonishingly accurate Middle English. Under the guidance of a spirit entity named Patience Worth, she produced sixty novels, plays, and poems, including a 60,000-word epic poem, all in perfect Middle English, a language Curran could not have known.[187] Patience Worth survived the death of her body and was intellectually and artistically vibrant 500 years later.

The fact that the messages came through in languages the mediums did not know demonstrates that they originated from the personalities living in the life after this life and that the mediums were not psychically reading someone. There was no individual related to the people in spirit present when the messages came to the mediums.

Do Near-Death Experiences Reveal that Consciousness Survives Bodily Death?

Answer: Early on as the body dies during a near-death experience, consciousness should stop functioning. Instead, the person's senses become more acute, memory functions perfectly, pain

> goes away, trauma and fear disappear, and the person has experiences of things not accessible to the comatose, nonfunctioning body. The person's Mind is entering the next realm of life alive and well.

Today medical science is able to revive people who are nearly dead, with little or no brain functioning. When they come back from the brink of death, many have remarkable accounts of feelings of calmness and peace, moving upwards through a tunnel, meeting deceased loved ones, encountering a being of light, experiencing a life review, and feeling a return to the body, often very reluctantly. These are near-death experiences (NDEs).

Those who have studied NDE accounts conclude that the phenomenon cannot be explained as a purely physical event. Cardiologist Dr. Michael Sabom at the Emory University School was skeptical about the NDE experience. With an associate, Sarah Kreutziger, he interviewed patients in his own hospital. He reported, "Having been on both sides of the argument, I now believe that the near-death experience is not simply the result of misfires within the dying brain, but that it is a spiritual encounter."[188]

Michael Schroeter-Kunhardt, MD in psychiatry, conducted an extensive study of near-death experiences. He concluded, "The large body of NDE data now accumulated point to genuine evidence for a non-physical reality and paranormal capacities of the human being."[189]

Experiencers sometimes learn information about deceased loved ones they could not have known if they had not seen or met them while in the NDE. Bruce Greyson, formerly a professor of psychiatry at the University of Connecticut, now Chester F. Carlson Professor Emeritus of Psychiatry and Neurobehavioral Sciences at the University of Virginia, described the following case.

> The author Maggie Callanan in her 1993 book, *Final Gifts*, wrote about an elderly Chinese woman who had an NDE in which she saw her deceased husband and her sister. She was puzzled since her sister wasn't dead, or so she thought. In actuality, her family

had hid her sister's recent death from her for fear of upsetting her already fragile health.[190]

In another study, the researchers recorded the account of an NDE case with information the patient had no knowledge of and didn't understand until ten years later. During an NDE, a patient reported that he saw his deceased grandmother. Standing next to her was a man he didn't recognize, who was looking at him full of love. More than ten years later he learned that his mother bore him out of wedlock with a Jewish man during World War II. This man was deported and killed. When he was shown a photo of his biological father, he recognized him as the man he had seen ten years before during his NDE.[191]

Does the Way the Universe Is Set Up Provide Any Evidence It Is Being Created Specifically for Us?

Answer: The universe of experiences in Our Universal Intelligence has characteristics fine-tuned to give us what we need to thrive and learn lessons. There is virtually no chance such a universe could have evolved by chance in a physical realm outside of Our Universal Intelligence. One estimate is that it would take 820 trillion years (58,610 times the estimated age of the universe) for such a world to have evolved using the materialists' properties of a physical universe.[192]

The universe in which we are having experiences was made uniquely for us. That fact is another indication that we are immersed in a temporary experience that is simply one stage in our eternal lives. When we have finished our tasks here, we transition to the next experience that will be made uniquely for us.

The energy and matter are the scenery in which we have experiences and learn lessons. Thus, we would expect that this combination of matter and energy would fit our needs for survival and growth, both intellectually and spiritually. In fact, it does more than simply fit. It is so perfectly matched to our needs that even minor deviations from the carefully engineered design would have rendered life in the universe impossible. It is matched to us in ways that are far beyond chance.

The fact that the universe is so remarkably matched to us resulted in Stephen Hawking, the renowned theoretical physicist, coining the term "Anthropic Principle" to describe it. He wrote, "The odds against a universe like ours emerging out of something like the Big Bang are enormous. I think there are clearly religious implications whenever you start to discuss the origins of the universe. There must be religious overtones. But I think most scientists prefer to shy away from the religious side of it."[193]

The existence of our universe, with galaxies and stars, is actually quite unlikely, with the odds against a universe that has produced life like ours being immense. These are some of the remarkably precise conditions the universe has that, if any fluctuated a small degree one way or the other, wouldn't allow humanity to live on Earth:

- If the strong force that acts on the quarks, neutrons, and protons of the atomic nucleus were just slightly *weaker*, the only element that would be stable would be hydrogen. No other elements could exist, and humankind couldn't live.

- If the strong force that holds the nucleus of atoms together were just a bit *stronger*, then the universe would be made up of atomic nuclei containing just two protons, so hydrogen would not exist to create water and the stars and galaxies would have evolved in ways that wouldn't support life.

- If gravity were just a little *stronger*, the average star would have only 10 to 12 times the mass of the sun and could exist for only a year, not enough time for humankind to live and grow.

- If gravity were just a little *weaker*, then matter would not have assembled into stars and galaxies, and the universe would be cold and empty.

- "Entropy" is the second law of thermodynamics. Things disintegrate—they fall apart over time. But that means our universe began with order and is gradually becoming less orderly. No one knows why there was order at the beginning and not chaos.

- At the "big bang," the initial rate of expansion would have had to have been chosen very precisely for the rate of expansion still to be so close to the critical rate needed to avoid re-collapse. This means that the initial state of the universe must have been very carefully chosen if the hot big bang model was correct right back to the beginning of time. It would be very difficult to explain why the universe should have begun in just this way, except as the act of a God who intended to create beings like us.[194]

- The gravity pull of the sun and moon perfectly stabilize the Earth's tilt of the rotation axis that results in a stable climate. The moon's size is just right to cause ocean tides that mix nutrients from the land and oceans to make life possible. The Earth is just far enough from the sun so water can stay liquid, with temperatures such that human beings can live, and a size sufficient to have an atmosphere.[195]

- The Earth is set up remarkably precisely to provide the water and oxygen the planet needs to support life. It has what amounts to an "oxygen machine," as explained by researchers in the journal *Nature*. Large amounts of oxygen are stored in a mineral called "majorite" deep within the earth. Some of the majorite is continually rising to the surface on convection currents. As it rises, pressure and temperature decrease and the oxygen is released. That gives the Earth oxygen, and may be responsible for some of the water so necessary for life.

- The Earth's magnetic field is set precisely so it helps keep the water and oxygen-rich atmosphere from being blown away by solar winds.[196]

Another indication that the Earth has been set up specifically for us is that evolution doesn't explain the emergence of life from chemicals. The emergence of life by accident would have required that amino acids, the building blocks of life, be joined together in chains of hundreds of thousands of units to form proteins, and then proteins would have had to have combined into the single-celled creatures we call "life." But evolution works through mutations of cells, by accident, resulting in the fittest surviving and passing along their mutations as adaptations. So the cells would have had to have existed first to have such evolution, and they couldn't evolve by themselves without some intelligent design. Work in a laboratory to produce the amino acids required to sustain life has not been successful:

> When, in 1953, Stanley Miller, then a graduate student at The University of Chicago, produced a few amino acids through purely random reactions among chemicals found naturally throughout the universe, the scientific community felt the problem of life's origin had been solved. Far from it. Subsequent experiments have failed to extend his results. Thermodynamics favors disorder over order. Attempting to get those amino acids to join into any sort of complex molecules has been one long study in failure. The emergence of the specialized complexity of life, even in its most simple forms, remains a bewildering mystery [to the Darwinian evolutionists].[197]

The same kinds of remarkable engineering are present in galaxies. For human beings to be able to live in a particular galaxy, it would have to have exactly the right mass, type, age, and allotment of heavy elements. Our Milky Way Galaxy has that fine tuning.[198]

The earth is also uniquely situated with distinct properties that allow conscious beings to discover how the universe works. That fact is explained by the authors of *The Privileged Planet: How Our Place in the Cosmos Is Designed for Discovery*.[199] Our universe is set up not only to allow human beings to exist, but also to allow us to have maximum opportunities to make discoveries about it.

The authors explain that the moon is just the right size and just the right distance from the Earth moving in just the right orbit to cover the sun precisely so we can have perfect solar eclipses—the moon exactly covers the sun from where we're standing. As a result, we've made discoveries about the sun's corona and the warping of light by gravity that couldn't have been made without this incredible set of matched conditions.

We're also situated perfectly in the Milky Way Galaxy so we can observe and make discoveries about the universe. We have front-row seats. There's very little dust where we're located to absorb light from nearby stars and distant galaxies so we can see the remarkable images, such as the Hubble image on the cover of this book. We're far enough from the center of the Milky Way Galaxy, and the galaxy disk is flat enough, that our view of the distant universe is not excessively obscured. We can see a wonderful diversity of nearby stars and other galaxy structures. And because of where we're situated, we can see the unique cosmic microwave background radiation that led us to realize that the universe is expanding and finite in age.[200]

All of that is engineered with such precision that it would be impossible for it to have occurred by chance as a result of an explosive expansion 13.7 billion years ago that materialists describe. These precise placements are within a universe with vast expanses of space where the sun, earth, and moon could have been formed anywhere by chance when the solar system was born 4.5 billion years ago. One analogy is that expecting to get our uniquely designed living environment out of an accidental explosive expansion in the universe is like expecting to get a dictionary out of an explosion in a printing shop.

The impossibility of all these factors' coming together accidentally to produce the scenery for our eternal selves has led an increasing number of scientists to suggest "intelligent design." They are quick to point out that this concept doesn't suggest a God, especially the God envisioned as a big old man in the sky. It simply means that some intelligent organization seems to be necessary for the universe to exist as it does to support human beings:

> The sudden appearance of the correct biocentric parameters "out of nothing" is essentially tantamount to a miracle because there is evidently no other way to account for this perfect life-giving format by random processes alone.[201]

Charles Townes, co-inventor of the laser and Nobel Prize winner, wrote that the discoveries of physics "seem to reflect intelligence at work in natural law." Francis Collins, director of the Human Genome Research Institute, declared, "A lot of scientists really don't know what they are missing by not exploring their spiritual feelings." Michael Turner, astrophysicist at the University of Chicago Fermi Lab, wrote, "The precision is as if one could throw a dart across the entire universe and hit a bull's-eye one millimeter in diameter on the other side."[202]

The materialists' conception of a universe with this fine tuning that is perfect for us has been likened to expecting to get a dictionary out of an explosion in a printing shop. Materialism has no satisfactory answer for why this realm is so perfectly designed for us. However, we know Our Universal Intelligence is giving us experiences of scenery that are being provided for us so the dramas of our eternal lives can play out and we can grow spiritually. When we end our experience in Earth School, we make the transition away from it and into the next realm where we will have more experiences.

Doesn't Darwinian Evolution Prove We Evolved by Accident?

Answer: People are not evolving to be fitter so they can use their evolved abilities to dominate others and spread their genes. Humankind is maturing to use our free will to subordinate our needs to the needs of others. We are evolving to be more loving, less aggressive, and more anxious to see others thrive than to dominate others. Our lives are purposeful, intelligent, and planned, not accidents in time in a physical universe that evolved by chance.

Darwinian evolution asserts that organisms evolve to become more sophisticated because they experience chance mutations that result in favorable adaptations. So, lungs developed because aquatic creatures were more likely to survive if they could get oxygen from both the water and the air. Sometime along the way, around 400 million years ago the materialists say, the float bladder of a fish opened to the air and enabled the fish to gain oxygen through its membrane. That was a mistake in the fish's physiology that actually gave it an advantage over other fish that couldn't take in oxygen from the air. As a result, it and its descendants thrived.

This is the principle of "natural selection" described by Charles Darwin. Natural selection favors the fit, strong, clever, self-seeking, and ruthless. These aggressive, self-seeking individuals will be more likely to live and bear progeny, perpetuating the adaptations they experience that made them more fit.

The evolution in spirituality we are seeing is actually making humans less able to compete in the world. We aren't fitter, stronger, more self-seeking, and more ruthless. We are, in fact, willing to give up our own possessions, be transparent and honest, focus on others, and give without reservation. We would expect that Darwinian evolution would squash such weak creatures.

Large numbers of people are becoming increasingly compassionate and other-centered, even as society remains self-absorbed and materialistic. Spiritual growth, in other words, is not the result of a genetic mutation; it is a result of the fact that we are spiritual beings having a physical experience, and our true natures are overpowering physical realm instincts as we reduce their influence on us. Being loving and compassionate is not a trait that natural selection would reward. The people who are successful today in life as it is now are those who are aggressive, self-focused, devious, and manipulative. They crush the people who are giving, loving, and compassionate. Spiritual growth toward love, other-centeredness, and giving rather than taking defies Darwinian evolution. It seems that the design of the universe is such that we are evolving toward becoming gentler, more loving, and more other centered. We're evolving to have unconditional love.

Darwin would roll over in his grave if he were there; but he's not.

Then What Are We?

Answer: We are eternal beings having Earth School experiences as one of the episodes in our eternal life.

Our eternal self exists apart from energy and matter. It's outside of the body and outside of the Earth, meaning consciousness (the Mind) is elemental. It exists independent of matter and energy. As a result, our consciousness survives the death of the body.

Knowing that to be true is important to your spiritual growth. If you believe you are limited in time and space to this short lifetime and the bag of flesh you see in a mirror, then you will be less interested in loving others, being a servant to others, loving Our Universal Intelligence, feeling your inner self has worth, and conserving nature. You'll try to get all you can get because life is short and you have only one time around. Knowing that you are an eternal being having the Earth portion of your eternal existence is critical to spiritual growth. And if everyone has that knowledge, then society as whole will grow spiritually as well.

Part 3

Reasons for What Happens to You in Your Life and Your Afterlife

Information in this section of the book is summarized from *Reasons for What Happens to You in Your Life & Your Afterlife: From Speakers in the Afterlife*, published in 2021. The book contains 570 citations supporting the statements. The information that follows generalizes from the specific details in that book without direct quotes or citations. For the sources, quotations, and more detailed information, please refer to the book.

5

What Is Earth School?

Answer: Everything we experience during our lives from birth to our transition at the death of the body is Earth School. Earth School is experiences in Our Universal Intelligence that we as individuated members of Our Universal Intelligence are participating in. It does not exist in space outside of our Minds.

Before our entry into Earth School, our Higher Selves and Souls wanted to have specific experiences that would help us grow in wisdom, love, and compassion and feel the range of emotions resulting from Earth School experiences. We chose to participate with other Souls in Earth School experiences in the twentieth and twenty-first centuries because this is the realm and the time affording experiences through which we can learn and grow.

Earth School is not made up of matter and energy apart from Our Universal Intelligence. It did not come into existence 4.5 billion years ago and will not be incinerated when the sun expands and burns it to a crisp in 5 billion years. That is all just part of the story resulting in playing out causes and effects in a realm that exists only as now experiences in Our Universal Intelligence for our Earth School Minds' benefit.

Earth School consists of accessible experiences from Our Universal Intelligence. The fact that earth is a world of experiences doesn't mean it isn't substantial—it is. Matter and energy are the fabric of Earth School. But the threads and weave of the fabric are entirely Our Universal Intelligence.

Some suggest that this experiential world is an illusion, called "maya" in Buddhism and Hinduism. Earth School is not an illusion in the sense of being a hallucination. Still, the basis of matter and energy is different from the commonly held belief that matter and energy exist independent of Our Universal Intelligence. The matter and energy that seem to make up Earth School are only experiences accessed by our Minds, which are individual manifestations of Our Universal Intelligence. Read *There Is Nothing but Mind and Experiences*[203] to find out why we know that is true.

The current environment of Earth School is a realm of experiences with time, space, continuity, cause and effect, and beginnings and endings that Earth School Minds may choose to experience. It is a crucible, with self-centered, insensitive people and loving, giving, other-centered people. The environment allows us to make choices among the options to be more selfish or more giving. In that way, we can grow to become loving, compassionate, and other-centered while we enjoy all the experiences available in Earth School today.

Where Is Earth School?

Answer: What we experience as Earth School is the set of experiences in Our Universal Intelligence that all people are having together. It has no location in a space outside of Our Universal Intelligence, any more than we can say the city we see in a dream is in space somewhere. We have experiences in our Mind that are Earth School. They have no location.

As a result of the experiences of space, time, and causality, we have the impression Earth School is on a planet in space, but Earth

School is only an attunement of Our Universal Intelligence to the experiences we commonly are having, such as our bodies, the sun, streams, mountains, and animals. This realm, including Earth, all the planets, stars, and galaxies, is in no place; it is a state of Mind in Our Universal Intelligence.

Earth is just the experiences we are having. We have attuned ourselves to the Earth experiences in Our Universal Intelligence so we have the unique experiences of Earth School together. If we were attuned to some other of the millions of realms in Our Universal Intelligence, we would have different experiences, and there we would be attuned to the same sets of experiences so we would have the conviction that we were in a separate world. But we are not on a world in space. We are experiencing a world.

Who Created Earth School?

Answer: The experiences we are having together comprise Earth School. The experiences come to our Minds because we are members of Our Universal Intelligence. The stable set of experiences we have was established in the Minds of those who came before us, and we perpetuate the experiences by now expecting and contributing to them. Earth School was not "created" as something outside of Our Universal Intelligence.

The question must be in the present tense: "Who is providing the experiences of Earth School?" The past tense is appropriate only for a universe made of matter and energy outside of us. There is no world outside of our Minds that was created and now exists somewhere in space. There are only the experiences we have in the point of now that are accessible from Our Universal Intelligence.

Who determines the experiences we have in Earth School? We do. We are having the experiences because we want and expect them. We are experiencing an Earth School available to us in Our Universal Intelligence that we expect to be available because of our learning about Earth School from childhood. We are creating the Earth School experiences at a level much more fundamental than our sluggish day-to-day consciousness. At that deeper level, we are accessing the experiences that create our reality because we as individuals and as a whole humanity grew up to expect them. We grew up accessing the experiences of all who preceded us that create the Earth School reality, and we expect the experiences we have tomorrow will be of the same stable Earth School environment.

It is like this. When you recall and relive an event you very much enjoyed, you are accessing the memories from Our Universal Intelligence. You expect the event to be as you experienced it, so it comes to you with the details you recall. You are given the reality of the event in your Mind based on experiences accessible in Our Universal Intelligence. You ask for the memory experiences and Our Universal Intelligence creates them to be what we expected.

In the same way, our world unfolds naturally as we expect. We don't intend the experiences as we do when we want to recall and relive an event, but our need for stability, familiarity, and predictability is the same as the intention. We are given what we expect as a natural course. What we expect is what we grew up with and the changes that have happened since then. The experiences that have been made accessible in Our Universal Intelligence are the experiences of a realm experienced by the people who came before us. Their experiences created realities in Earth School life much like our memories create a mental reality. We don't have to ask for our moment-by-moment reality to be created as we ask for a memory to come to Mind. The reality of experiences unfolds naturally because we expect it in Earth School. The experiences creating our reality are simply there just as we need them.

We know that is how reality is created for us because of the example from the life after this life. In the life after this life, people don't need to eat, but if a person wants to eat, food is simply there. They don't have to ask for it. It is there because Our Universal Intelligence is aware they want it. There, we have bodies in our prime, usually from our 20s or 30s. We don't have to ask for the bodies. Our Universal Intelligence knows the bodies we would prefer and they are created for us.

In the same way, we learned from childhood that we could open a door and walk into our childhood home, where we experience all the furniture, wall treatments, and rooms we experienced from childhood.

These all happen as experiences in our Minds, not in an outside world. We learned to expect the experiences because they were in Our Universal Intelligence based on the experiences others had with the house that are now accessible in Our Universal Intelligence. When we opened the door and walked into the house, these experiences came to us naturally, without having to request them. Because of our expectation that the house would be as we expect it to be, Our Universal Intelligence makes the experiences of the house available to us without our asking for them. They are simply made available.

Just as we access our memories in our Minds and they play as we expect, we go through our daily lives accessing the experiences of houses, streets, animals, mountains, forests, weather, and people accessible in Our Universal Intelligence because the experiences, much like memories, have been created by those who preceded us as they experienced Earth School.

We chose to attune ourselves to the experiences available in Our Universal Intelligence for the twentieth and twenty-first centuries in Earth School. We access the experiences attuned to this time and place because we grew into the common experiences of Earth School from childhood. We could have grown up as ancient Egyptians or pygmy tribespeople in the Congo basin. We would have accessed different experiences with different people who had the same experiences as we were having that unfolded naturally from Our Universal Intelligence.

Out of the billions and billions of experiences we could have, drawn from all times and all realms in the cosmos, we are accessing the narrow sliver that fits with our brief lives in Earth School. Every experience that ever was or ever will be is accessible to us because we are Our Universal Intelligence taking on roles as individuals in Earth School. Even so, our Minds stay in character and access only those experiences that give us continuity, stability, and cause and effect in our sliver of Earth School. We don't realize we are accessing the right experiences, and we usually don't ask for them. As we play our roles in Earth School, our lives unfold as we access the right experiences to make what I call "myself" in the world I experience as Earth School.

These experiences that naturally unfold in Our Universal Intelligence create the type of world we live in. We are perpetuating a world that is shaped by the spiritual beings we have grown to be. All of us, together, are bearing fruit from the trees we grew into from childhood. Our world has available for us only the fruit from the experiences we have all created. If we live in a world of fear, self-absorption, tragedy, suffering, disease, conflict, and violence, it is because we are creating it, moment by moment. If we live in a world of love, compassion, joy, comfort, and other-centeredness, it is because we are creating it.

We have the ability to change the experiences, thereby changing the world.

How Do We Create Our Reality in Earth School?

Answer: We create the reality of Earth School in seven ways.

1. We planned the general framework of our lives in Earth School before our births. Our Universal Intelligence is giving us the general circumstances of what we planned. Nevertheless, we have free will to reject any part of the plan if we so decide.

2. We have control over our responses to experiences. We can change the programming we received in childhood to create our own, unique interpretations of experiences and responses. We can interpret other people as being loving and lovable (although flawed), and our experiences as opportunities for happiness. We have the opportunity to control our interpretations.

3. We make ourselves happy or miserable by choosing to dwell on happy or miserable thoughts. The reality we create in Earth School can be one in which we see love, peace, and joy in all things or we see rejection, discord, and unhappiness. What we choose to see in what we experience results in our emotional worlds.

4. We create our body experience. At a very deep level, we change our body experiences by our expectations. We make ourselves sick and fatigued or energetic and healthy. Read the full explanation in pages 162-166 of this book and in *There Is Nothing but Mind and Experiences*.[204]

5. We create the life we decide to live with what we intentionally put in it. If we fill our lives with people, things, and experiences embodying fear, competition, manipulation, self-absorption, anger, and violence, our world will feel like it's filled with fearful, competitive, manipulative, angry, self-absorbed, violent people and we will live in the miserable, dysfunctional world we've created. Living in atmospheres with negativity is like swimming through polluted water.

   On the other hand, if we fill our lives with people, things, and experiences embodying love, peace, and joy, our lives will be more loving, peaceful, and joyful. We will be loving, peaceful, and joyful with others and they will reciprocate. We create that atmosphere.

6. We are also creating reality as a collective. If humankind evolves to have only love, joy, and peace with each other, everything in Earth School will show the influence of those glorious sentiments. The stress illnesses will disappear. Violence will be no more. People will care for one another eagerly so there will be no misery or suffering. These positive characteristics of living together will come about because we will be creating a new, glorious reality and eradicating a reality filled with hatred, unhappiness, self-absorption, and discord.

7. Our Universal Intelligence is giving us the matter and energy at the fundamental level of the Earth School world because of what we have learned to expect in the world. This realm is available to us through Our Universal Intelligence as the perfect environment in which to love, learn lessons, and be happy—to fulfill our purposes in Earth School. Since we

have grown up in Earth School as it is, Our Universal Intelligence gives us continuity by maintaining the experiences we have of the Earth School environment. We don't have to ask for it—Our Universal Intelligence gives it to us without our realizing it. And so, we perpetuate the Earth School environment because we now expect it.

Those experiences we all access can be changed by our collective Minds, even the experience of mountains; but we will not come to the point of changing the experience of the Rocky Mountains. We instead accept the experiences we have in Earth School, manipulate experiences in it, and love, learn, and enjoy life within the experiences.

Yeshua bar Yosef, a great teacher whose name evolved into the English "Jesus," is reported to have said, "Truly, I tell you, if anyone says to this mountain, 'Go, throw yourself into the sea,' and does not doubt in their heart but believes that what they say will happen, it will be done for them" (Mark 11:23 NIV). Scholars have suggested this is a metaphor of sorts, but in his wisdom Yeshua meant that literally. We create our reality. Because we create the scenery collectively, we can't do something that violates others' experiences. The mountain will remain there. It is our deeply felt experience of the mountain together that gives us a mountain. Nonetheless, if we all expected the mountain to cast itself into the sea, it would be so.

Do We Have Any Responsibility for Helping Humankind Change?

Answer: We may have planned to come into Earth School for a time because of our desire to help humanity evolve. Or our plan may have been simply for our advancement and the advancement of others who planned this experience with us. In neither case are we responsible for helping humankind change as a burden we must carry alone like a savior or world leader. But our accomplishment of our Soul's plan will result in humanity's advancement in love, compassion, and wisdom by the measure we can add.

An important responsibility we have in Earth School is to evolve humankind. Humankind is in the situation it is in today because all the individuals, including you and me, are creating this Earth School as it is. If we want this time on Earth to be filled with love, joy, and peace, we must create a loving, joyful, peaceful world by being loving, joyful, peaceful individuals. It may seem that we individuals have little power over the other eight billion people on the planet, but all the people are individuals changing themselves and thereby changing the world. When we change, society will change. When society changes, all of us will live in the paradise that is Earth School imbued with love, peace, and joy. We have a responsibility to change society.

When we change society, those who enter Earth School after us will not have to abandon so much of their childhood teaching. Children will be well on their way to achieving higher levels of love, compassion, peace, and brotherhood because society will have given them experiences, interpretations, beliefs, and mores that they agree as adults are loving, compassionate, and other-centered.

Will Earth School End?

Answer: Earth School is only experiences in the consciousness of Our Universal Intelligence, which has no beginning and no ending. When people are finished having their experiences in Earth School, they attune to other realms to have experiences. If no one attunes to Earth School, it doesn't end; the potential Earth School experiences are simply not being experienced. The Earth School experiences are still accessible when someone chooses to experience Earth School with others who have also made that choice.

We are members of Our Universal Intelligence that will never end, so we will never end. We will change our attunement to other worlds of experience, but the "we" doing the changes are eternal.

Materialists, believing the universe is an accident in time independent of us, assume the universe began from a tiny singularity at the big bang and will eventually either collapse back into a singularity, or will continue expanding until the energy is dissipated, so it ends in a cold, lifeless universe. But the universe is only experiences we as individual members of Our Universal Intelligence have. It never "began" in the sense of being created. Instead, groups of people have become attuned to experiences that are Earth School experiences.

The "universe" is experiences we are accessing in our awareness from moment to moment. The universe doesn't "exist" in the sense of being matter, energy, and forces separate from people with separate people living in it. As long as there are people attuned to Earth School, they will continue to have Earth School experiences. Nothing can harm the individuals in Our Universal Intelligence. If people stop having Earth School experiences, it will be because we are all attuned to other realms. If we decide to tune into Earth School again, we will continue with the experiences we're having, but there will still be no realm of matter and energy that exists apart from individuals.

We are having experiences in Earth School to love, learn lessons, and enjoy the experience. Earth School will not end in a big crunch or lifeless cold. People will continue to experience an Earth School as long as it fits with people's goals for their lives.

Why Are There Beginnings and Endings?

Answer: We experience beginnings and endings in Earth School because we wanted to learn from the experience of enjoying things we receive and the sadness when they are taken away, the ecstasy of loving and the despair of losing the love, and limitations on the time of the presence of things in our lives, including the body.

Beginnings and endings seem like the natural order of things, but they are not. They are part of the Earth School experience. We experience things being created and annihilated. We have seasons with growth and destruction of the growth. We have birth experiences and death experiences. Earth School is the realm of change in which we experience beginnings and endings.

In the other realms of life, people grow in mental and spiritual stature but do not experience a death. They transition to higher realms, but never die. Flowers and animals flourish without dying. There are no ends; there are only transitions. Earth School has beginnings and endings to suit our time in experiencing and learning here.

Why Are There Cruel and Violent People in Earth School?

Answer: We chose to live in a world with cruel and violent people because their presence and actions have roles to play in our learning. This world, with extremes from cruel and violent people to loving and compassionate people, also allows us to be at any point on that continuum so we can advance in our ability to love, thereby advancing all of humanity by that measure.

This period in Earth School's history is a crucible with all types of people. Some have planned lives in which they have no conscience: they are psychopaths and sociopaths. Some have chosen to be in a family and environment with the potential for great conflict, abuse, and violence. Others have chosen to be in a family and environment filled with love, regard, and sensitivity.

In Earth School, we interact with the entire range of people, from those who planned insensitive, potentially violent lives to those who planned gentle, loving lives. As a result, we have great challenges, a variety of models of kind, loving people, and a wide range of opportunities for growth and helping others grow. We chose to enter Earth School knowing there are dangers, tragedies, and pain. We knew we would see maleficence, manipulation, greed, and inhumanity. But we also knew there would be the bliss of loving and being loved, feelings of happiness and delight, triumphs over challenges, ecstasy in learning and discovering, and great rewards. We knew this would be a time of discovery, advancements in spiritual wisdom and technological knowledge, and opportunities to love, grow, and enjoy life.

For us to experience growth to be increasingly loving, compassionate, and other-centered, we wanted to be in a world where we could have some measure of insensitivity and self-absorption so we could progress from where we were to be all we can be. Here we also can increase our empathy and sensitivity by helping people who are cruel, violent, and self-centered to grow from their lower levels of love and compassion into being more loving and compassionate. Earth School in the twentieth and twenty-first centuries has cruel and violent potentials so this growth can occur.

Do We Have Free Will to Choose as We Wish?

Answer: Yes. Throughout our eternal lives, we always have free will to choose as we wish, even when the decision is not in our best interest or the best interests of people around us. The faulty choice becomes another growth opportunity.

We have free will to choose what we want to become. We can thwart our life's plan by making choices that divert us from the path, but our guides and Soul take steps to adjust our experience so we are likely to travel the right path. Their guidance does not interfere with our free will. We can choose to live a life of personal growth by becoming more wise, peaceful, loving, and happy, or we can continue to tolerate stunted growth, discord, discontent, and unhappiness.

The reactions that are loving and compassionate or cruel and insensitive come automatically from our subconscious repertoire of interpretations of experiences. Yet we have the ability to examine and work at changing the automatic reactions so we are loving, compassionate, and other-centered. We can choose to live lives full of love, peace, and joy even though we started our lives with examples and teaching from the environment we grew up in that resulted in our tendencies toward being self-absorbed, violent, cruel, insensitive, and unhappy.

We are exercising our free will when we challenge our beliefs and circumstances with the help of our guides, loved ones, and Soul.

Their counsel does not interfere with our free will. It enhances our decisions.

On the other hand, people who feel they need to maintain rigidly a belief system and lifestyle based on their early childhood in Earth School are not exercising their free will. They are prisoners of their childhoods, blindly following what comes from the subconscious formed by their parents and society. A primary goal of our lives in Earth School is freeing ourselves from the shackles of the erroneous beliefs we learned as we grew up in a spiritually backward world. We have the free will to do that.

Does the Person's Soul Plan the Exit Point?

Answer: Yes, the person's Soul plan includes more than one exit point. The Soul and guides then select an exit point depending on the person's progress in Earth School.

There is a consensus based on contacts from people who have gone on to the next stage of life that the Soul plans more than one potential exit point before enrolling in Earth School. Loved ones left in Earth School need never feel there should have been something they could have done to stop the transition. When the appointed time comes, the transition will occur regardless of what measures are taken.

The exit point chosen by the Soul and guides is at a time based on the person's progress in achieving their life goals. There is also evidence that the exit point can be changed if the Soul and guides feel something must be learned before the exit happens. There are many verified accounts of people not wanting to transition while certain others are present or while anyone is there. They pass quietly when someone leaves or in the middle of the night when no one is with them. Others hold onto life until they hear from loved ones that it's okay to pass. The Soul and guides can adjust the exit point.

Does Chance Exist?

Answer: Some things do happen by chance. Not everything is in the life plan.

Since we plan our lives before entering Earth School, some ask whether our lives are predetermined or whether things can happen by chance. The answer is that some things do happen by chance.

Why Is There Time?

Answer: There is a time of sorts in the life after this life, but not like our time. We have time with minutes, days, and years because Earth School functions require us to have a flow of time to accomplish activities. Other realms do not need such a strong sense of time.

Time as we know it is part of the scenery in Earth School. Time in other realms is not quite the same as time in Earth School. People living in the life after this life say they don't have the sense of time we have in Earth School. There is no sun, so there are no years or days. There is no moon. There is a twilight at times, but never dark nights. People don't count time. They do get a sense of time when they return to Earth School, and they receive our thoughts, so they know when birthdays and anniversaries are coming up. Otherwise, they don't keep track of what we call time.

There are no clocks there, and no one refers to "o'clock" (meaning "of the clock") when deciding when to meet. They simply have the commonly held thought when it is time to meet. Our preoccupation with time in Earth School is part of the Earth School experience, not a condition of the cosmos.

As we have experiences in the now, the environment and circumstances change. Because the environment is different in one point of now from the previous now, we say there has been a time period over which the change occurred. Change results in a sense of time. Without change, there would be no sense of time.

We have a sense of what we call the past because we can access memories of experiences we have had in Earth School. We construct what we believe will happen in the future from our memories of experiences that happened in the past that we project into the future. Our sense of time, in other words, is entirely in our Minds. If we had no memories of experiences, we would have no sense of time.

We need the arrow of time from past to present to future so we can function and learn in Earth School. We learn lessons and change over time through an accumulation of experiences. As children, we learned the rules of Earth School. We needed time to do that. As adults, we abandon much of what we were taught and grow to be more other-centered, loving, compassionate, and wise. That takes new challenges and learning over time. As a result, time is an important component of Earth School.

Why Is There Space?

Answer: We need the sense of space to be able to function in ways that allow us to learn lessons, love others, and enjoy the Earth School experience. The sense of space is entirely in our Minds, not in a world outside of us.

Experiences must be apparent in space. The experience of sight requires a sense of space. The experience of touch requires a non-touch when space intervenes between the toucher and touched. The experience of sound requires atmosphere between the sounding event and the ear experience. The experience of taste requires movement through space to have the mouth experience. Smell requires the experience of an odorous source that is acquired in space. These are all experiences. We could have the experiences without the intervening space, but to have a body in Earth School that has experiences, we must have a sense of space.

Our Minds and Our Universal Intelligence do not require space. When we think of a waterfall, the image comes to Mind, but there is no space in our Mind. We have the sense of space between us and the waterfall, but there is no space when we access the memory. Space isn't necessary. But the actual experience of the waterfall in Earth School requires that we have the sense that the waterfall is some distance from us to see the breadth of it. That is part of the waterfall experience.

When we sit in a theater watching a movie with gangsters speeding through the streets of Chicago, we sense the space the car is traveling through. But there is no space. There is only a two-dimensional screen. We don't have to transport Chicago to the theater to have our sense of space during the chase. Our Minds have the experience of the car and fill in the space before and after it. The experiences come without space or time. We add them.

We walk through space in Earth School and get into cars or planes to travel through space. But in the next stage of life, people think of being in a location and are instantly there. They can return to visit their families in Earth School by simply intending to be with them. Space has no bearing on their activities. On the other hand, because they are recent graduates of Earth School and still need and want a sense of space, they do navigate in space and see at a distance. That is purely because their Minds are comfortable with space after having lived in Earth School with space.

6

Why Is Earth School Set Up as It Is?

Answer: We have chosen to enter Earth School at this time because it has characteristics that will enable us to grow in love and compassion, develop wisdom, and enjoy the time we have here. It is set up as it is because we need it to be so.

Earth School is a mix of the most backward spiritual elements and the more advanced. There are hostile, selfish people and loving, caring people. People can choose between being self-absorbed and self-serving and being other-centered and other-serving. As a result, in this realm people can grow from being self-absorbed to being loving and other-centered. We can see the effects of being cruel and selfish or being kind and giving so we learn from the presence of both extremes.

Why Is Earth School Set Up So People Have So Much to Be Afraid Of?

Answer: The media, entertainment, politicians, news commentators, film producers, and companies that benefit from fear selectively present messages and images that make people afraid. The steady diet has created a population of people living in fear. Earth School is not set up to induce fear; people are cultivating fear for their benefit.

Earth School today has the most extensive, pervasive networks of communication in the history of humankind. In the eighteenth century people would learn about life from a small circle in their geographical location, perhaps a hundred acquaintances in a lifetime. They might hear someone read reports about events that happened in some other location, but most people had no interest in the "news," and those who did learned about a very small number of events outside of their location. None of this information was as dramatic as video is today. It was all verbal. Very few people ever saw a murder. Today, the average child has seen 8,000 murders by age 10.[205] The portrayals are highly graphic and realistic.

Among the large numbers of events the media and entertainment could choose to present to people, they selectively present messages and experiences that induce fear, desire, greed, and basic negative human responses such as anxiety and rage. Politicians, news commentators, film producers, and companies want to create an emotional reaction so people want their products or services. They are intent on having all people feel fear, outrage, and separation from other groups so they can benefit from the panicked responses. The beneficiaries receive money, position, or control when people tune in to their video presentations, elect them, or buy their products. They are motivated to make people feel separated by fear, outrage, and greed.

The result is an Earth School today dominated by fear, anxiety, and dissatisfaction with what people have in life. People living in Earth School have spent every day since childhood receiving a constant flow of these messages adeptly designed to make them fearful, anxious, suspicious, unsatisfied, and greedy.

The state of fear people feel influences all of humankind. We are all Our Universal Intelligence creating this reality by our expectations at a subconscious level of what the reality should be. When we feel fear for any of a great variety of reasons, we create a world of fear. We pass that fear on to those around us, especially children. They grow up in fear.

Suicide is the second leading cause of death for children, adolescents, and young adults ages 15 to 24.[206] For every suicide, there are at least 100 suicide attempts.[207] The average feeling of happiness decreased for the Gen Z generation from an already low 2.15 on a three-point scale in 2006 to 1.97 by 2017.[208] By 2016 and 2017, both adults and adolescents were reporting significantly less happiness than they had in the 2000s.[209] The Australian Youth Mental Health Report found that one in four young people ages 15 to 19 has experienced a "probable mental illness," meaning depression or anxiety or both.[210]

Fear results from the illusion that we are separate from one another, rather than seeing others as one with us in Our Universal Intelligence. Fear and this feeling of separation from others are root causes of the problems humankind is experiencing today.

On the other hand, living in a world of fear allows us to learn the folly of feeling fearful and to grow to reject fear and embrace love. Only in this world with its extremes resulting from fear can we triumph over fear by learning how to be content, confident, loving, and other-centered. We have chosen to be in Earth School at this time because the triumph over fear is possible.

Are People in Earth School Going to Be More Spiritual in the Future?

Answer: Yes. Humankind is steadily evolving to become more wise and spiritually mature.

Earth School is undergoing monumental changes now. In the West, until the seventeenth century, Christianity and the Church held power and controlled people's Minds. The result was unspeakable cruelty and repression of individual thinking. Only the Church's dogma was to be accepted as truth.

In the seventeenth through the twentieth centuries, science and technology came to dominate people's view of life. People were told their individual thoughts were irrelevant and naive. Truth was in the cult of science and scientists were the priests. Society, schools, and institutions viewed the truths of objective science as all that was worthwhile in life. Individual beliefs and development in matters of Mind and spirit, personal perspectives not taught in books, were regarded as irrelevant.

But now, beginning in the last decades of the twentieth century, mass media allowed people to see other perspectives on reality. They began to experience through video media new and wonderful perspectives on life and the life after this life. Their eyes were opened. Masses of people began to experience a new sense of spirituality that had no name and no organization to give it identity.

While the Church demonized communication with loved ones living in the life after this life, people have always had experiences showing their loved ones are alive and anxious to communicate. The warnings of the Church, and the general societal belief that there is no certainty of an afterlife, are breaking down. Humankind is changing its nature. Children especially are more open to the greater reality and what we call psychic experiences. The most gifted of these children are called the "indigo children."

Affiliation with religion is on the decline, but professed spirituality is increasing. A Pew research survey of American adults found that between 2012 and 2017, five short years, the number of adults who reported themselves to be "not religious" rose from 35 to 45 percent. However, the number of people who reported themselves to be "spiritual but not religious" rose from 19 to 27 percent during the same five-year period.[211]

Humankind is changing. We have come into this period of Earth School's history to participate in the change.

What Could Earth School Eventually Become?

Answer: Humankind is evolving Earth School. We are together creating it based on our collective level of wisdom and spiritual maturity. As humankind evolves to have more love, peace, and joy, the world will become a world imbued with love, peace, and joy. However, we chose to enroll in Earth School while it is still in turmoil, early in its spiritual revolution.

We did not choose to participate in the Earth School experiences that will be available in the next centuries. In those later Earth School periods, people will be more loving and other-centered. We are the laborers laying the foundation for that glorious Earth School. As our Minds grow, the conception of Earth School held by the participants evolves. When the conception changes, the environment changes because we are creating the Earth School environment through what our Minds expect to be here.

As humankind grows to be more loving, compassionate, and other-centered, the thoughts, feelings, and interactions of the people in Earth School will become more loving, compassionate, and other-centered. We will live together in love, peace, and joy.

The list below is what Earth School will be like then. We cannot conceive of this reality now. It may seem like kum-ba-yah, New-Age, make-love-not-war talk, but we know from the nature of the life after this life and the best of Earth School as it is today that these will be the characteristics of this new Earth School. Some characteristics are markedly similar to the characteristics of people living in agrarian societies before the Industrial Revolution, when extended families relied on one another to sustain life.

- People will take for granted that everyone lives on after the body dies and people will actively communicate with loved ones in the next stage of life easily and regularly.

- People will not seek fulfillment and happiness in things and activities. They will be most fulfilled when they make those around them satisfied and happy. They will be devoting themselves to others with little thought for themselves. That doesn't mean they won't have needs and desires, simply that the needs and desires won't result in their taking from others by theft, manipulation, or threat. The others will give freely.

- People will live a minimalist life. There will be no wealth disparity because there will be no wealth.

- People will be more interested in helping others have their needs satisfied than in having their own needs satisfied. Giving will be valued more highly than acquiring.

- There will be learning, but not schools where children are forced to learn facts. There will be gatherings of people, including children in which all learn to become confident in themselves. Children will be encouraged to be all they can be with their unique abilities. There will be no uniformly required behaviors, expectations, judgment, report cards, or failure. They will grow from early childhood to take positions as valued, functioning members of the family and society who offer what their talents can most easily, enjoyably, and successfully give to others at every age. They will learn to be loving and compassionate.

- Children and adults together will explore their inner selves and understand their psyches. No knowledge will be regarded as better or more valued than each person's self-discoveries. Humankind will continue to advance intellectually, but the inner person will always be valued more than technological and industrial advancements.

- People will feel free to spend time on activities that may seem frivolous and unproductive, for years if they want to. Other people will encourage and support them.

- No work activity will be regarded more highly than any other. The person who prepares food will be held in as high an esteem as the person who helps people heal.

- There will be no business owners and employees. All people will work at the businesses to ensure they serve clients, consumers, and themselves. They will share in any rewards. Some people will have the role of overseeing the entire business. Others will do more laborious tasks, such as cleaning the business. Neither will be in a more senior position or held in higher esteem.

- There will be no money. Money is a means of giving someone something of value in return for their services or goods. People will freely, joyously give their services and goods without expecting something in return.

- There will be no need for fences, locks, guard dogs, surveillance cameras, and all the other things we need today to keep people from stealing what we call ours. No one will feel the need to steal. The owner will freely give whatever it is the person wants or will help the person find another source if the owner wants to keep whatever the other person wants.

- "My" and "mine" will be heard much less frequently, replaced by "ours" and "everyone's."

- People will celebrate developing and becoming proficient through activities that now are regarded as competitive. There will not be the level of competition present in activities today. Everyone will help others improve and become competent.

- There will be no wars or turmoil. People in more developed areas will strive to help those in areas that are less developed or have more undesirable living conditions.

- There will be no killing of people or animals for any reason.

- There will be no police or other entity that protects people from each other. People will not violate others' rights.

- There will be no insurance. When someone suffers a loss, all of society will rush to help the person recover.

These characteristics of a heaven on earth seem unattainable. We look at them through twenty-first-century Earth School eyes. "I could never leave my doors unlocked. Someone would steal my things." "If we support people doing what they want, we'll have lazy bums we have to support." When all of humankind is loving, compassionate, and other-centered, these concerns we have now in Earth School will dissolve.

We didn't choose to enroll in Earth School at that time. We chose to be here during the turbulent times when humankind is still struggling with greed, authoritarianism, selfishness, manipulation, war, discrimination, and elitism. We are doing the heavy labor of lifting ourselves out of this quagmire and thereby lifting humankind toward the higher position of that heaven on earth.

Why Is Everything Constantly Changing in Earth School?

Answer: For us to have circumstances that enable us to learn and grow, we must confront new experiences with our evolving understanding and capabilities. As we mature physically, spiritually, and mentally, changes in Earth School experiences allow us to apply our new maturity to learning lessons and cultivating our love and compassion for greater growth.

Things and people must come and go. Nothing is permanent. As we encounter changes that are challenging to us, we learn and grow through overcoming or adapting to the challenges.

If we do not meet the challenges, adapt to the changes, and stride into the future confidently, open to the change, we will be stuck in a world that no longer exists. We will feel like aliens in each new world because we have not adjusted our Minds. Since the past is no longer available, we can inflict upon ourselves feelings of loss, depression, hopelessness, discontent, and anger toward the new world.

The world of an infant is different from the world of a 5-year-old, which is different from a 13-year-old's world, which is different from a 21-year-old's world, which is different from the world of a 60-year-old. In one period in Earth School we live many different lives, with different affiliations, perspectives, attitudes, expectations, personalities, repertoires of skills, and levels of love and compassion. We are continually living new lives as new people. Each new life within our Earth School life is ushered in by the ending of the previous life. In each new life, we face new experiences and challenges for us to deal with using our newly formed perspectives, attitudes, expectations, and personalities. It is not a law of the eternal cosmos that we should be born, live our lives, and graduate from the realm we are in. Those changes are created for the Earth School experience.

If things didn't change, we would never have the lives we have today. We wouldn't have been challenged to adjust and grow from infancy into childhood into adolescence and from there into adulthood. We would have learned nothing from the Earth School experience. Change is the necessary component of Earth School that allows us to mature and learn.

Are There Forces and Entities Dedicated to Promoting Humankind's Progress?

Answer: Yes. We are told consistently by people speaking from the life after this life about the fervent, concerted effort to help humankind advance in wisdom, love, and compassion. Those entities involved are continually influencing individuals for the benefit of humankind, although few people realize they are being influenced.

There are strong forces in the realms that are in common with the earth realm that are endeavoring to lift humankind out of the distressing conditions in which we find ourselves. People speaking from the life after this life and other realms or dimensions speak often of their deep desire to help humankind learn to love, have compassion, and live in peace.

Mahatma Gandhi, speaking from spirit through Leslie Flint on June 21, 1961, explains these forces. You can hear Gandhi speaking these words from spirit at www.earthschoolanswers.com/Gandhi1/.

> We on this side, for a long time, have striven to build between our world and yours, a bridge—whereby man could climb to heights and find that peace which your world could give. We know that it is only in this truth, only in this realization of communication, between the so-called dead and the living, that lies the salvation of your world.[212]

Michael Fearon, a biology master at Taunton School, England, who was killed in 1944 in World War II, spoke often to his mother during Leslie Flint sessions. Fearon describes the efforts by people on the other side to help humankind.[213] You can listen to Michael speaking these words at this link: www.earthschoolanswers.com/fearon1/.

> We come to break down the barriers that lie between men. To break down the barriers that man has created by racial intolerance and hatred, by creed and by dogma. We come down that we might, in some measure, bring all peoples together as one family, under one God. We have a purpose and a mission. . . .
>
> We come that we might, in some measure, make your world a better place to live in for the people that follow after you, that they be born free in their mind to live and to love and to learn and to understand the things that are of God. We have great purpose in coming.[214]xxx

Are Any of the Forces Working for Humankind's Benefit from Other Worlds?

Answer: Yes. We know with certainty that spiritual beings are living in other realms, sometimes described as other planets, spheres, realms, or dimensions.

Beings we call "extraterrestrials" described by people living in the life after this life have been in contact with individuals on earth for some time. The Afterlife Research and Education Institute (AREI) Circle of the Masters of Life is a physical mediumship circle. During the meetings, we have been told that people from other realms are in the team in spirit working with us. Three Arcturians and an Andromedan on our team have visited our circle and conversed through the circle sitter who is our channel. They tell us there is a Galactic Federation of 57 groups that meet to explore ways of helping humankind.

We understand from people living in the next realm that UFOs or UAPs are entities reaching out to our world from different sources. They are spiritual, with high standards and attitudes of life and want to be of service to help humankind. Sir Thomas Beecham, who was an English conductor of the London Philharmonic and Royal Philharmonic orchestras during his life, spoke from spirit of the UFOs during a Leslie Flint session. You can listen to Beecham speaking these words at www.earthschoolanswers.com/beecham/.

> It's very distressing the way the world is now, we're very concerned about your world. My goodness me, and you know there are thousands of souls returning from the various worlds of the spirit. Now you take these UFOs as you term them these entities that are reaching your world from different sources and you know I have to explain this there is a reality in that . . . There are entities on different planets who have a higher standard and attitude of life and condition of life whose desire is to be of service and to help because there's great fear, well not fear that's not the word, but great concern about the state of your world you know.[215]

Sir Oliver Lodge, a British physicist and writer, spoke from spirit in a Leslie Flint session responding to a question by George Woods, sitting with Flint, about "flying saucers." You can listen to Lodge speaking these words at www.earthschoolanswers.com/lodge/.

> **George Woods:** Sir Oliver, could you...I wanted to ask you something now you've come through. About these

flying saucers; are they true or not true? Are they...do they come from other planets?

Oliver Lodge: But of course there are other planets, who are endeavoring to make contact or are curious or interested in your world. Just the same as your world or scientists, certain scientists, and peoples are interested in other planets. Of course they do exist, and of course there is a lot of nonsense, no doubt, talked and a lot of things which don't apply.

But of course there are entities, souls, who are trying to break through in a scientific way from other planets into your world and who are in a position, and I would say in some senses, more advanced and are trying to make contact in their own way. But, I think I can say with absolute truth, that of course they are very apprehensive.

In another Leslie Flint session, a man named John Grant described from spirit the concern of these other entities with humankind's motives and experimentation. You can listen to Grant speaking these words at www.earthschoolanswers.com/grant2/.

But in some shape or form, there is a manifestation of many forms of life in and around the Earth, reaching up and outwards to the varying other worlds, upon which certain worlds, entities do live of a much higher order than man himself. And these too, from certain spheres or planets, have at varying times made contact with Earth. But they have been denied, to a certain extent, the opportunity to converse with man.

I am not suggesting here that there have not been isolated instances of souls from other planets, who have not, in some way or other, manifested themselves mentally...uh, there are contacts that have been made of a mental nature and, in consequence, appearances of individual souls from other planets have manifested.

But, generally speaking, for a very long time there have been manifestations around the Earth of mentalities from other planets who are concerned, very much concerned, at the motives of man and the experiments of man . . ..[216]

Are Any of the Entities Concerned with Humankind in Other Dimensions?

Answer: Yes. There are descriptions of entities living in other dimensions on earth and on other planets that are not visible to us but are concerned with humankind's welfare.

The man named John Grant who spoke in a Leslie Flint session described in the previous answer spoke of the entities living in other dimensions not visible to us. You can listen to Grant speaking these words at www.earthschoolanswers.com/grant3/.

> [There are] astral worlds around the Earth, invisible to the human eye.
>
> You see, man assumes anything that is visible is a real thing...uh, the moon it is a reality because it is visible, it is tangible and soon he'll be landing upon it and...as indeed are other worlds, of which as yet knows nothing.
>
> But these are the so-called visible worlds, but the invisible worlds—these are invariably, though not always, the more highly evolved worlds—these are the worlds of the mind and of the spirit and these are the worlds which man has not seen and cannot see, because he is of a different substance and a different composition.[217]

Are There Forces and Entities Seeking to Retard Humankind's Progress?

Answer: Yes. Everything is Our Universal Consciousness. In consciousness, there are thought forms created from the negative energies of hate, discord, and fear widespread in the Minds of people on earth. The thought forms don't want humankind to progress because if hate, discord, and fear cease they will no longer exist. So they do what they can to retard our progress toward evolving a loving, compassionate world.

There are forces and entities seeking to retard humankind's progress. Speakers from the life after this life say that there is no such thing as hell in the religious, pit-of-everlasting-fire notion, but there are dark thought regions where evil dwells and works to retard humankind's progress. Humanity has created the condition. The evil thoughts and actions by these thought forces and entities result from the power of negative human thoughts and actions.[218]

These forces are directly antagonistic to the purification of humankind. They stand in the way of humankind's progress and establish blocks to retard and thwart it.[219]

Many people do not believe such entities exist. They believe them to be primitive, religious superstition. But ignoring or denying them is "an open device of the evil ones for [our] bewilderment."[220] We can resist the influences of these entities by remaining on a higher spiritual level in our daily lives, with more love, compassion, and wisdom. Eventually these thought forms will vanish, banished by love.

Are There Unseen Entities Affecting Us Individually?

Answer: Yes. Some are inspiring and guiding us, such as guides, angels, our Souls, and our loved ones. Others are earthbounds whose bodies have died but they stay in the earth realm moving among us. Some earthbounds have the ability to affect people and objects by moving things, making noises, or otherwise creating disturbances.

Earth School is composed of experiences: sights, sounds, touches, smells, tastes, and bodily sensations. We interact with people

Many Beneficial Entities Are Around Us to Help Us

we can see, hear, and touch. These experiences give us the feeling that is all there is to the world. However, we know that is not true. There are unseen entities that are also part of this world. They exert their influence upon us from their unseen positions. They are all around us, all the time. Explanations of some of these entities follow.

Many Beneficial Entities Are Around Us to Help Us

As we go through our lives in Earth School, we are continually being given guidance and help from our Soul, guides, helpers, angels, loved ones in spirit, and entities that have an interest in our well-being and development. We rarely realize we're being aided. We have inspirations or insights that suddenly come to us to solve problems or act. The guidance is sound, so we act upon it, not realizing its source. At times other people around us in Earth School are influenced in ways that help us. All Souls, guides, helpers, angels, and loved ones are working in concert to help us as we go through our years in Earth School.

"Ghosts" Can Be Just Memories on the Ether

There are also visual experiences of entities we term "ghosts." These ghosts are described by those in the afterlife as being impressions on the memory of the "ether," the spiritual atmosphere surrounding earth. When emotional, traumatic events occur, the ether may retain a memory of the event. Later, sensitive people may be able to see the memory act out. These ethereal memories have no spirit attached to them, can move only in the ways the living person moved when the memory was created, cannot communicate, and are completely harmless. That is why hauntings often involve a spirit seeming to perform actions repeatedly, with no communication between the apparition and the witnesses. When the conditions between the earth's atmosphere and the ether are just right, the memories may play out like a movie so more than one living person witnesses them. That is what happens when people witness a battle scene being played out by what people call "ghosts." There is no living spirit there when the memory is in the ether.

Some People Will Not Leave Earth and Become Earthbound

There are myriad unseen people living in the Earth School environment without bodies called "earthbounds." They no longer have a body, but their spirit remains on earth. Being still attuned to earth, they can walk, sit, ride, attend gatherings such as church services, and otherwise participate in activities unseen by people still living on earth. If they advanced to the next level, they would leave the earth realm and participate in that level's experiences and activities. Their advancement is an act of will, however.

People may be earthbound because of feeling shocked after a sudden traumatic death, because of false religious beliefs about the afterlife, because of a desire to vicariously enjoy earth's pleasures, or because of intense emotions of anger, fear, love, resentment, jealousy, guilt, or remorse. These sentiments keep the person fixated. They live in the earth environment in a dimension where time does not really exist.[221] As a result, the earthbound may be so totally immersed in the illusion, unable to see alternatives, that the person may stay in that state for centuries. Counselors and others continually work to try to get through to them, but since the earthbounds are still in the earth realm, they do not see or hear the counselors, just as people in Earth School do not see or hear guides or loved ones.

Sometimes people living in Earth School called "rescuers" are able to help the earthbounds realize what has happened to them to open their perception to the counselors and loved ones who have been trying to reach them.

Earthbounds leave the Earth School environment when they realize they are no longer in bodies or when they come to appreciate the benefits of going to the next stage of their eternal lives and giving up on the reasons they tarried on earth. The transitioning out of the Earth School environment into the environment of the life after this life is termed the "second death." It would be better to call it the "second transition." There is no "death" involved.

The transition from one attunement to another is entirely in the Mind and seamless. Earthbounds have free will and may decide to stay in the Earth School environment as long as they want to stay. As a result, some earthbounds remain in that condition for hundreds or thousands of years.[222]

Earthbounds May Have Unfinished Business Holding Them Back

Some earthbounds stay in the Earth School environment because they have unfinished business. They could want to stay near a loved one who is ill or grieving. Children lament that they cannot go on because their parents are grieving so much.

Earthbounds May Fear What Comes Next If They Leave Earth

Some earthbounds accept the mythology of the church, so they are afraid if they leave the earth realm they may go to purgatory or hell. Neither exists.

Others who were materialists in their earth life are certain there is no life after the bodies dies, so they're afraid if they do something that shakes the balance of the position they are in, they will fall into the abyss of nothingness.

Earthbounds Can Be Very Frustrated at Not Being Noticed

As the earthbounds travel on earth, they can become very frustrated at not being seen or heard. They may try to move objects or make noise to get people's attention. They are not malicious, however. They are just annoyed that they are close to people and the people take no notice of them.

Poltergeists can be earthbound people who are not able or willing to change their mental condition to allow themselves to leave Earth School. They are almost always simply trying to attract attention and are frustrated that no one can see them or respond to their communication. As a result, they may bang on things, move things about if they can, and otherwise disrupt Earth School.

A woman named Dorcas who came through in a Leslie Flint session described how she delighted in scaring people. She said, "I used to play pranks. I used to do all sorts of things. I used to get quite a great deal of fun and pleasure out of that; opening and shutting doors, and throwing coal and all sorts of things, breaking mirrors, and frightening people."[223]

You can hear Dorcas explaining what she did in more detail at www.earthschoolanswers.com/dorcas/.

Earthbound People Stay on Earth to Participate in Earth Religious or Other Such Activities

Other earthbound people remain in the Earth School environment to continue practicing the rituals they practiced while in bodies, such as religious practices. They may practice old religious rituals, holding on to the religious dogma. They cling to the old beliefs in fear that to doubt would be sacrilege. They go into church and mingle unseen with other people, hear the same old teachings, perform the familiar rituals, and continue in the old mental attitude until some realization guides them into the knowledge that they can move on. They do not progress and obtain knowledge and advancements until they break away from the old beliefs and creeds.[224]

Earthbounds May Stay on Earth to Influence People

Some people will not leave the earth environment because of their attachment to the materialistic experiences on earth. They influence the weak and vulnerable to carry out acts through which they receive vicarious pleasure. Those who loved to drink alcohol and enjoyed the atmosphere of bars hang around those establishments, hovering over the people there, enjoying the pleasures vicariously. They are gleeful over the downfall of the person they have attached themselves to. The streets are dotted with spirits who find their joy in wrecking souls and dragging them down to their own miserable level.[225]

Angry, hostile, and violent people staying in the Earth School environment will actively influence people in Earth School who are angry, hostile, and violent. They enjoy the vicarious experiences that result. They cannot control them or make them do anything against their will, but when a person is in a weakened condition, such as being drunk, they are more easily influenced by these earthbound people.

These earthbounds who have not progressed can have such an influence over someone mentally or physically weak that it seems the person is possessed, but people can only be influenced, not possessed.

People who are earthbound often are unable to make connections other than to the people still living on earth. As a result, they may "attach" themselves to someone.

Earthbound Influences Often Cause What Is Mistakenly Called Mental Illness

Some in the next realms of life have also said clearly that these earthbound spirits are the cause of many cases diagnosed as psychosis, paranoia, depression, addiction, manic depression, criminal behavior, and phobias. The earthbounds cannot "possess" a person, but people who are sensitive to the other realms of life and easily influenced can become the focus of earthbound spirits who wish to use them to have vicarious experiences. The voices people hear, the cravings, and the impulses to do things are the result of these influences.

Twentieth-century Swedish-American psychiatrist and psychical researcher Dr. Carl A. Wickland, a member of the Chicago Medical Society and American Association for the Advancement of Science and a director of the National Psychological Institute of Los Angeles, explained that "Spirit obsession is a fact—a perversion of a natural law—and is amply demonstrable. . . . to be an ignorant or mischievous spirit, whose identity may frequently be verified."[226]

Today there are psychiatrists who specialize in treating people negatively influenced by entities. Among the most prominent are psychotherapist Dr. Edith Fiore, author of *The Unquiet Dead: A Psychologist Treats Spirit Possession*, and psychotherapist Dr. William Baldwin, author of several books, including *Spirit Releasement Therapy: A Technique Manual*.

Children May Be Influenced by Earthbounds

Many young children have mediumistic abilities because their Minds are in the state that is associated with meditation and creativity in adults, called the alpha or theta states. As cell biologist Bruce Lipton explains, in the first seven years of a child's life, the child's Mind is in a receptive, learning state. This state registers in the body experience as alpha or theta brainwaves. In this state, children are open and naively receptive. They are being programmed to live successfully on earth.[227] Poltergeists are often associated with children and adolescents because this openness is the same as medium ability. The entities can draw from this energy to act in the physical realm.

If children use a device such as a Ouija board, they can hear from earthbound people who intentionally deceive them. In those cases, the lower-level spirits can provide misleading and disruptive messages. In no circumstances, however, can a lower-level spirit possess someone.

Are There Such Things as Negative Thought Forms That Affect Us Individually?

Answer: Yes. When many Minds on earth are filled with animosity, hate, fear, and resentment, they contribute to creating a world of animosity, hate, fear, and resentment. Negative thought forms have a life of sorts and do affect people.

In the Earth School environment there are unseen influences or forces that have an effect on people. I hesitate to call them "beings" or "entities." Although they have no personality, as such, they do have motives and perform actions that may disrupt people's lives. They are described as "thought forms" that are created from the accumulation of negative thoughts. Thoughts have much more power than people realize.

Annie Besant and Charles Webster Leadbeater wrote *Thought-Forms*, a book describing the emotions, thoughts, and actions that forms may take. Besant described them as "ensouled thought forms" and "destructive elementals."[228]

7

Why Is There Evil and Suffering in the World?

Earth School is a crucible of negative and positive energies. Since we're here together now, it's apparent we wanted to love, learn, and have experiences in this troubled environment. There are reasons for Earth School's level of what are regarded as evil and suffering. In this chapter, I explain evil and suffering in the world.

Why Is There Evil in the World?

Answer: There is no evil in the world. There are only people with free will performing actions we regard as evil because they harm others. When humankind matures to live in love and compassion, what we call evil will disappear.

We regard some act or person as evil when that person causes others mental or physical suffering, including murder, mass killing, ethnic cleansing, genocide, enslavement, kidnapping, torture, rape, destroying a person's spirit, and inducing fear. Volcanoes are not evil. Tigers are not evil. Even viruses and bacteria that kill people are not evil. They all cause suffering, but they have no intent to do harm. Evil is only in what people do to each other.

We regard actions as evil when someone chooses to cause others to suffer. We do not regard as evil a toddler's destructive act because the child is not making free-will choices as an adult does. Before sentencing in a trial, a judge determines whether the perpetrators are capable of understanding their actions, regardless of the offense, because we assume a person unable to make free-will choices cannot be held accountable for their actions. Such a person's actions that harm others are not deemed evil. We do not regard as evil the action of causing a car accident that results in injury or death. The accident didn't result from a free-will choice to cause injury or death.

As a result, we can say that we regard as evil the free-will choice to cause suffering.

What we regard as evil differs dramatically among ages and cultures. The people and activities we judge as evil depend on the mores of the group we belong to. In India, more than 5,000 brides are killed annually because their dowries are considered insufficient.[229] The families don't see this as evil. In Nigeria, the Yoruba people once saw as evil the birth of twins because they believed it meant the woman had engaged in sex with two men around the time of conception.[230] The God of the Old Testament ordered 160 killing sprees with a specific enumeration of 2.8 million deaths. Satan, on the other hand, was responsible for only 10 deaths.[231] We do not call the God of the Old Testament evil, but we do call the Satan figure evil. What people regard as evil is very much dependent on their belief system.

When people use their free will to perform acts that harm others, we regard the free-will choice as evil if it violates society's mores. Evil is not built into the fabric of the world. People choose to do evil things. The question is not "Why is there evil in the world?" The question is "Why do people choose to perform actions that harm other people?"

If we are to eradicate the actions we regard as evil, we must help all people grow to be loving, compassionate, other-centered, sensitive to others, and unwilling to harm others physically or psychologically. For that to happen, the false sense of separation among people must fall away. We are not separate; we are one Mind with each other in Our

Universal Intelligence. Only the shell we take on to act in Earth School is separate from other people's shells. We, the Souls taking on separate bodies, are one Mind. When people come to realize that truth, there will be no more activities or people we would call evil.

Why Is There Suffering in the World?

Answer: Suffering results from what we learned in a spiritually backward society that teaches us falsehoods we must grow out of. Because of our beliefs in the falsehoods, we make ourselves suffer. Rejecting the falsehoods by realizing the truth will allow us to live every day in love, peace, and joy without suffering.

A perennial question people ask as they try to understand our lives in Earth School is "Why is there so much suffering in the world?" The answers to the question come from understanding what suffering is and how suffering happens. There is suffering in the world, but its causes and outcomes are not what people believe them to be. The answers to why there is suffering in the world lie in six areas people regard as suffering:

Suffering from having our loved ones pass away
Suffering from losses and life changes
Suffering from people harming other people
Suffering from starvation
Suffering from illnesses
Suffering from psychological problems
Suffering from physical pain

The questions about why each of these forms of suffering are in the world are answered in the pages that follow.

My Important Heartfelt Note to You

In the explanations of suffering that follow, I describe what life will be like when humankind matures out of self-absorption, fear, and conflict into love, compassion, and peace for all people. When I write that suffering and pain can be alleviated when humankind matures I don't want you to feel I'm saying we could stop our personal suffering if we just put our minds to it. We can't. It's too soon. But we can advance up the slope a little during our lifetimes toward the summit of living free of suffering. In our lives today, as we grow in understanding we will live healthier, happier lives and we will bring humankind closer to the time when all people live together in love, peace, and joy with no suffering.

Why Does This Life Have Mass Death Atrocities?

Answer: All deaths of the body are individual, involving the person and the circle of loved ones around the person whose body has died. The numbers of people whose bodies have died and the manner in which they died are unimportant. The death of the Earth School body by any means is a natural end to the Earth School episode of our eternal lives.

A perennial statement people make is "I don't believe in God because God would not allow the Holocaust" or "God should have warned people about the Twin Towers terrorist attacks." I don't believe in a big male in the sky who would make choices about who lives and who dies either. But the question remains: Why does life have atrocities involving the bodily deaths of millions?

There have always been atrocities, some far greater than those perpetrated by the Third Reich and Himmler, the architect of the Nazi Final Solution. Many involve painful, drawn out deaths in which families watch each other die. North Korea has subjected people to slavery, torture, starvation, shootings, gassing, and human experimentation. The death toll is estimated at over 3 million. In the

Khmer Rouge holocaust an estimated 3 million people died from mass executions, torture, forced labor, malnutrition, and disease during internment—25% of the population. The Congo Free State atrocities killed as many as 10 million from mass murders, mutilations, and starvation. The Japanese Wars killed as many as 14 million civilians and prisoners of war. Somewhere in the range of 4.5 million Chinese died from starvation during horrible conscription campaigns. Stalin is estimated to have killed 20 million of his own people through famine, purges, labor camps, and massacres. The estimates for Mao Zedong's terrible reign is as high 70 million, many from starvation.

Death of the body is the way we end our period of experiences in Earth School. Bodies die from cigarette smoke, automobile accidents, murders, suicides, overdoses, and other avoidable causes. Death of the body is a natural part of life, whatever its cause.

However, bodily death is individual, involving each person and those around them. All our bodies must die to end our tenure in Earth School. But the frail, temporary body is of no worth compared to the value of the love and compassion we have for those in our circle during the brief time we have on earth. Who we are and how we live with others is all that is important. The body is insignificant. The manner of bodily death or how many people come to the end of their lives because of this atrocity or that preventable act isn't important.

Bodies die in a great many ways. So the question isn't how many people's bodies die from cigarette smoke or murder or automobile accidents or atrocities. The question is how is each person living with the circle of people in their sphere of influence until that moment when the exit comes? We must have the perspective on life that what happens to the body is of no consequence, and the number of people who have their natural, planned exit from earth from any specific cause is unimportant.

The true atrocities in our lives are the psychological or physical abuse inflicted by others. We must devote our love, compassion, and intervention to that one child or spouse or elderly person who is suffering at the hands of another.

Why Do We Have to Suffer from Having Our Loved Ones Pass Away?

Answer: Sadness at a loved one's graduation is natural. All the things familiar about life together on earth have ended. We will suffer less grief and for a shorter time when they realize with conviction that our loved one is alive and well, only a thought away, and we will be again on the same plane in a short time.

A prominent reason people suffer to the point of becoming ill is the passing of someone close to them, such as a child, spouse, close family member, or close friend. Suffering from a loved one's transition from earth will cause grief and sadness but should not cause long-term suffering. We feel great sadness that a loved one has graduated from Earth School ahead of us. But the sadness does not have to result in debilitating or long-term suffering. The transition from Earth School results in suffering only if we believe at some level that

~ The person may be gone forever, lost in the abyss of eternity.

~ We will never have contact with the person again.

~ The person is in some other existence we cannot reach or understand and may be unhappy or in dire circumstances.

~ The person is in the ground or in a mausoleum.

We bring suffering on ourselves by misunderstanding the transition from Earth School. We can reduce the suffering by changing our understanding. We do not die.

These are the truths about the transition from Earth School:

1. The loved one who has transitioned has changed form but is still with us.

2. The loved one is happy, enjoying life, and growing, just as if they had gone off to live an exciting life in another country.

3. The loved one is accessible to communicate. The person still in Earth School just has to be willing to take the time to learn how to communicate.

4. In a very short time, there will be a wonderful reunion when all are in the same realm, living fulfilling lives together.

5. The exit was part of pre-birth planning by the person, the family, and all others involved.

Why Does the Body Have to Die?

Answer: The body is just a focal point for us in Earth School so we can have experiences with others, like an avatar. We are never the body. As a result, when it is time for our graduation, those remaining on earth will no longer have the lifeless body as the point of contact for us. The person is freed from it to live and communicate without the constraints they had put on their body in their life plan.

Death of the body is just a way to make the transition into the next stage of life, like going from infancy to childhood, childhood to adolescence, adolescence to young adulthood, and young adulthood to maturity. The exit from Earth School is a natural transition into the next stage of life.

Somehow we must have a situation in which the body ceases to function so the transition can occur. Everything in Earth School has reasons, causes, and effects. As a result, the body must be shed for some reason: old age, illness, accident, homicide, suicide, or other such event.

Our leaving the body behind is like getting on the plane to go to a new country to live for a few years until our family can come there and all live together. If someone we love gets on a plane to go to the new country, we may be sad but we don't grieve as if we will never see them again. We don't go on Sundays to the airport and put flowers at the TSA gate.

In the same way, if we realize our loved one was never a body but did display a body overcoat for a period of time, we can feel joy and comfort knowing our loved one is alive, healthy, happy, and waiting at the arrival gate for us to come through when we make our own trip to that destination.

Why Would the Souls of a Family Plan an Early Exit for a Child?

There are many reasons the Souls of a family and the child's Soul plan a child's exit from Earth School. For the family planning the child's brief life before their entry into Earth School, the planned exit is not traumatic. While outside of Earth School with full understanding of what will happen, all see Earth School as a short time in eternity in which to learn lessons. The early exit is part of the lessons being learned by the child, the parents, and others who are part of the child's circle. All agreed to it during pre-birth planning.

The Soul that is the child may have wanted the benefits of having this particular mother personality for the time the child was on earth, and during the pre-birth planning the mother Soul agreed. Sometimes short lives are planned when a Soul wants to accelerate its growth. All lives are interconnected and there are myriad reasons a Soul may choose to have a short life, and the planning for all people bears upon the final decision to have an early exit point. We don't know the reasons for it, but we can be assured that it was in the Soul's plan.[232]

Eventually, Humankind Will Not Grieve and Suffer When a Loved One Transitions from Earth

When humankind matures in our understanding of life and the transition called death, the feeling of suffering resulting from a loved one's transition will disappear. A loved one's transitioning before us will result in sadness because the person is no long available in the body we knew, in the same realm we are in, but we will realize how natural and normal the transition is, and that soon we will again be on the same plane together. Death should not result in suffering.

Why Does This Life Keep Making People Suffer from Losses and Life Changes?

Answer: Life doesn't make us suffer. If we invest our feelings of happiness and well-being in things and people, we will inevitably make ourselves suffer when the things and people are not available, we are afraid and fearful that we will lose them, and we feel despair when they leave or are lost. To stop making ourselves suffer, we must feel fulfilled and happy with who we are, whoever is with us, and what we have.

People cause themselves to suffer over life changes. Something they have been accustomed to having, have relied upon, or love, cherish, or value has gone away, or the person is faced with loss of the old and familiar when new circumstances emerge from life changes. These stressors include divorce or separation, jail term, being fired, changes in the health of a family member, sex difficulties, negative financial conditions, foreclosure, children leaving home, business readjustments, change to a different job or line of work, increased arguments with a spouse, a large mortgage or loan, change in responsibilities at work, trouble with family or in-laws, trouble with a person in authority, or minor violations of the law.

Any of these changes in life circumstances causes suffering when the person is fearful of the change, has difficulty adjusting, and is stuck yearning for the past condition.

Losses and Life Changes Do Not Have to Result in Suffering

A person chooses to suffer when losses and life changes occur, but the suffering is not in the changes; it is in the person's reactions to the changes. If we cling to things and what was, we will inevitably suffer when the things disappear and what was is no more. We will continually fear that we may lose what we have and be extremely controlling to be sure we continue to have it. If we make ourselves feel uncomfortable when life changes and we lose what was, the discomfort may be suffering, but we are making ourselves suffer.

The problem with feelings of happiness that can only come when we have what we desire or avoid what we fear is that the happiness is dependent on having or avoiding something. Feeling happy because we have gotten something or have eliminated something is just another face of unhappiness. As long as we invest our happiness in having or avoiding things, we will be miserable because we can't always have what we want or avoid what we don't want. The result is a life filled with unfulfilled desires, fears, and squandering everything of ourselves and those around us to get what we want or avoid what we don't want. That is not lasting happiness.

The key to not feeling suffering from losses or threats is to realize nothing in Earth School is of any value except our love, compassion, and feelings of peace and joy with people, especially those we love. Everything else is disposable. When we realize we are in a temporary period of life, that nothing is permanent, and that clinging to things will cause unhappiness because things will go away, then we can adapt to changes and look forward to the new world we are entering. We can close the door on what we had and look forward to what will be. If we continue to look backward, yearning for what was, we will be discontented with life and feel hopeless. We will make ourselves suffer.

Accepting changes as they occur, with the confidence that in the end we are cared for, results in little or no stress and unhappiness when changes and losses occur. As people grow to be other-centered, we will increasingly support one another during times of change and stress. We will also be comforted if we know our guides and loved ones are supporting us, rejoicing with our triumphs, and aiding us in our challenges. They will help us adapt to these changes and find joy in what comes to us. We must learn to regularly communicate with them and learn how to receive their counsel.

Suffering from life changes is not a necessary characteristic of Earth School.

Why Does the World Have Suffering from People Harming Other People?

Answer: A primary reason the world has suffering is that people harm others, are insensitive to others, and have little love for others. When humankind learns to live together in love, peace, and joy, people will no longer harm each other. Instead, all people will ardently seek ways to serve and help others. We will live in a world of love, peace, and joy when we have a change of heart and mind.

Suffering results from harmful things people do to other people: adult rape, childhood sexual abuse, violence resulting in bodily harm, witnessing the murder of a loved one, witnessing or being the victim of atrocities, witnessing or being the victim of domestic violence, physical abuse, emotional maltreatment, neglect causing bodily and mental anguish, serious accident, natural and manmade disasters, and removal from a secure environment such as a home or family

These traumatic experiences can be devastating. The victim relives the experiences in memories triggered throughout the person's lifetime. When the person re-experiences the traumatic memories, the recalled experiences have the same effect as the traumas that resulted from the original experiences. Each re-experience causes a new memory experience itself, so the traumatic memory experience remains at a high probability of being triggered by some stimulus during the Earth School day. Suffering continues.

Suffering from People Harming Others Will Be Eradicated

The suffering people cause for other people is not necessary in our lives. It is what people do to other people, not something inflicted on us by a god or the structure of Earth School. People will no longer harm other people when humankind awakens to the realization that we are spiritual beings, one with each other, who can live together in greater love, peace, and joy through kind, compassionate acts. The dysfunctional motives and actions people have learned from their childhoods in today's spiritually backward society will fall away.

We can change humankind, but it will take time. We must keep our focus on the goal and move people within our sphere of influence toward being loving, peaceful, and joyful at every opportunity. Eventually, when enough people are moving humankind forward, we will see the traumatic events and resulting suffering from them disappear.

Suffering inflicted by people on others is not woven into the fabric of Earth School. We are inflicting it upon ourselves. It is a temporary condition that will be eradicated as humankind evolves. We are contributing to that evolution when we are loving and compassionate with the people in our circle of contacts.

Why Does the World Have Suffering from Starvation?

Answer: Some people choose starvation during their pre-birth planning for a variety of heartfelt reasons important to them and those in Earth School with them. More importantly, hunger and starvation result from what people do to other people. When humankind grows to share a natural, pressing need to satisfy all people's needs, hunger and starvation will disappear.

Every five seconds a child dies of starvation.[233] The U.N. estimates 793 million people are today starving around the world.[234]

Perhaps the worst image of suffering is the photograph of a starving child in the Sudan trying to get milk from his starving mother's breast, but she has no milk because she herself is starving. The mother will watch her child die slowly and then will die herself.

It may seem that suffering is an integral, permanent characteristic of Earth School because it is so widespread, but it is only widespread because people are inflicting it on other people. The causes are poverty, inequality in wealth and standards of living, religious turmoil, corruption, and government actions. To alleviate suffering in the Earth School realm we must have societies that have evolved away from political corruption, religious conflicts, dysfunctional government activities, and inactivity by people with the resources to alleviate the starvation. They must be replaced by compassion for the plight of starving people, commitment by governments to helping their people, and engagement of people with the resources in alleviating the poverty causing starvation.

Poverty and the resulting starvation could be eliminated if the wealthy countries were willing to divert a small amount of their wealth to eliminating it. Jeffrey Sachs, one of the world's leading experts on economic development and the fight against poverty, explained, "The cost to end poverty is $175 billion per year for 20 years. This yearly amount is less than 1 percent of the combined income of the richest countries in the world."[235] That figure is only 19 percent of the United States military budget in 2021.

Another estimate is that global hunger could be eliminated by 2030 if the wealthy nations devoted $33 billion a year to its eradication.[236] That is only 3.5 percent of the United States annual military budget.

Poverty and starvation are inflicted on people by other people or are the result of inactivity by people with the resources to alleviate the poverty. Suffering from starvation is not a condition woven into the fabric of the world.

Suffering from Starvation Is Freely Chosen in Pre-birth Planning

As terrible as the situation is, the starving mother watching her child die from starvation could have entered Earth School to be a martyr whose circumstances could stir people to have compassion and the drive to help alleviate the suffering, or could be someone whose Soul has resolved to understand the depths of despair that result from the starvation. The possibility is not as preposterous as it sounds. "Hunger strikes" are a common event. Mahatma Gandhi underwent 17 episodes of hunger fasting, sometimes to near death with no indications he would relent. An Indian revolutionary named Potti Sriramulu did starve himself to death in 1952 for political reasons. In the 1981 Irish hunger strike, ten republican prisoners in Northern Ireland chose to starve themselves to death.[237]

Many people have chosen starvation to death as their path. Jain monks have a practice called Sallekhana in which the person fasts to death. The practice has been observed by men, women, and even royalty for centuries. Each year, up to 500 followers of Jainism starve themselves to death.[238]

In the same way, people planning starvation for their lives before birth would have had the clear perspective that the Earth School experiences would be only temporary, and they would be choosing them of their own free will. Just as people now living in Earth School are choosing to starve themselves, any individual may have accepted the fate of starving as part of the Earth School experience.

We must not judge why people are going through the experiences they have chosen to go through. We chose to have experiences at this time in Earth School because we need something this period gives us. It could be that we felt the need for suffering from starvation or to experience love and compassion for people experiencing the suffering. Or it could be that humankind needs to grow through realizing there is widespread suffering being inflicted by people upon other people so humankind changes to be more loving and compassionate. We entered Earth School at a time when we could co-create a reality with these circumstances. We chose this time and we chose our circumstances. Now the question is what did we intend for our Earth School selves to do with what we regard as suffering from starvation that is present now?

Why Is There Suffering from Illnesses?

Answer: We bring most illness on ourselves through lifestyle, negative thoughts and actions, and an epidemic of people with no lasting, loving relationships. Conversely, people living healthy lifestyles with loving relationships and positive belief systems experience less illness. Illness will be less common when humankind creates a world filled with love, peace, and joy.

Debilitating illnesses—especially neurodegenerative diseases such as Alzheimer's, Parkinson's, ALS (amyotrophic lateral sclerosis, or Lou Gehrig's disease), multiple sclerosis, muscular dystrophy, motor neurone disease, and others—cause suffering because the person loses mental or physical capacities over time, often succumbing to the disease.

Humanity Brings Much Illness on Ourselves

Disease is humbling. It reminds us we are a community, dependent on one another, and that our period in Earth School is short. Disease continues to teach people not to be so tied to the objects in Earth School, but to focus on what is important in life: our love, peace, and joy with each other.

However, we create the diseases that afflict us. Our attitudes, beliefs, and frame of mind create disease. Bruce Lipton, a cell biologist on the faculty in the Department of Anatomy at the University of Wisconsin School of Medicine and author of *Biology of Belief*, explains that if someone believes they will have a disease, they may develop it. Disease-inducing negative thoughts, called the "nocebo effect," operate unconsciously and are almost always related to self-critical and disempowering beliefs acquired from parents, family, and even doctors, before the age of seven.[239]

We are creating illnesses because of the stresses we live under and our attitudes and beliefs about victimhood and pressures and the competition for life.[240] We are creating the disease in ourselves that people call "suffering."

You can view a video of Dr. Bruce Lipton describing how our thoughts create illness at www.earthschoolanswers.com/lipton/.

Elizabeth Blackburn, winner of a Nobel Prize in medicine, explains that chronic stress, negative thoughts, and pessimism shorten our lives. They damage our body, hasten our aging, and wreck our immune system. She explains that the deleterious effects are from the "telomere effect." Telomeres are the chromosomes located inside the cell's nucleus, which contains our genes and genetic information. In her book *The Telomere Effect: A Revolutionary Approach to Living Younger, Healthier, Longer,* Blackburn explains that negativity, hostility, pessimism, and a lack of presence were proven to shorten longevity and lead to accelerated aging.[241] We shorten our lives by our beliefs and state of mind.

A study by Sheldon Cohen at Carnegie Mellon University found that people who are happy, lively, or calm or exhibit other positive emotions are less likely to become ill when they are exposed to a cold virus than those who report few of these emotions. When they do come down with a cold, happy people report fewer symptoms than would be expected from objective measures of their illness.[242]

What we call suffering from disease results in large part from our belief systems and lifestyles.

Harmful Body Conditions Can Result from Our Expectations

Another reason we know our Minds bring illness to the body experience is that our body experience changes from psychological suggestion. Accounts in the literature describe people's physiologies changing when they are given the suggestion that something is true about their bodies. When a person's interpretations of experiences or beliefs change, the body experiences may change to match. Bodily suffering results, in large part, from what we are creating in our body experience.

In one study reported in the *American Journal of Psychiatry*, a combat veteran was placed in a hypnotic trance. He was then told he was back in combat and a shell had just exploded, dropping a small particle of molten shell fragment on his hand. When he came out of the trance, the veteran complained of a pain in his hand as though he had a cigarette burn. Four hours later a full blister about one centimeter in diameter appeared on his hand, just as though the shell fragment had landed there. Of course, none had. His beliefs and expectations changed the experience of his body.

On the day after the burn had healed, he was again put in a hypnotic trance and told that his right hand was perfectly normal but his left hand was anesthetized and drained of blood. When he was brought out of the trance, a needle prick to a finger on his right hand caused him to wince, and he bled. But when a finger on his left hand was pricked, he felt nothing and no blood emerged from the wound.²⁴³

The beliefs resulting from interpretations changed the combat veteran's body experience. The body experience is in the Mind, as are all experiences, not in a world outside of the person. There are no bodies in worlds outside of the Mind. Since the body experience is in the Mind, changes in beliefs and expectations can result in changes in the body experience. What we regard as illness from suffering results from our inflicting illness upon ourselves by our attitudes and beliefs.

We Change the Body Experience When We Expect a Change

In the placebo effect, a person can be convinced something is true, and the body experiences will reflect whatever the suggestion is.

Patients with Debilitating Knee Pain Healed Themselves

In a Baylor School of Medicine study reported in the *New England Journal of Medicine,* patients with severe and debilitating knee pain were divided into three groups. Surgeons shaved the damaged cartilage in the knees of Group 1 patients. Surgeons flushed out the knee joints of Group 2 patients. Group 3 patients received a fake surgery: surgeons made incisions and bandaged the knees, but performed no surgery. The three groups had no knowledge of which procedure had happened to them.

All three groups went through the same rehabilitation process. The result was that the placebo group improved as much as the other two groups that had had surgery. The authors concluded that the health care industry should rethink how to test whether surgical procedures for the relief of symptoms are more efficacious than a placebo.²⁴⁴

Mr. Wright Heals Himself, Then Succumbs When He Loses Belief

In another example of beliefs affecting the body experience, psychologist Dr. Bruno Klopfer describes a patient named Mr. Wright with an advanced lymph-node cancer called lymphosarcoma. Wright's neck, armpits, chest, abdomen, and groin were filled with tumors the size of oranges, and his spleen and liver were so enlarged that two quarts of milky fluid had to be drained out of his chest every day.

Mr. Wright learned about a drug called Krebiozen that was being used to treat this specific type of cancer. He begged his physician, Dr. West, to give him the drug. Dr. West reluctantly injected him with Krebiozen. Ten days after the first dose of Krebiozen, Mr. Wright left the hospital cancer free.

Two months later, Mr. Wright chanced upon a copy of a study reporting that Krebiozen was a fraud; it is worthless for the treatment of cancer. Upon reading it, his cancer quickly returned in full force.

Dr. West knew his patient was failing, so he tried an experiment. He announced to Mr. Wright that he was giving him a new variant of Krebiozen called "ultra-pure Krebiozen." Actually, he injected Mr. Wright with harmless saline solution. Sure enough, the tumors melted away and the fluid in his chest disappeared. He was once again cancer free.

A short time later, the American Medical Association announced that without a doubt, Krebiozen was utterly worthless. Mr. Wright saw the study and his cancer returned. He died two days later.[245]

Mr. Wright's interpretations of the experience of being injected with Krebiozen changed him physiologically. Such is the power of our beliefs and expectations resulting from our interpretations of experiences.

Anita Moorjani—From Death's Door to Health by Changing Beliefs

Anita Moorjani, author of *Dying to Be Me*,[246] lay slipping in and out of consciousness in the hospital, succumbing to a four-year battle with cancer. Her tumors had grown to the size of lemons throughout her lymphatic system; her brain and lungs were filled with fluid; and her skin had lesions weeping with toxins. She fell into a deep coma. Her husband was told she would not live through the night.

But as she lay dying, she began to lose attachment to her body, feeling as if she was no longer a part of it. She felt her Mind expanding beyond space and time. Joy filled her spirit. She sensed the presence of her deceased father and her best friend who had died of cancer. Others also surrounded her. She felt the overwhelming love of a being she knew was God, but not as a person—as a state of being.

She experienced a life review and realized she was creating her cancer by her fears of displeasing others and not measuring up to their expectations. She was part of a traditional Hindu family in a foreign land, struggling and failing to manage conflicting cultural and religious expectations. She was fearful of everything. "Only when I realized my own magnificence, my own perfection, my own self worth as a beautiful child of the universe, was I able to let go of fear and embrace life with all its uncertainties, ambiguities, joys, sorrows, and challenges. Seeing myself as perfection, as an exquisite manifestation of life, led to my healing," she said.[247]

She was given the choice by the God presence to leave earth then or return to her life on earth. She chose to come back, embracing her new understanding of her life. She awoke from the coma with newfound purpose and resolve to be true to herself, live the life she wanted to live, and heal herself. Within weeks, she was released from the hospital without a trace of cancer in her body.

Our beliefs can bring disease upon us. Our beliefs can cure us.

The Bodies of People with Multiple Personalities Change When They Change Personalities

People's beliefs and expectations create their reality, including their illnesses. Physiological changes occur when people with multiple personality disorder (now called dissociative identity disorder) believe they are another personality with a different physiology.

A drunk person can instantly become sober when the personality changes. Scars, burn marks, and cysts can appear and disappear. Some multiples must carry two or three different pairs of glasses because as the personalities change the visual physiology follows suit. One personality can be color-blind and another not. Even eye color can change. Tumors appear and disappear. The voice pattern for each of a multiple's personalities can be different, a feat that requires such a deep physiological change that even the most accomplished actors cannot alter their voices enough to change basic voice patterns.[248]

Sybil was a psychiatric patient who had dissociative identity disorder with 16 distinct personalities that emerged over 40 years. One of her personalities was diabetic, while another was not. Sybil's blood sugar levels would be normal when she was in her non-diabetic personality, but when she shifted into her diabetic alter ego, her blood sugars immediately rose and all medical evidence demonstrated she was diabetic. When her personality reverted to the non-diabetic counterpart, her blood sugars immediately normalized.[249]

In another example, a patient showed up at a doctor's office with one eye swollen shut from a wasp sting. As the patient was in the office, he changed to another personality and the pain and swelling quickly ended. When the patient returned home, the personality that suffered the wasp sting came back and the pain and swelling returned with a vengeance. The patient went to an ophthalmologist who attested to the fact that the patient indeed had an eye swollen shut from a wasp sting.[250]

We are affecting our body experiences every day. What we believe deeply, without reservation, about our body experience is what the body experience becomes. The literature on healing attests to the fact that the body experience can become what we want it to become. Our belief makes us whole. This is another demonstration that what people term suffering from disease is, at least in most cases, a result of what people are doing to themselves and others.

If humankind had the confidence that our lives are eternal, we are loved, and we are cared for by unseen hands, people would feel contented, happy, and confident they do not have diseases. Suffering from disease would be greatly reduced or eradicated.

Disease Is Not a Permanent Characteristic of Earth School

Humankind is creating disease in Earth School because of our self-absorption, greed, insensitivity, and cruelty. We are told by people living in the life after this life that there will continue to be disease as long as humankind is lacking in love, compassion, and sensitivity. When all people are loving, compassionate, and sensitive, disease will disappear.

While there is still disease in the world, a loving, compassionate humankind will make people's lives more comfortable. And the thought of the body dying from a debilitating disease will not have the impact it has when a materialistic belief system predominates. People will look forward to the next stage of life when they are healthy and vibrant.

Eventually, when humankind is loving, peaceful, and joyful, disease will no longer be the force it is today.

Why Do People Suffer from Mental Illness and Disabilities?

Answer: The people experiencing mental issues have chosen to experience them as part of their life plan, for the sake of others or to learn lessons themselves. Even so, mental illness and disabilities will have less of an impact when the society we are evolving gives all people support and unconditional love. And when society matures spiritually, there will be fewer unseen entities exacerbating mental illnesses.

People with mental illnesses do not need to suffer to the extent they do in society today. When humankind evolves to being caring and sensitive to others in all circumstances, individuals with mental illnesses will be accepted and cared for more readily because humankind will be more compassionate and other-centered. We can alleviate suffering from mental illness.

Another reason we know suffering from mental illness can be reduced or eradicated is that many mental illnesses are created by the influence of entities intent upon controlling people still living on earth. Dr. Carl Wickland, who was chief psychiatrist at the National Psychopathic Institute of Chicago, became convinced that many of his patients suffering from mental illness had unseen entities attached to them that influenced them in their addictions, proclivities toward antisocial behavior, alcoholism, madness, and even murder.[251]

As with the other sources of suffering in Earth School, these mental illnesses are in large measure the result of humankind's condition. When people become more loving, compassionate, and kind, these negative entities will have no ability to influence people. They are able to influence only people who are already predisposed to drunkenness, mind-altering drugs, angry outbursts, crime, and arson. When society has matured away from the negative influences, there will no longer be easy prey for the entities. They will no longer exist because they are created and sustained by negative emotions. There will also be fewer earthbounds to make mischief because people making the transition from the earth realm will have stronger spiritual grounding and an understanding of our nature as one Mind with one another.

Why Do People Suffer from Accidents That Cause Painful Injuries or Loss of Function?

Answer: Accidents and injuries are normal parts of life. Some are in the person's pre-birth plan. Whether the losses resulting from accidents are devastating depends on the person's attitude toward the loss and what is important in their life, not the experience or resulting disabilities.

It seems unfair that someone must live a life disabled by an accident or illness. Everyone, it seems, should be able to live a full, healthy life with no disabilities. However, suffering because of the loss of abilities results from interpretations of the experience, not from the disabilities. We will experience little or no suffering if we understand that the accident or illness and disability were part of careful planning by the person in the accident, the family, and all others involved. Everyone agreed to this event and the results before beginning the Earth School experience. All knew there would be limitations on life because of disabilities but chose to have the accident or illness out of love for each other, for reasons that may be unclear, but which we can be reassured are for everyone's benefit.

People also have the choice of accepting the disabilities with optimism and happiness, realizing we have abilities rather than being defined by the disabilities. Optimism and happiness depend on the person's beliefs and attitudes, not the nature of the disability. Having a disability does not mean the person must suffer.

Why Does Life Have Suffering from Physical Pain?

Answer: Pain is the body's way of telling us something is wrong and must be attended to. People without pain sensors receive no warning about debilitating, life-threatening illnesses and physical damage. When pain goes awry, usually people can mitigate the pain through their control of it and attitude toward it.

Pain is a unique form of suffering everyone experiences. However, pain can overextend its function and leave the person in great discomfort or agony. Debilitating pain is probably the worst form of suffering because it is constantly present and may have no remedy.

Pain does not have to dominate a person's life and create suffering. Pain is experiences in the Mind, not in a body. The Mind feels pain and attributes it to something happening in the body, but the pain is only in the Mind. Pain, like emotions, is irreducible, meaning we cannot dissect it to tell what it is made of. We can only say, "I feel pain" or "That hurts." Pain is an experience.

However, people's mental conditions affect the severity of the pain. People have control over their pain. In one study, clinical and experimental participants with different types of pain obtained substantial pain relief from hypnotic techniques.[252] According to the Arthritis Foundation, "Studies show that more than 75% of people with arthritis and related diseases experience significant pain relief using hypnosis."[253]

A professional hypnotherapist and psychotherapist hypnotized himself before an 83-minute procedure in which the base of his thumb was removed and some joints were fused to alleviate his suffering from arthritis in the hand. He said he was aware of the consultant tugging and pulling during the operation, but felt no pain."[254]

Pain does not have to result in suffering in most people. It can be mitigated, and the diseases that cause pain will become less prevalent when humankind changes to live in love, peace, and joy.

What Makes Us Feel Suffering in This World?

Answer: What we call suffering is something we take on ourselves. Experiences don't make us suffer. We make ourselves suffer because of our interpretations of experiences.

One person in a circumstance may suffer from the events while another feels less disturbed. One person may feel suffering when a loved one transitions from Earth School, while another may be very sad but realizes the loved one has just changed form and is still present; there will be a wonderful reunion when both are in the same realm. Whether there is a feeling of suffering depends on the person's interpretation of the event. Suffering is completely personal.

We must find life and joy in what we now have and what is now happening. No change can result in unhappiness and suffering if we are confident in who we are and assured that our lives have purpose. Every change is an opportunity to learn lessons and have a more fulfilled life. We just have to find out what the opportunity is.

Did We Choose to Have Events in Our Lives That Are Causing Us to Suffer?

Answer: We chose events in our lives that could result in our making ourselves feel suffering, but suffering is not inevitable and the reactions to events do not have to result in a deep, lasting experience of suffering. Whether we suffer when tragic events occur and how long we suffer depends on our progress in learning the truths about ourselves and life.

We planned our lives before our births in intimate cooperation with the others who are now in Earth School with us. We may have chosen circumstances and events that seem unfair and are tragic, but we did so knowing that only these extremes could help us learn the lessons we decided we wanted to learn. Suffering is never a punishment. There is no punishment in Our Universal Intelligence that is the source of creation. What we call suffering is always so we can learn lessons, help others learn lessons, or help humankind grow in love, compassion, and understanding.

The Souls of the families of children with disabilities and the children's Souls have chosen the disabilities to help one another learn lessons they decided they wanted to learn in Earth School before they were born. The parents are silent heroes, and the children's Souls describe their choice to live with disability in which they can achieve their life goals without full capabilities.[255]

One woman received the message from her guide about the reason for choosing deafness: "Deafness is not a handicap. It is an opportunity. It provides a subtle shift in focus that is necessary for personal and profound spiritual growth. Deafness is not one's fault. It is a choice. Like every other choice, it provides the opportunity to experience life in exactly the way that is needed for one's purpose."[256]

Our lives were not intended to have suffering. We should be living lives full of love, peace, joy, optimism for the future, comfort, and good health. When events occur that disrupt our lives, we should be able to adjust to them, secure in knowing we are spiritual beings living through temporary circumstances so we can learn lessons, and that we are supported by those around us who have learned to be other-centered and unconditionally loving.

Is There Any Way Humankind Can Bring About a World in Which There Is No Suffering?

Answer: Yes. The world is what we make of it. If all people felt and displayed love, compassion, and concern for others, humankind would alleviate all of what we regard as suffering.

All suffering results from ignorance about the transition called "death," clinging to things, unwillingness to adapt to and thrive with change, people harming other people, and an attitude toward events that creates the suffering. Earth School will eventually evolve to the point at which there are none of the forms of suffering because of changes of heart and mind among all its citizens. In this heaven on earth where people ensure others do not suffer, there will be no violence to create suffering. Grief when a loved one leaves Earth School will be replaced by sadness at the separation, but with confidence that the transition is just a temporary separation and the loved one is available now to communicate. Living life with disabilities will not be suffering because all others will value and love the person, mitigating the shortcomings from the disability by satisfying the person's needs. The person with a disability will focus on their abilities, not the disabilities, and will lead fulfilled lives. People will not mistreat each other. Employees and management will treat each other with love, kindness, and respect. Everyone will be happy, content, and satisfied in their jobs.

Suffering is not a necessary part of the Earth School experience. It is prominent in the Earth School experience now because humankind has not yet evolved to be loving, compassionate, and other-centered. We bring suffering on ourselves.

We chose to be in Earth School at this time because society, our families of origin, and the others we live with all would create and experience suffering as a natural course of living at this time. Within this suffering, we knew we would be able to learn the lessons we planned to learn.

8

Why Am I Here?

Answer: Only in the environment of Earth School can we have the unique experiences that will enable us to fulfill the purposes for our lives. When humankind is populated by people who also have grown to fulfill these purposes, we will live together in love, peace, and joy.

We enrolled in Earth School to have experiences that will evolve us into being loving, peaceful, and joyful. We might wonder why Our Universal Intelligence doesn't simply give us the end results—create us to be unconditionally loving, peaceful, and joyful on the spot, without going through the struggles of Earth School to change and grow. And why does Our Universal Intelligence expect our imperfect, impatient, impudent Earth School egos to grow into loving, peaceful, joyful beings?

The answer is that only by living in a world with disturbing experiences that compel us to change can we grow from having mistrustful, cynical thoughts to experiencing wonderful feelings of trust and optimism; from having feelings of being conditionally loved or rejected to experiencing the exuberant feelings of being loved and accepted with no conditions or expectations; and from being self-absorbed to finding joy in helping others as they go through their own struggles.

We can realize why we enrolled in Earth School by understanding who we have been at our beginning level of development in love, compassion, and wisdom and who we are becoming through Earth School experiences. We begin Earth School by being taught that loving others and feeling love from them are conditional and tainted with mistrust and selfish expectations. Most people mistrust others and feel they are separate from the rest of humanity. Earth School teaches us an understanding of the nature of reality and our place in eternity that is fraught with misinformation, superstition, fear, and ignorance. Most people are cynical about life and resigned to feeling that depression, disappointment, and unhappiness are the way life must be—*c'est la vie*.

Through the unique experiences available in Earth School we can have a change of heart and mind that overcomes those negative conceptions of who we and humanity are. We can learn to be unconditionally loving and enjoy the experience of living with others who love without expectation or judgment. We can learn to trust others and believe those we love would never judge, manipulate, or deceive us. We can learn we are spiritual beings, manifestations of Our Universal Intelligence that is the source of all creation. We can become confident that unseen arms enfold us in love and guide us into learning lessons and being confident that we are supported in every struggle we encounter. We can learn to be happy in our Earth School lives for the pure sake of being in this paradise of experiences with people we love, with no requirements or reasons necessary for our happiness.

These wonderful fruits of life in Earth School result from having unique experiences only Earth School can provide. Our Souls choose Earth School so we can

- Experience the feeling of loving and being loved

- Develop a compassionate nature that loves others and desires to express it

- Learn lessons that give us more knowledge, wisdom, tolerance, trust, and other traits we desire

- Learn to accept and love others without judgment

- Learn to love ourselves and feel our own worth and competence
- Help others grow in love, compassion, and wisdom while they enjoy Earth School experiences
- Help humankind live together in love, peace, and joy
- Realize we are spiritual beings who do not die
- Grow to feel happy with no reason for it
- Enjoy the pleasure of joyful experiences
- Feel competent and capable in endeavors that bring us bliss
- Become self-determined, confident, independent, and capable of making choices
- Have clear goals and a sense of purpose
- Enjoy the sensual experiences available to us on earth
- Come to trust the support and guidance given to us by guides, helpers, and loved ones in the life after this life

9

Who Am I?

Answer: I am the Soul taking on a temporary Earth School Mind. My Soul is an integral part of my Higher Self that comprises many Souls who have had and are having experiences with Earth School Minds. And I am Our Universal Intelligence, wholly the manifestation of the creative and sustaining energy of all that is.

We are brought up to believe we are the temporary characteristics of our Earth School stories: our bodies, personalities, and activities. When someone describes who they are, it sounds like an ad on a dating site: "I am a single 25-year-old dental assistant who likes to travel and lives in the city with my cat and a goldfish." She was none of those things 10 years ago and will be none of those things in another 10 years. They can't be who she is.

She might describe her physical characteristics: height, weight, color of eyes and hair, and racial characteristics. But we know they aren't her either. When she graduates from Earth School and leaves those things behind, she will still be the same person. And even while she is in Earth School, when we talk with her we aren't talking to her epidermis, nose, eyeballs, hair, or ears. We're talking to the inner person who is apart from her body.

She also isn't just the person she seems to be now in the Earth School environment. The primary, permanent characteristics of who she is are in her Soul, Higher Self, and membership as an individuated member of Our Universal Intelligence. Describing herself using only Earth School characteristics confuses the role she has temporarily taken on with who she is in her eternal life.

As we go through our daily lives in Earth School, experiences enter our awareness and leave instant by instant. The experiences are not who we are. What is permanent is the aware individual temporarily immersed in Earth School, having experiences that change us so we grow to be more loving, compassionate, and wise. Nothing in Earth School defines who we are.

We do not enter Earth School or enter a body. We simply begin having the experiences of Earth School and the experiences of a body made available by Our Universal Intelligence. During the whole time, we, our Soul, our Higher Self, and all of Earth School are manifestations of Our Universal Intelligence. No part of us "incarnates" somewhere outside of Our Universal Intelligence with a spark or piece of who we are remaining with the Higher Self. Our Souls and Earth School Minds are individual manifestations of the one Universal Intelligence. We have simply attuned ourselves to the Earth School experiences others are having. We are not the bodies we seem to be in Earth School.

How Am I My Higher Self, Soul, and Earth School Mind in Our Universal Intelligence?

Answer: Our Higher Self or Oversoul, Soul, and Earth School Mind are all one in Our Universal Intelligence. It is as though Our Universal Intelligence was dreaming our Higher Selves who were dreaming the numerous Souls and Minds living in Earth School. We are individuals in all those dreams. But the dreams have substance and real individuals interacting in real events.

After years of pondering the enigma of how God is related to the substance of a physical world, the quantum physicist Amit Goswami came to an epiphany that explained the relationship fully: "There is nothing but God. There is nothing but God."[257] There is nothing but Our Universal Intelligence. Our Higher Selves are Our Universal Intelligence enabling experiences in a great variety of roles in different environments, including Earth School. Our Souls are the individuated members of our Higher Selves who are having the experiences of the individual roles through the Earth School Mind. The Earth School Mind is the activity of the Soul that grows in Earth School to learn how to think and act so the Earth School Mind can grow in love and wisdom through experiences. We are all that.

What Is Our Universal Intelligence?

Answer: There is nothing but Our Universal Intelligence.

We must set aside the Anglo-Saxon term "God." The word has too many connotations created by the West's saturation with the Judeo-Christian religions. Foremost is the assumption that there is a personality or being with the range of human emotions that creates a world separate from himself (masculine pronoun). There is nothing but Our Universal Intelligence. I do not use "Universal Mind" because "Mind" suggests a person with personality and human traits such as our Earth School Mind. Instead, Our Universal Intelligence is the ground of being, the source, that manifests in what we call matter and energy. Everything is Our Universal Intelligence in different forms, including all experiences and our Earth School Minds. We are wholly that. There is nothing but Mind and experiences in Our Universal Intelligence. They are our reality.

What Is My Higher Self or Oversoul?

Answer: Our Higher Selves are conscious aspects of Our Universal Intelligence. We as individuals in Earth School are the Higher Self allowing the limited focus of one of its innumerable Souls to nurture its individual Mind by having Earth School experiences.

The Higher Self is like we're experiencing a movie. While we are in Earth School experiencing the movie, feeling ourselves to be the characters in the movie, we are still the Higher Self sitting in the audience enjoying the movie. We are both the actor and the spectator. There is only one being. We've just voluntarily decided we will allow ourselves to have the Earth School experiences so we can learn lessons and enjoy the experiences.

We are able to interrupt the movie by relaxing ourselves out of the focus on this experience and coming back into who we really are as expressions of the Higher Self. The actor and the spectator experience the one Self we always are. We are still attuned to Earth School, so when we come back from the relaxation we resume our roles by having Earth School experiences.

Our Higher Self is like the experiences of our bodies. We can focus on our left foot to see what it is experiencing. While we are focused on our left foot, we don't sense what our right ear is experiencing. We can focus on the experiences of only one body part at a time. The Souls that are the Higher Self are focuses within the Higher Self, just as our focus on a body part is integral with our Mind. The Soul is not separate from the Higher Self. The Soul is just a focus within the Higher Self. As a result, a Higher Self comprises a great number of Souls that are all the Higher Self.

When we talk of "incarnating," there is no "re-incarnating," meaning an Earth School Mind comes back to Earth School. We remain individuals after we have developed in Earth School, forever. Instead, many Earth School Minds that are aspects of a single Higher Self have come into Earth School and had experiences the Higher Self benefits from. Reincarnation is explained more fully later in this book.

An analogy will help you conceptualize the Higher Self. Imagine you are 75 years old looking through a picture album of your life. You see a picture of yourself as an infant, then as a 5-year-old, then as a pre-pubescent 12-year-old, then as an adolescent, then as a 25-year-old, then as a 50-year-old, and finally as a 75-year-old. As you look at the pictures, you remark, "That's me when I was an infant. That's me when I was 5 years old. That's me when I was 25 years old." In all cases, you know every one of those people is you. They now make up who you are as the person you are at your present age.

But they were all very different. Your body and Mind as an infant were quite different from your body and Mind as a 5-year-old, and greatly different from you as a 25-year-old. From birth to 24 months you didn't know that an object existed if you couldn't see it. It disappeared when it left your sight and a new object appeared when you saw the object again. From ages 2 to 7 your thinking was based on intuition and experience, with little logic. You couldn't grasp cause and effect, time, and comparison. From ages 7 to 11 you developed your mental abilities but couldn't think abstractly or hypothetically. It wasn't until your mid 20s that your Mind was able to analyze problems that have no right answers, such as moral dilemmas. Not until after your mid 20s were you able to see yourself as an actor on the stage of life and evaluate how satisfied you or your employers, partners, and others were with your performance and their impact.[258]

The Higher Self is like you as the person you are now with all these individuals in you whom you have become. The Higher Self has many Souls with Earth School Minds that make up the Higher Self. Each is just a different aspect of the Higher Self. The difference between the analogy and your Higher Self is that every one of those individuals that make up the Higher Self still lives on as an individual. Each continues growing to higher spiritual and mental levels. But these individuals still are members of the Higher Self. The Higher Self has learned through the experiences of each of these selves.

Many people report profoundly moving experiences in communications with their Higher Selves, but we must remember that this communication is not with a separate entity. It is relaxing into a dialogue within ourselves like the one we have when we're speaking aloud to ourselves as we review alternatives to make a decision; the speaker and listener are one. The Higher Self knows the plan the Earth School Mind in Earth School is living out and was involved in developing the plan through the Soul.

What Is My Soul?

Answer: The Soul is each person at the level of the Higher Self. The Soul is integral with the Earth School Mind but is healthy, lucid, and intelligent, even though the Mind in Earth School may be constrained by mental or physical limitations and disabilities. The Soul knows the life plan and participates in guiding the Earth School Mind through life experiences.

The Soul planned the Earth School experience with guides, other Souls who would be in Earth School at the same time, and other beings who came into the planning as necessary. The Soul is not separate from the Higher Self or the Earth School Mind. All are one, taking on different roles in the individual's growth. The Soul is like the adult we are who would be able to care for the infant we were who was growing in Earth School. Both the infant and adult are one individual, just with different perspectives about the life the infant is embarking on. The Soul knows the life plan and takes an active role in helping the Earth School Mind achieve the planned life goals for this period in Earth School.

There is no "merging" of the Earth School Mind and Soul after the person leaves the Earth plane. They were never separate. The Soul is not one personality and the Earth School Mind another personality. They are the individual in different roles as the Earth School Mind, Soul, Higher Self, and Our Universal Intelligence. That is very difficult for our Earth School Minds to envision because during Earth School we have the limited perspective that all things are separate: people, our Minds, and the different roles we play in Our Universal Intelligence. We envision them as four separate beings at different levels. There are no separate beings; all are one, taking on different roles.

What Is My Earth School Mind?

Answer: Our Earth School Mind comprises all the knowledge, memories, abilities, personality, attitudes, fears, loves, and all the rest of what we recognize as "me." They all developed while we were in Earth School to prepare us to be able to transform ourselves into the person we come to realize we want to be. Our Earth School Mind does not know our Soul's plan for our life.

We start as Earth School Minds that are *tabula rasas*, blank slates, and grow to learn how to navigate in Earth School. At the moment when we have our first experience, we can say we have entered Earth School. It is a state of Mind.

The Mind develops from nothing into the person who can make free will choices to grow to become more wise, loving, compassionate, and other-centered. The Earth School Mind has all the characteristics determined in pre-birth planning, such as physical characteristics, disabilities, and mental capabilities. The pre-birth planning comes to fruition as the person's Mind develops. However, none of the disabilities and limitations affect the Soul, which is always whole and mentally capable.

The Earth School Mind has been called the body/Mind because it includes the reactions and senses of the body as well as the characteristics we normally associate with a Mind. But the distinction is misleading. Rather than think of body and Mind as separate entities, we must speak only of the Earth School Mind. There is no body component, only a body experience in the Earth School Mind.

10

Why Did My Soul Select Earth School for My Life?

Answer: Our Souls decided to enroll us in Earth School to learn, grow, and enjoy experiences; to help others learn, grow, and enjoy experiences; and to help humankind evolve in wisdom and love. Only in the Earth School environment as it is today could we have the experiences that would enable us to achieve our growth goals.

Our Universal Intelligence is the basis of all reality. The Higher Selves as members of this all-encompassing Universal Intelligence are continually evolving and maturing. To be able to have a wide range of experiences that evolve an increasingly wise, knowledgeable, loving Higher Self, individual Minds mature in one of the millions of realms where the individual Minds are able to have experiences that allow them to learn lessons, love, feel the joy of being loved, and enjoy experiences.

The experiences and the growth from the experiences can come only in an environment in which the individuals have childhoods that prepare them for their lives, changes in circumstances that bring challenges to overcome and learn from, people who are self-absorbed and insensitive as well as people who are loving and other-centered, and the free will to decide to become what we desire to be.

The Higher Self comprises many individual selves that have graduated from Earth School and other realms. Each has had unique experiences that have added to our Higher Selves' wisdom, love, and compassion. The lives were planned carefully to bring desired understanding and experiences.

There are three primary reasons the Higher Self decides to bring an individual into an experiential realm:

- To learn, grow in love and compassion, and enjoy experiences
- To help others learn, grow in love and compassion, and enjoy experiences
- To help humankind evolve in wisdom, love, and compassion

The individual may be part of a Soul group that includes individual members of other Higher Selves. Michael Newton reports that the Soul groups have between three and twenty-five members.[259]

The Higher Self decides to put a new individual into the situation of having experiences by accepting the limitations of a narrow life circumstance, rather like falling asleep and dreaming. In the dream, the individual has vivid, real experiences, with sights, sounds, touches, smells, and tastes, but there is no world outside of the dream that results in the sensed experiences. All of it happens in Our Universal Intelligence.

The Higher Self has decided to select a school with circumstances such as those in Earth School so the Soul can learn, grow, and enjoy life. Our Higher Selves have selected Earth School for us.

Why Did My Higher Self Decide to Enroll Me in Earth School?

Answer: Our Souls and Higher Selves chose for us to have experiences in Earth School with other individuals because Earth School has the circumstances our Higher Selves and Souls knew we would need to learn lessons, grow in love and compassion, and enjoy rich experiences.

Our presence shows we carefully selected Earth School because it has time, space, beginnings and endings, technology, pleasurable experiences, challenges, opportunities to love, and the pain of loss. Earth School is perfectly suitable for us to engage in the activities we know will result in the learning we want to have. The speakers from the life after this life tell us there are millions of other environments described as realms, spheres, and planets. A Soul could choose to have the Mind engaged in any of them for growth experiences. These other realms may involve a planet that has etheric zones or dimensions that are in the planets' environments but not visible or detectable by the senses of people now living in Earth School. When we look at the planet, we may not see the environments in which spiritual beings of many kinds are living.[260]

There are also invisible worlds that generally are of a higher order of advancement. They have at varying times made contact with Earth. But they have been denied, to a certain extent, the opportunity to communicate with people.[261]

Our Higher Selves could have chosen any of the other realms for the experiences that would achieve our goals for the Higher Self's development. Our Souls chose Earth School because of the circumstances that will allow us to live a blissful life, give love and receive love, learn lessons, help others learn lessons, and help humanity evolve.

Why Did I Choose This Time in Earth School's History?

Answer: Our Souls knew what would be happening in the evolution of humankind on earth in the twentieth and twenty-first centuries. We wanted the experiences of conflicts, trials, and disturbance in the world today so we could grow above the turmoil to greater levels of wisdom, love, and compassion.

We knew we were entering a time in Earth School's history filled with danger, tragedy, self-absorption, greed, wars, political upheavals, loss, and disease. We knew there would be people who are cruel, greedy, hostile, and violent, as well as people who are loving, other-centered, and giving. We knew this is a spiritually backward time when people do not understand the death of the body and are selfish, greedy, and self-absorbed. We wanted to live our lives with the struggles inherent in life in Earth School today.

Did My Soul Plan What Would Happen to Me in This Earth-School Experience?

Answer: Our Souls planned the contents of our Earth School experience before we began our time in Earth School, but we do not know the plan. We have free will, so we may act in ways that do not follow the plan, or we may divert it to other paths because of our preferences during the Earth School experience. Our Souls and guides will counsel us and help us learn the life lessons along the new path.

The pre-birth planning was quite detailed, involving guides, our Souls, and sometimes higher-order beings. Our lives are not sequences of accidents in time. We chose the family of origin, mental and physical capabilities and limitations, events that would shape our Minds and allow us to learn the lessons we chose to learn, and the potential exit points when we would graduate.

We did the planning in dialogue with the others who are in our sphere of contacts and influence in our lives, and with our guides, Souls, and higher-order beings whose role is to ensure we learn the lessons and have the experiences we planned to have. We grew up in Earth School to take on all of Earth School's positive and negative characteristics so we could encounter the challenges we have chosen to live through and learn from them.

However, we are also the Soul that is not constrained by the Earth School Mind. Our Souls are knowledgeable about who we are in eternity, the lessons we have set about learning, the events we have planned, and the others who have chosen to enroll in Earth School with us to learn lessons and help us learn our lessons.

We have free will in Earth School. As we live our lives, we may choose not to engage in the experiences and not to learn the lessons we had planned before being born. Our lives are not predestined. If someone else changes their plan in ways that affect our plan, our guides, Soul, and others will inspire us into different actions to help us return to the process of learning the lessons we want to learn and of being happy.

How Did My Soul Plan My Life?

Answer: The deliberations as our lives were planned occurred with great care in considering alternatives and settling upon life characteristics and events that would give us what we uniquely need in Earth School. The planning group included the Souls of the people who would be involved, guides, and sometimes higher-level Ascended Masters.

For answers to this question, I recommend reading Rob Schwartz's books, *Your Soul's Plan* and *Your Soul's Gift*. Much of what follows is inspired by those books.

Our Souls plan the experiences that will enable us to learn lessons in cooperation with the group of beings functioning as a planning group. The composition of the group changes as people are added for specific activities. The group comprises Souls who will have Earth School experiences with us, guides available to come into the discussions as necessary to give the planning group help, our Souls, and occasionally, higher-level Ascended Masters, but they limit their involvement because the planning must be completed on the level of the Souls who will enroll us in Earth School.

Our Souls planned our lives first by deciding on the circumstances of our lives. We chose our families, friends and colleagues, physical and mental capabilities and limitations, gender, neighborhoods and home environment, prosperity or lack of prosperity, schools, careers, addictions, and other conditions of life. Our Souls then planned life events that would help us confront challenges and have learning experiences that would enable us to learn the lessons we chose to learn.

The plans do not include actions such as murder, suicide, and violence. We enroll in Earth School to learn how to love, not participate in violence. We do take on roles that may tend toward violent acts, but in the hope that through love, we will rise above violent tendencies.

The planning group sits in a room talking about what the Soul is interested in learning and how each entity can participate. They explore life-event alternatives, evaluating what might happen in the person's life if a life-event occurs and how that will affect the learning and other events in the person's life. The learning experiences are planned with great care.[262]

The planning group plans events and circumstances with life challenges the person must deal with and overcome. The challenges are intended to help the person learn the lessons the Soul and other planners want the person to learn. The greatest challenges were chosen because of the important lessons the Soul wanted the person to learn. They may not be able to triumph over the challenges the first time they encounter them. The person's Soul and guides may alter upcoming events during the person's life in Earth School to present the challenges again. However, as with everything in our eternal lives, we have free will to choose not to go through the struggle of overcoming the challenges. There is no judgment for not confronting or learning from the challenges.

Are Any of My Planned Life Challenges More Important than Others?

Answer: Yes. Most people have a primary challenge that dominated the considerations and decisions during the pre-birth planning.

The primary challenge may be learning compassion, humility, trust, other-centeredness, sensitivity, or other positive learning. If a person's life seems to be dominated by challenges and growth in an area, that likely is the area of the primary challenge. The individual will feel guidance about the circumstances in which the primary challenge appears, and growth will occur each time the person faces the challenge.

Because it is so profound, the area of the primary challenge is the area of life that may not be successfully addressed. But even when the challenge does not result in the desired outcomes, some learning will occur, and the learning will continue in the life after this life.

Did My Soul Consider and Reject Any Plans for My Life?

Answer: Yes. The planning group considers a variety of alternatives suitable to all who will enroll together in Earth School and chooses the plans that will be of most benefit to everyone.

The planning group is able to see the alternative paths the person may take during the Earth School experience. The planning discussions consider alternatives and the Souls of all involved discuss how one individual's plan will affect the plans of others entering Earth School at the same time.

The experiences are not pre-destined. The person has free will and may choose a path not in the pre-birth planning. The planning includes contingencies for these detours. The person's Soul and guides are engaged in working with the person every moment of the lifetime, so when detours occur, the person can be guided through influences and circumstances to choose an alternate path that will arrive at the desired learning.

How Did My Soul Plan for Me to Learn Lessons?

Answer: One of the foremost ways the planning group plans for learning the desired lessons is through opposites.

In learning through opposites, the Soul plans for the person to be in circumstances and experiences characterized by the opposite of what they want to learn so they can experience that opposite condition and learn to value and appreciate the missing sentiment the Soul and Higher Self want to understand more fully. For example, a Soul that wants to understand humility may have the individual born into a family that is arrogant because of its wealth and position. In that circumstance, the person is able to become offended by the family's treatment of employees and others, thereby realizing the importance of being humble rather than arrogant. That person may then choose to lead a humble life without wealth and position.

Do the Souls of the People I Live with Know about and Go Along with My Plan?

Answer: The Souls of all people involved in an individual's life participate in the planning. They understand the roles of the Earth School Minds and the lessons they may learn because of the circumstances. Our Earth School Minds are not aware of any of our plans.

Since all in the planning group will be playing parts in each other's Earth School experience, there is lively discussion about the plans for each Soul's life and the effect planned events will have on each person involved. Throughout all the deliberations, all realize that "Life is based on love and service. There is nothing else."[263]

Some life plans that the planning group prepares for a person have lessons that benefit the entire group. All participate; all share the struggles; and all experience the learning.

Some members may take on the personalities, motivations, and inborn tendencies that make them more unruly, insensitive, cruel, and disliked. During the planning process they are greatly affected by the roles they must plan and want to make sure those on whom they will inflict the negativity are willing to allow it. All are aware that everything that will happen will derive from love. In our Earth School lives, we must realize that those who seem most insensitive and cruel, who may have antisocial personalities and impoverished consciences, have chosen to take on those roles out of love for the people most affected during the Earth School experience.

Some in the life planning agree to take on lives that are less for their own learning than to be part of the learning someone else is experiencing. In eternity, delaying personal growth is just for an instant, and even then, there are lessons the self-sacrificing individual will learn. That person may lead a life in which they are reviled and otherwise have negative experiences. They are willing to go through those experiences for the love of the others who are learning lessons from the relationship.

Does Anyone Plan a Life of Service to Humankind?

Answer: Yes. Some Souls have chosen to enter Earth School because the planning group realizes humankind needs the special messages and abilities the person will bring to all in their circle of influence and beyond.

Some Souls have decided the personal life lessons that might be learned during a period in Earth School are less important for that lifetime than performing activities that will have an impact on others. Because these individuals are bringing messages that may not be popular, they may experience trials and have to overcome obstacles. In some circumstances, an entire Soul group may enter Earth School to have an effect on humankind.

Does Any Soul Plan a Life Devoted to Serving the Needs of One or More Others?

Answer: Yes. Some Souls plan to enter Earth School primarily to be in roles that will help others grow and learn lessons.

Souls who want to learn how to be of service to others may pair with Souls who want to experience the limitations resulting in the need for care. The Earth School Minds will learn to feel hopeful, secure, and content with who they are when others take care of them. The person serving may be a parent caring for a disabled child. The disabilities and their severity are planned. Both will achieve their life goals by cooperating in the Earth School experience.

When My Life Has Interruptions, Did My Soul Plan the Interruptions?

Answer: Some life lessons can be learned best as a result of interruptions such as divorce, sudden disability, or loss of something of great value. By understanding and growing through the turmoil and discomfort of the interruption, the individual will grow in wisdom and understanding.

Life planning includes experiencing painful interruptions of aspects of life that are important to the person, such as divorce, loss of a job or career, financial downturns, and loss of abilities, talents, and skills. There are reasons for the interruptions. The person's life circumstances may have served their purpose and are no longer necessary, or the person may be moving on to another circumstance that will teach other lessons. A door may have to shut for another to open. When the interruptions cause turmoil and sadness, the person most likely has lessons to learn to restore a sense of well-being.

Did My Soul Plan for Me to Experience Afflictions, Accidents, and Tragedies?

Answer: Yes. Afflictions, accidents, and tragedies are some of the teaching circumstances our Souls have chosen.

Illnesses such as AIDS, cancer, ALS, dementia, Alzheimer's, and the disabling results of accidents are all chosen for some reason. For all of them, the person can meet the challenge and live a life that is rich and full. The afflictions and unfortunate circumstances don't create hopelessness, sadness, and despondence. Those are states of mind. The Soul that has chosen for the person to have an affliction or experience an accident or tragedy has done so to allow the individual to learn lessons. The person must understand the experiences in this way and overcome the challenges to be happy in Earth School.

The person who is ill or injured and the people caring for them all have challenges that, if met successfully, will result in spiritual and mental strength. Those strengths will raise the person's sensitivities and the sensitivities of humankind by that measure. The Soul and Higher Self will be enriched by the triumphs when the person with the afflictions learns to live a full life in love, peace, and joy. In pre-birth planning and during life struggles, the person's Soul and the others involved in planning all see the wisdom and necessity of the affliction, injury, or tragedy. The Earth School experience is short compared to the length of our eternal lives, but the lessons learned will have an impact on the Higher Self and the Soul's learning.

Tragedies are part of life planning. During planning, the Souls involved in the tragedies are careful to plan them so the person has much guidance and support during the traumatic time. The lessons will be difficult, but the person will be given all the support necessary to learn from the adversity, including help from guides and others who are entering Earth School with the person.

Could My Soul Have Planned a Life with Less Structure So I Have More Freedom?

Answer: Yes. Some Souls choose less structure. They want the Earth School Mind to have more latitude in making choices during the person's Earth School experiences.

We are always guided and helped by our Souls, guides, helpers, and loved ones, so we're not left to fend for ourselves entirely even if our Souls planned for us to have less structured plans. Our lives will achieve our goals even when we have less structure in them. If one choice doesn't work, we will be given opportunities to make other choices. In the end, however, we always make our own choices. We always have free will.

For those people who choose a less structured life experience, others in the group who enroll in Earth School with them may take on the role of educator, parent, or counselor to help them through the experience. The person facilitating the experiences will help the person with a less-structured plan to make good choices and learn from the experiences.

Other Souls planning the Earth School experience may want their Earth School selves to have more of a planned, rigid structure and may choose a circumstance, such as a disability, that cannot be altered. They may believe the person needs the rigidity to ensure the person learns the lessons set out in the plan.

Does My Life Plan Include Special Opportunities to Enjoy Life?

Answer: Enjoying the sensual pleasures of Earth School is one of the reasons our Souls chose the Earth School realm to have experiences. Yes, our Souls plan for us to have pleasurable experiences.

The planning also includes events the Souls would like to experience because of their desire to have rich, fulfilling lives. Our time in Earth School is not just to learn lessons. We are to enjoy all the exciting opportunities and new experiences Earth School has to offer.

Does My Life Plan Include Exit Points?

Answer: Yes. The life plan includes exit points.

Rob Schwartz's sources explain what I have read in other sources: there are "always three or four or five possibilities. No one has just one exit door."[264]

The person will have an exit regardless of changes in circumstances such as getting medical attention quickly. If the person's body is in dire straits but they are not at their exit point, circumstances will be set in motion for them to survive. No one still on earth needs to feel that if they could have, would have, or should have done something differently the person would still be on earth. The exit would have occurred regardless.

On the other hand, some people have been given hours, days, or even years to postpone the exit because of some heartfelt need the Soul and others in the planning group honor.

Could My Soul Have Planned That I Would Be Violent and Murder Someone?

Answer: Violence and murder are not part of pre-birth planning. We enter Earth School to learn to love.

The individual may have taken on characteristics that might make them prone to violence, such as an antisocial personality or psychopathology. Life circumstances, such as being abused and traumatized in childhood, might be such that they would lead the person to be more likely to commit violent acts. But the decision to murder or take one's own life is a free-will choice the person makes that is outside of the pre-birth plan.

The others involved in the life also know there is a chance this person may become violent. They take on their roles in this Earth School experience accepting that possibility, in love, because they know the person must learn the lessons they have chosen, including learning how to reduce violent tendencies and love freely.

Our Souls enroll us in Earth School to learn how to love. We are not enrolled to engage in violence and conflict.

Is Suicide in the Person's Plan?

Answer: No. Suicide is not in any Soul's plan. Someone may take on a personality with such burdens and turmoil that there is a chance the person could truncate their life. The hope in the plan is that the person will learn to overcome the challenges so suicide does not happen.

We understand from the Masters of Light, the team working with AREI's physical mediumship circle, that people do not plan a suicide. It is a free will choice that truncates the person's plan.[265] Suicide is not in any Soul's plan. It is an unplanned free-will choice, although a person may choose to be born into stressful circumstances with a personality prone to suicide. They have life goals involving overcoming these tendencies or allowing someone else to learn to love and care for them so the tendency toward suicide doesn't evolve into carrying out the act.

When someone ends their life or there is a murder, the life plans of the others involved with the person may be affected. In that case, their Souls and guides work to change the circumstances in their Earth School environments to increase the likelihood they will shift back into alignment with their pre-birth plans. The person may still decline to accept the realignments.

People who end their life are met with great empathy, love, and concern by loved ones who are living in the next stage of life. There is no judgment or condemnation, but sorrow that the person chose to leave Earth School early is felt by the person, the loved ones already in the life after this life, and the loved ones still in Earth School.

How Did I Enter Earth School?

Answer: A better word than "enter" is "begin my experiences." "Enter" suggests there is a world with bodies that exists apart from Mind and that our Minds enter a body in it. But there is only

Mind and experiences. We attune to the experiences of Earth School from the moment we are able to have experiences.

The body is always just a body experience, not some object. Until a person has body experiences after birth, the fetus is merely a potential body experience. The Soul never "enters" the fetus. That is a conception based in materialism. There is no material world. There is only Mind and experiences. There is no material fetus for the immaterial Mind to enter.

The commonly used term for beginning Earth School experiences is to "incarnate," a word derived from Latin meaning "be made flesh." We must abandon this common term for beginning our Earth School experiences. We don't incarnate in the sense of becoming objects on an earth globe made of matter and energy that is apart from Our Universal Intelligence. Instead we are Souls who attune our Minds to the commonly held story of Earth School at this time to have experiences.

"Entering the Earth plane" is also not an appropriate phrase. It suggests a material world that is independent of Our Universal Intelligence. It is better to talk about attuning to the experiences others are having that are in Earth School. When our Souls have our Earth School Minds attune to the experiences others are having at this time in Earth School, Our Universal Intelligence gives us experiences we have together: houses, rivers, stars, weather, and all the other experiences we have in the Earth School Mind. There is no physical plane with physical houses, rivers, stars, and weather that exists when no one is there. All of the experiences are happening in our Earth School Minds that are unique attunements of Our Universal Intelligence. The pre-birth planners, including our Soul, could have attuned our Minds to a million other realms, but we have chosen to attune to Earth School together.

We begin Earth School when the Soul turns its focus to the story being played out in Earth School that is in the Minds of all the current participants. The Earth School Mind then begins to develop. We fit into the Earth School environment by sharing in the sensory experiences people already in Earth School have, available from Our Universal Intelligence. We don't think about it or make it happen. The commonly held understanding among all who are in Earth School about the environment shapes our perception of Earth School. The common sensory experiences are accessible by each of us through Our Universal Intelligence. We share the same dream.

The Mind then develops from nothing into the person who can make free will choices to grow to become more wise, loving, compassionate, and other-centered. However, the Earth School Mind and the body experience have all the characteristics determined in pre-birth planning, such as physical characteristics, disabilities, and mental capabilities. The pre-birth planning comes to fruition as the person's Mind develops. However, none of the disabilities and limitations affect the Soul, which is always whole and mentally capable.

We start as Earth School Minds that are *tabula rasas*, blank slates, and grow to learn how to navigate in Earth School. At the moment when we have our first experience, we can say we have entered Earth School. It is a matter of a state of Mind.

Did I Have Other Lives Before and Reincarnated into Earth School?

Answer: Reincarnation is misunderstood. It doesn't mean someone keeps coming back to Earth School to learn lessons. We remain the individuals we are in the next life and the continuation of our lives after that, but the framework or life essence we have can become the framework for a new life.

We are told consistently by sources in the next life that we as individuals retain our individuality when we graduate from Earth School. All our experiences are part of the Higher Self's evolution, and we continue to grow in wisdom, love, and compassion after our graduation from Earth School. Other individuals of our Higher Selves attune to Earth School instead. We and the Higher Self learn from the experiences of these other people.

In our pre-birth planning, however, another life in the Higher Self may be the basis for the life we plan. Our Souls may want to learn something not fully learned in that previous life, or counter some actions in that other life during our life, or in some other way want our life to augment or continue something of the other life. We grow up in Earth School as our unique individual self that continues to live in the life after this life as the same unique self. But lives are intertwined because of the desire among us in the Higher Self to have experiences based on that other life. In the Soul-planning meeting, the planning group "leafs through" the various individuals who are part of the Oversoul or Higher Self to decide whether to learn new lessons based on previous learning or bring previous learning into the new Earth School experience.

This affiliation between an individual and other individuals in the Higher Self is where past-life accounts come from. In a past-life regression, someone in this life recalls another life that is affiliated with the person. Aspects of that other person are part of the individual currently in Earth School.

What Happens to an Individual Whose Potential Body Is Miscarried, Aborted, or Stillborn?

Answer: Unborn children who are loved are born in the life after this life and grow into adults. They are available to communicate with us and we will have reunions with them when we make our transition.

The Soul that will dedicate itself to having an Earth School Mind is involved in the conception and development of the fetus body experience from before the conception occurs. The Higher Self has arranged for the Soul to attune to Earth School as an Earth School Mind. However, if the fetus body experience is no longer viable, for whatever reason, the Higher Self does not devote the Soul and Mind to that fetus. That just means no Mind has experiences using that potential for body experiences that we call the fetus. The Higher Self, Soul, and other members of the planning group may simply find another family suitable to the Soul's plan.

Nothing can harm the Soul. When a fetus is aborted, it is just that no Earth School Mind is having experiences using the body experience of this fetus. Nothing is "killed" when the fetus doesn't come to term.

However, a mother's love for the individual who would grow into a person with the body experience of a fetus that is aborted, miscarried, or stillborn is a loving inspiration that results in the individual's being born in the life after this life and growing up there. The love is for the individual, not the experience of flesh that is a fetus. That individual is alive, available to communicate, and anticipating a loving reunion with the mother and others when they go on to the next stage of life.

You can hear a woman living in the life after this life explaining how she discovered she had two children, Sybil and Peter, when she entered the next life, but she thought she had no children because of two miscarriages: www.earthschoolanswers.com/children/.

In the trial of medium Helen Duncan who materialized deceased servicemen who had described military secrets, a woman testified that she talked with her materialized son who had miscarried at five months: www.afterlifeinstitute.org/helaine/.

11

How Can I Have a Life Filled with Love, Peace, and Joy?

Answer: We are creating lives filled with love, peace, and joy or loneliness, separation, turmoil, depression, and unhappiness. We create our reality.

Our life is the way it is because we are creating it that way. Everyone goes through experiences that could be interpreted with feelings of despair, hopelessness, fear, and victimization. Yet the same experiences could be interpreted with feelings of well-being, confidence, inner strength, and self-assurance. We create our reality from the way we interpret and respond to the experiences in our daily lives.

How Can I Be Happier in My Life?

Answer: Happiness is the sign that a person is content with life as it is. To be happy we must remove the influences that are resulting in our discontent.

Being happy means having emotions that are very pleasurable. We cannot define happiness further. There are apparent changes in body chemistry, but the changes in body chemistry are only part of the Earth School story. They happen after the feelings of happiness have already been experienced by the Mind.

Happiness is not a goal. It is a sign that the person is content with life as it is, feels loved, feels no threats or negative influences, and feels life has a purpose. Happiness is our natural state. We can speak of "unhappy," "disease (dis-ease)," and "discontent (dis-content)," meaning the natural state of happiness, ease, or contentment is being blocked. We do not refer to happiness as "un-miserable" or to health as being "un-ill." The natural state is to be happy and healthy.

For a person to change from being unhappy to feeling happy, the person must discover what is blocking the natural happiness they should feel.

Where Do the Feelings of Despair or Joy in My Interpretations of Experiences Come From?

Answer: Society's dysfunctional teaching and models programmed us as children to have episodes of despair and unhappiness throughout our lives. We can deprogram ourselves and discover that love, peace, and joy are ours if we learn to view life and other people differently.

The child is a *tabula rasa*, a blank slate. A child must learn to function successfully by internalizing knowledge, attitudes, judgments, and capabilities as they are modelled and taught by the family of origin, religious and educational institutions, and society. In the first seven years of a child's life, the child's Mind is in a receptive, learning state. This state registers in the body experience as theta or alpha brainwaves. In this theta or alpha state, children are open and naively receptive. They are being programmed.

This unusually receptive state is so the child's Mind can be molded into the Mind the person will need to function successfully in Earth School in preparation for learning life lessons and growing in love and compassion. The cell biologist Bruce Lipton estimates that 95 percent of what governs our lives is the programming from childhood rising from the subconscious.[266] You can see a video of Bruce Lipton explaining this at www.earthschoolanswers.com/bruce/.

When we emerged from childhood, we were equipped to make the decisions and perform the actions that would enable us to function in Earth School so we could learn lessons, enjoy the Earth School experiences, and grow in love, compassion, and wisdom. Yet after learning the basic functions for life in Earth School, we were not unique individuals making our own decisions about who we were and who we wanted to be. Our functioning was based on what our family of origin, religious and educational institutions, and society programmed us to be. We were living someone else's life.

All people have a constant stream of experiences. Whether the person feels despair or joy depends on the childhood programming. But we do have free will, so we are able to change the programming and lead lives full of joy most of the time. We don't have to preoccupy ourselves with striving to make a good future. We can enjoy the present as it is. There is no preparation for life. There is only life.

What Are the Mistaken Ideas about Life We Have Learned During Our Childhoods?

Answer: We begin life as a blank slate, with no beliefs, knowledge, or abilities. We spend our early years learning to function in life by adopting the beliefs and assumptions about life that society today is teaching children. Unfortunately, we learn mistaken, primitive perspectives from a naïve, spiritually backward teacher.

Our family of origin, school, religious organizations, and society in general teach primitive, destructive superstitions about our place in eternity and the life after this life.

- Our loved ones who have "passed away" are buried in the ground or are stone-cold dead in a mausoleum. To visit them, we must go to the cemetery and stare at the ground, but we can't talk to them. They're dead.
- We don't know where we go after the body stops functioning. It's a great mystery no one has the answer to. Religions have only the most primitive, vague references to an afterlife that offer no insights into the realm we enter after the body stops functioning.
- The only important goal in life is to buy bigger, better, more expensive, more opulent things. We must get good grades in school and go to college so we can get a good job and make money to become a successful consumer. That's our life's goal. Work long hours and take extra jobs and earn more money to buy more things and pay the loans incurred from buying them. What we have is never enough.
- Schools are places where we are taught to be obedient, memorize facts in the schoolbooks, and get good grades. Nothing of value comes from looking within to discover insights. Memorize facts in canonized books. It is futile to explore personal paths and dreams.
- We must obey the authorities instead of partnering with them. Society places great value on the rule of law. There is little value in considering the spirit of the laws.

- Children who are uninterested in or incapable of learning school lessons are failures. Talents in areas other than the schoolwork don't count.
- We have no control over our lives. We are victims of fate in a world that makes us unhappy and miserable.
- People must not "waste time." Everyone must be productive. Doing something not regarded as productive is frowned upon.
- A caste system determines whether our occupation is important. Doctors and lawyers do important work and should be revered as demi-gods. House spouses are not really working. Fast-food workers are losers. People who are not working are worthless burdens on society.
- People who own companies can tell the people who actually do the productive work that results in revenue whether they can work, how much they receive, under what conditions they will work, when to work, when to eat, and how to work. Companies are feudal systems, not democracies. It is right that owners receive vastly more money than the workers who produce what the company sells.
- People must guard the things they call "mine." They must cling to them to keep others from taking them away. They must not give away the things they call "mine" unless they don't care about the things anymore.
- Life is a competition. We win by beating other people. We celebrate winning with trophies and accolades. Losing is not tolerable, so we give nothing to the losers except notations of failure and firing the coach.
- War is honorable. Wars are necessary, highly regarded state activities. People in wars are heroes. The deaths and ruined lives from post-traumatic stress disorder and physical disabilities caused by war are not important.

- Killing animals is great sport.

- Government killing of people in wars and executions is acceptable.

- We must strive to make our own way in life using solely the training and skills we receive in school and work activities. We're on our own. There are no insights from any other source coming into our Minds. The ideas of guides, angels, and helpers giving us insights is woo-woo nonsense.

- We must have insurance to cover losses because other people are not going to help people recover what they lose.

As long as people continue to live based on these erroneous beliefs taught in childhood, they will not be able to grow into the unique people they were destined to become. They will remain ineffectual duplicates of the people who influenced them in childhood. They will be filled with fear and feelings of inadequacy.

We begin our lives with spiritual and mental deficits.

Could I Make My Life Happier and More Enjoyable If I Abandoned the Mistaken Ideas?

Answer: Yes. Your Soul's plan was that you would learn how to confront life's struggles during childhood, but for you to be all your Soul planned for you to become, you must use your free will to leave behind much of what you learned as a child and be born into the new life waiting for you as an adult.

What children are being taught in Earth School is failing humankind. We are creating the world that is bringing people hopelessness and misery. Society, our families of origin, and organizations such as schools and religions teach children to believe they are flotsam and jetsam, bobbing about in an unsympathetic sea that flings them onto the rocks of suffering and misery. Children are taught to see themselves as victims in a cold, mindless world they cannot control or appeal to.

The repertoire of memory experiences, interpretations, emotions, strategies, sentiments, and norms we acquired during our childhood create the reality we live in as adults. Reality is not outside of us or being inflicted upon us. The primary change in perspective we must make as we cast off Earth School's mistaken teachings is to realize we are creating our world. If we are miserable, it is because we are making ourselves miserable. Misery is not imposed on us. Happiness is freely available when we realize we are not victims and change our lives to be what we want our lives to be. If we do not confront and change the interpretations of experiences we learned as we grew up, we will continue to live someone else's life. Intellectually and physically we will be adults, but emotionally and spiritually we will remain children.

To grow to have a fulfilled, successful, happy life we must confront and change the interpretations of experiences we learned as children that have kept us prisoners of childhood. We must break out of prison.

We must then choose the person we want to be and confidently grow into being that person. We planned our lives carefully before our birth to learn the lessons we have come to learn; to grow in love, compassion, and wisdom; to enjoy life's experiences in comfort and happiness; to help others as they learn, grow, and enjoy life; and to help humanity evolve toward becoming loving, peaceful, and joyful. To achieve these pre-birth planning goals, each of us must use our free will to evaluate and accept or discard many things we learned in childhood so we can discover who we are and change ourselves to be the person we have decided we want to be.

Why Are People So Full of Fear Today?

Answer: People are being taught life has much to fear by individuals and organizations that benefit from the presentation of fearful displays and the discomfort their teaching inspires.

Earth School today has the most pervasive networks of communication in the history of humankind. In the eighteenth century people would learn about life from a small circle in their geographical location. They might hear someone read reports about events that happened in some other location, but most people had no interest in the "news," and those who did learned about a very small number of events outside of their community. None of this information was as dramatic as video is today. It was all verbal. Very few people ever saw a murder. Today the average child has seen 8,000 murders by age 10.[267] The portrayals are graphic and highly realistic.

Among the large numbers of events the media and entertainment could choose to present to people, they selectively present messages and experiences that induce fear, desire, greed, and basic negative human responses such as rage. Politicians, news commentators, film producers, religions, and companies want to create an emotional reaction so people want their products or services. They are intent on having people feel fear, outrage, and separation from others so they can benefit from the panicked responses. The beneficiaries receive money, position, or control when people tune in to their video presentations, elect them, or buy their products. They are motivated to make people feel separated by fear, outrage, and greed.

The mass media today are doing humanity a great disservice by exposing people from a young age to violence, cruelty, and sensationalism. The result is an Earth School today dominated by fear, anxiety, and dissatisfaction with what people have in life. There are only two inborn fears: fear of loud noises and fear of falling.[268] All the rest of the fears are from interpretations of experiences taught by word or example during childhood in Earth School.

How Can I Change the People around Me So They Make Me Happy or Stop Making Me Unhappy?

Answer: You have the keys to your own life but are locked out of being able to change others. You will find lasting happiness only when you use your free will to make changes in yourself and your life without expecting others to change.

The people around you may be creating a system in which it will be difficult for you to live in love, peace, and joy. You control whether you make yourself miserable or happy, but when you are in difficult circumstances, with unloving and insensitive people, in a job or other situation you dislike, or with groups of people who ridicule and belittle you, being happy and avoiding unhappiness are difficult. You enrolled in Earth School knowing life would be difficult, but that doesn't reduce the strain of living through the difficulties.

We must not expect people around us to change or for our life situations to adjust to our needs. Our actions to bring love, peace, and joy into our lives must involve only our own words, thoughts, and behavior. Any statement about our happiness that begins with "I will be happy when . . ." followed by someone or something that must change betrays expectations that will result in continual frustration and unhappiness. Instead our statement must be "I will be happy when I . . ." followed by what I must do to change myself or my circumstances.

We must not justify our expectation that others behave as we want because we feel we are being victimized. We are victims only if we rely on someone else for our feeling of well-being. Victimhood is a self-inflicted condition. People can be victims only when they believe they are victims, do nothing to change themselves to alleviate their feelings of victimhood, and behave as though their human rights have been violated by those they regard as the oppressors. To be a victim the person must fail to exercise their ability to control their own destiny, regardless of the words, thoughts, or behavior of others.

People who see themselves as victims needing others' sanctions and enforcement to produce their feeling of well-being are not willing to exercise their self-control to change themselves to adapt to what they regard as victimizing words, thoughts, or behaviors. They keep themselves immaturely dependent upon others to take care of them.

If someone is in a situation that is aversive to them, an intellectually, spiritually, and morally mature person will change their attitude toward the situation, change their role in the situation, or leave the situation. We are victimizing ourselves if we do nothing to change our attitude, role, or presence in the situation. We most likely will be unsuccessful if we expect that things and people around us must change so we feel less victimized.

A primary malady of societies today is that many people feel those around them must adjust to their expectations and neuroses for them to feel happy. They believe they not only have the inalienable right to be happy, they have the inalienable right for others not to make them unhappy. When they identify with a group they see as being victimized, they assert that other groups of people are the oppressors and insist on controls to reduce the oppressors' offensive words, thoughts, or behavior.

Unfortunately, institutions and governments support their sense that they are victims; legislate controls over thoughts, words, and behaviors the self-victimizing groups feel are offensive to them; and erode all people's inalienable right to freedom of thought, word, and deed by that measure. Government and institution controls and sanctions stunt the individual's growth to becoming a self-confident, emotionally mature adult. The self-victimizing individuals are continually looking for someone or some institution or government control that will decrease their self-inflicted sense of victimization by controlling the thoughts, words, or behaviors of others. When the institution or government shares that immature view of relationships, it results in control of thought, word, and deed by sanctions and legislation, resulting in actions that are themselves oppressive. Such sanctions and legislation contribute to keeping humanity from evolving into being loving, accepting, and nonjudgmental.

In a society developing in spiritual maturity, evolving toward the other-centered, compassionate world that can be in humankind's future, those people who have evolved in wisdom and maturity will naturally not act in ways that are offensive to others. Those who have not matured to the level of wisdom and maturity will be censured for their behavior by the wiser, more mature members of society, not by a controlling institution or government. In that healthy society, those who might have taken on the role of victim will mature into being able to disregard the inflaming words, thoughts, or behavior of some as the rantings of individuals with immature intellectual and moral senses. In so doing, they will foil the immature efforts of a backward few by rising above their actions in their reactions. They will mature, and as a result, society will mature.

The answer to "How can I change people around me so I am happy?" is that we must rely on ourselves for happiness, without expecting people around us to make us happy.

Why Does It Seem My Disturbing Situations Don't Change?

Answer: The familiar, stable routine of situations keeps us in them even if they're disturbing, so we keep experiencing the same issues even though we want things to be different. To change them we must have the courage to break out of the familiar routine and chart a new course.

To change ourselves or our positions in disturbing situations, we must understand that all involved are playing roles in a system. The system is stable as long as everyone plays the role they are expected to play by others in the system. A stable system doesn't mean it is a system that is good for all involved. These systems and the roles individuals play may be quite dysfunctional. For example, a family may comprise a verbally abusive father; a submissive, depressive mother; and children who separate from the family by withdrawing, rebelling, or abusing substances. The system is dysfunctional but will remain intact and functioning as long as everyone stays in their role. If we are to live our lives in love, peace, and joy, we must either disrupt the system, adapt to it in healthy ways, or leave it.

Eric Berne, in his groundbreaking work *Games People Play: The Psychology of Human Relationships*, referred to disrupting the dynamics of the system as "foiling the system."[269] We foil the system by changing our role to be healthier for us, regardless of the expectations others have for our role. For instance, the submissive mother with an abusive husband can foil the system by changing from being submissive to being assertive about her rights. We cannot expect the other people involved to change their roles. They might make changes if we confront them or involve them in counseling, but we must not rely upon their change to bring about our happiness.

In any such situation we must mature into making known our love and regard for all involved, regardless of the disturbances and conflict that have characterized the relationships. The purpose is not to inspire them to change. It must be a genuine outpouring of our underlying love and compassion for all involved.

Then we can adapt to the system in healthy ways. For example, we might adapt to the behavior of others in the system by changing our expectations so we are not dependent on them to fulfill our expectations. When all else fails, we may have to leave the system. People have difficulty leaving systems because, while dysfunctional, systems are familiar and satisfy everyone's needs for stability. Thoughts of leaving can be uncomfortable. Yet leaving an unhealthy system can be good for all involved because it changes the roles in the system dramatically. It certainly will be healthy for the person who chooses to leave.

If we change our role, we will upset the system. The others involved may be quite disturbed. But we are not responsible for their happiness any more than they are responsible for ours. They must make their own adjustments to the changes in the system. We must take care of our own needs. We can then help them in love to make their own adjustments so they eventually grow into mature adults who are responsible for their own happiness.

That may seem heartless to a person caught in a system in which other family members have taken on roles that make them dependent on the person for feelings of well-being and happiness. Feeling that our role is to make someone else happy is the hook that keeps us in a situation in which we cannot ourselves be happy—our preoccupation with trying to make someone else happy is at our own expense. We can help others grow into having healthy expectations of behavior and the self-confidence to find happiness in themselves, not others. But that maturity will not develop as long as we are enabling their dependence on us.

Can I Find the Security, Feeling of Belonging, and Identity I Want in Specific Things and People?

Answer: You can find lasting, stable security and feelings of belonging and identity only by building your trust and confidence in yourself. Things and people are easily lost, leaving the person who relied on them lonely, unhappy, and in turmoil.

We must abandon the models and teaching from our childhood that taught us we can be happy and fulfilled only if we acquire and hold onto things, activities, and affiliations that will give us the feeling we are secure, loved, and successful.

To lead healthy, happy lives and grow in our ability to love and show compassion we must engage in the scary, painful activity of giving up the need for things, activities, and affiliations. Only then can we establish our own unique, new identity that will remain, strong, vibrant, and full of self-assurance as each of the things we had been investing our identity in inevitably pass away.

The attachment to things, activities, and affiliations is referred to in Buddhism as *dukkha*. The result of *dukkha* is suffering. Attachment to things, activities, and affiliations results in suffering when we don't have them; when we have them and constantly worry they will go away; when we are preoccupied with controlling circumstances so they won't go away; or when we are devastated because they do go away. The solution to *dukkha* is to stop clinging to anything in the physical world. We must see that the things, activities, and affiliations we thought were important have no lasting value. They will not give us enduring happiness. In the end, striving for them, worrying about losing them, and inevitably losing them makes us miserable. When we stop clinging to things, activities, and affiliations, the craving for them disappears. We are happy without a reason. The cessation of the *dukkha* is *nirvana*, the condition of being peaceful and happy with no reason for it.

That also will enhance our relationships. As long as we feel that to be happy, life and the people around us must give us things and attention we need to be happy, we are placing tremendous burdens on the people in our lives. When we cling to people for our happiness, some will acquiesce and give us what we insist we need, but with a measure of resentment. Others will simply leave. When we are content with what we have without feverishly striving to acquire more, and when we place no demands on the people around us to feel and behave in ways that give us microbursts of happiness, we will live lives with greater freedom and happiness and people will feel freer around us, more interested in us, and happier being with us. They will love us for who we are.

The answer to the question "Can I find the security, feeling of belonging, and identity I want in specific things and people?" is "no." We must learn to be happy within ourselves only, with no specific thing or person that gives us a feeling of happiness. Then when we have the thing or person in our lives, we can feel joy without fearing loss or being devastated when the thing or person goes away; we are still joyful.

Why Is It Difficult to Be Open to Examining My Childhood Teaching and Accepting Alternatives?

Answer: We were told the path we learned to travel as children is the only safe and right path, so it is difficult to divert to our own path. It is more comfortable to avoid anxiety by staying on the old, familiar path. To become all we were destined to become in life, we must learn to trust that clearing our own path will lead us to a destination more wonderful than we can imagine.

When we confront who we are, we must be willing to uncover our deep-seated beliefs and examine them as an observer, outside of ourselves, realizing we may uncover things we're uncomfortable with discovering that are impeding our mental and spiritual growth. That brings anxiety. To become all we can be, we must face the anxiety by courageously examining our deeply entrenched beliefs and welcoming change, realizing that only through change can we fulfill our life's destiny.

We fear giving up on the beliefs because we feel we'll be out of control, as though we're speeding through life at 120 miles an hour and if we relax our grip on the steering wheel something awful will happen. We are afraid, so we control and resist change to feel safe.

We must not allow fear to dominate our lives. Learning to be comfortable with life as it is, regardless of the challenges it brings to us, ensures we will always be happy with no reason for it. There is a person full of peace and joy waiting for us to arrive. That person is us, after we strip away the layers of teaching acquired during our childhoods and discover the alternative beliefs and knowledge that will give us freedom and bliss.

Can I Find All I Need for My Life in Some Religion?

Answer: We must find our own path in life by looking within. Religions provide maps that require people to go along someone else's path to someone else's destination.

It's been said that every religion has a glimmer of the truth about spirituality, but that isn't true. A religion is a rigid set of beliefs members must adhere to. All required sets of beliefs stultify the progress toward becoming the person we can become.

Because of their rules for members, religions stand in the way of having spiritual experiences and growing to be loving, compassionate, and other-centered. Carl Jung wrote, "Religion is a defense against the experience of God."[270]

The answers we need for our lives are entirely within us. We need no external sources. We just have to strip away the false teaching from childhood, especially that instilled in us by religion.

The reliance on our own internal compass is not itself a religion. It prescribes no beliefs or doctrines from outside of the person. It asserts that everything a person needs is already in place. The person just needs to learn to trust and accept it.

Can I Give Myself Some Happiness with Drugs, Alcohol, Sex, or Work?

Answer: Drugs, alcohol, sex, work, or other diversions don't bring happiness. They dull the awareness so even the distorted feeling of happiness is unrewarding and empty.

The early teaching in our lives can bring great unhappiness, so people anesthetize themselves against the unhappiness through drugs, alcohol, sex, work, or even the meditation practice of pushing thoughts and feelings away. The anesthetics dull the negative emotions, but also rob the person of the opportunity to feel the emotion of joy. In the end, these futile attempts to deal with the discomforts that come from living life based on dysfunctional early teaching are counterproductive. They add to the person's burdens, psychologically and physically. And unresolved craving or worry is still there when the anesthetic wears off. Only by facing issues directly, rejecting what is causing the unhappiness, and adopting alternative beliefs can the person learn to be happy for no reason.

Is There Some Way I Can More Quickly Make the Changes in My Life to Become What I Want to Be?

Answer: Transforming from the person you are to the new person you planned to become is like growing from an infant to a child or a child to an adolescent. Growth cannot happen quickly.

When we are feeling something we want to explore, such as a trauma or disturbance, we must relax and go into it repeatedly, over time. We must see the disturbance as an object, not who we are. We have the new perspective in that moment, but the disturbing feelings will come back until, after repeated efforts, they diminish.

Our effort isn't to relieve ourselves of the disturbing feelings, although that will happen. It is to grow ourselves into realizing we are the "I" that is not in the Earth School Mind. We are the Soul that has an

Earth School Mind having experiences. Over time, as we face the disturbing feelings, we will realize that more and more. The feelings will decrease naturally. We can then condition ourselves to go to that state in which we see ourselves as the "I" that is greater than the Earth School Mind.

It takes time. There is no quick solution.

Does Society Have to Change for Me to Have the Maximum Love, Peace, and Joy in My Life?

Answer: Eventually society will mature so children can learn to love and care for others more than themselves. Now, however, society is spiritually backward, so we must make adjustments to live the live we enrolled here to live.

Society is the sentiments, beliefs, and norms held and enforced by groups of people. Just as we must abandon the teachings we acquired in childhood to become the person we wanted to become in our pre-birth planning, society must abandon its prevailing sentiments, beliefs, and norms to nurture an environment in which children grow to be loving, compassionate, and other-centered.

In the ideal future world people will not have to cast off the teachings from childhood in Earth School to grow into loving, compassionate, happy adults. When adults reexamine everything they were taught as children, they will find that they accept most or all of what they were taught. Only because society today is so spiritually backward is it necessary for adults to abandon what they were taught as children so they can find their path to spiritual maturity, love, peace, and joy in life.

Society must change so children can grow up in an environment with models and teaching that develop them into loving, peaceful, joyful adults.

At What Point in My Life Do I Start to Form Myself into the Person I Want to Become?

Answer: Now.

The fact that you are asking the question shows you are at the point or well along in the process of making yourself into the person you came to Earth School to become.

We enrolled in Earth School to learn lessons; grow in love, compassion, and wisdom; enjoy life's experiences in comfort and happiness; and help others as they learn, grow, and enjoy life. Our Souls planned an Earth School environment to accomplish those goals in concert with the others who would be involved.

We spent our early days in Earth School learning—from our family of origin, religious and educational institutions, and society—how to function in the Earth School environment, interpret experiences, and develop strategies to respond to experiences in preparation for going on to accomplish the goals our Souls established for us.

As we come into the maturity in which we are able to form ourselves into unique individuals, we must abandon much of what we learned from our family of origin, religious and educational institutions, and society because they are teaching children to be fearful, self-absorbed, materialistic, greedy, insensitive, competitive, conditionally loving, and ignorant about our true nature. The early teachings result in self-absorbed, lonely, unhappy, fearful adults who are ignorant about what happens when the body dies.

There is no specific point at which we begin the process of growing into spiritually mature people. Each of us has an epiphany at some time in which we realize what we have been taught to believe about life is wrong. The realization seeps into all our beliefs about ourselves and life. One by one the beliefs change. We begin to remake ourselves into loving, compassionate, wise people who are happy for no reason, know and love ourselves, love others, know who we are in eternity, and help others as they learn, grow, and enjoy life.

Each of us knows when that time comes.

How Can I Change When It Seems the World Is Continually Making Things Happen to Me?

Answer: Earth School experiences change continually. They present new opportunities that enable us at various stages of our lives to mature in love and compassion, and they provide the challenges we must face to be able to grow in wisdom and learn the lessons we came to learn. Our job is to face the changes confidently and learn from them, knowing we are guided by loving hands. In the end you will receive an A+.

We did not enroll in Earth School to allow life to happen to us. In Earth School we are the masters of our lives, striving to achieve our goals in the face of daunting challenges. We can change who we are, what we feel, and how we react to these challenges. We can choose to be happy and successful most of the time. We can be loving, compassionate, and other-centered so we have cordial, loving relationships. We just have to cast off the old person we were to grow into the new person we are becoming.

As we go through our daily life in Earth School, circumstances change, confronting us with new experiences. Some are challenging and difficult. Some cause dramatic changes that we react to with fear, grief, and depression. Others are full of joy, fulfillment, and ecstatic feelings of love. The key to becoming successful and happy in all circumstances is learning to persevere through the challenges and tragedies, grounded in knowing who we are in eternity.

Every new challenge, adversity, loss, and misfortune becomes a new problem we set ourselves to solving, knowing we will prevail and return to the happy lives we are intended to live. With each success, we grow in maturity, strength, humility, and love for those who walk with us through the trying times. When we confidently confront the challenges without shrinking from them by withdrawing, imploring others to rescue us, or anesthetizing the emotions with chemicals, work, or other diversions, we move a step higher toward the summit of our lives.

There is no single path every person must follow. No sacred text, religion, guru, or psychotherapist can decide for us how we must navigate through Earth School. We will make decisions every day and adjust our course as the circumstances change. There is no student manual for Earth School.

To grow to have a fulfilled, successful, happy life we must confront and change the sentiments, beliefs, norms, and interpretations of experiences we learned as children. We are in control of our lives.

How Can I Change Who I Am?

Answer: When we triumph over life's challenges, show our love and compassion for others, and become confident that we are eternal beings, we change ourselves so we live in love, peace, and joy and our body experience becomes healthy, youthful, and vibrant.

As we grow and change the interpretations and view of life and our place in eternity we learned as children, we become a different person. We are changing ourselves at the molecular level. Molecules, like everything else in Earth School, are based in Our Universal Intelligence and are continually changing and being renewed. Our new self is different at the molecular level from instant to instant. Love and compassion permeate our being so we feel more blissful, empathetic, loving, and compassionate as a natural outpouring from our being. We become love.

The high energy and bliss that results from our active display of love and compassion also causes our body experience to become healthy, full of energy, and youthful.

When we change so love and compassion characterize our being, we are aligning ourselves more closely with our Soul, which is always loving and compassionate. We are spending our days in Earth School using the skills and knowledge we learned in our early years to be successful in the Earth School environment, but we are transforming ourselves from that child into the loving, compassionate adult we planned to become before we were born.

Our loving thoughts and deeds affect the lives of people around us and the evolution of humankind. Thoughts and sentiments are energy. When we feel compassion, the energy infuses everything in our life and in the world around us. Each loving thought and deed is another measure of compassion added to the vessel of love that humanity is drinking from. When we are loving and compassionate, others become loving and compassionate, and the environment around us is imbued with the light and energy of love and compassion.

What Are the Conditions for Developing into the Person I Enrolled in Earth School to Become?

Answer: We have been blessed with all we need to grow into the person we enrolled in Earth School to become.

These are the conditions for developing into the person we enrolled in Earth School to become:

1. Be open to examining our beliefs and assumptions about life and adopting new beliefs.
2. Realize we are spiritual beings having an Earth School experience.
3. Know we are expressions of Our Universal Intelligence with all its qualities.
4. Realize our loved ones are alive and happy, although living in another location.
5. Know we have control over who we are and what we feel.
6. Feel the desire to become a loving, compassionate, other-centered person
7. Know we can change our lives to be filled with love, peace, and joy.

8. Know how the person we want to become differs from who we are now.

9. Face negative feelings and understand them and the interpretations that give rise to them.

10. Learn to feel, hear, and trust the guidance from our loved ones, guides, and others.

11. Learn to act upon the guidance we're given.

12. Learn who we are and to love ourselves.

13. Learn to be a loving, compassionate, other-centered person.

14. Have periods of relaxation, separation from daily life, and meditation.

15. Learn to understand our feelings

16. Fill our lives with experiences imbued with love, peace, and joy.

17. Learn to be happy with no reason for it.

18. Triumph and enjoy the success.

19. Help others as they learn, grow, and enjoy life.

12

Can I Communicate with People Living in the Life after This Life?

Answer: Yes. They are waiting for you to talk to them.

Our loved ones who have graduated from Earth School before us communicate with us regularly, although most people are not aware of their efforts. We are also in constant communication with guides, people interested in us, and angels during our lives. We just have to learn how to receive the communication at a conscious level. It is important for us to receive and respond to these communications because they continue the bonds in love and help us as we accomplish our life-plan goals in Earth School. We know we are loved and are not alone in Earth School, even if people on earth aren't helpful.

We also are part of the spiritual growth of our loved ones who are continuing to learn and grow in their lives after this life. They are increasing in love, compassion, and other-centeredness by helping those of us who are still in Earth School.

Are My Loved Ones Who Have Left Earth Before Me in Good Conditions and Happy?

Answer: They're fine. In fact, they're joyous. They are enjoying their lives in conditions more wonderful and beautiful than they could have imagined.

The most important concern for most people is whether their loved ones who have transitioned are all right. I can say with great assurance that they're happy and full of energy and vitality. Everyone who speaks from the next life describes their happiness at being without worries, healthy, feeling light as a feather, with a young body that has no aches and pains. They're delighted.

They're not worried about us unless we're grieving and unhappy. They only grieve if we're grieving. They are happiest when we're happy. They now know the truth that we and they are eternal beings. We'll live our lives and transition into the life after this life where we'll reunite. But in the meantime they know we must continue to learn lessons, and they know they can't interfere with our struggles; we must work them out ourselves.

They're busy learning and working. They have occupations and preoccupations, often what they wished they could have done in the earth realm but couldn't. They haven't forgotten us, but just as most of us leave our family members to go to work each day, those who are in the life after this life are busy. They aren't preoccupied with staying around us unless we are grieving deeply.

Those in the next life can help us take care of ourselves and learn our life lessons. We may have a sudden insight or a feeling of calm and peace in the midst of worrying or stress. Someone in the earth realm may contact us unexpectedly with a message we need to hear, or we may chance upon some information in a book or on television that helps us through a crisis. Any of these insights may have been brought about by the inspiration of that person in the life after this life we wish we could hear from. The assistance may not be in the way we expect or wish, but it assuredly comes to us.

Our loved ones often return to be with us when we think of them. They don't observe birthdays and anniversaries because there is no time, as we know it, in the life after this life. Even so, when they know the family is getting together, they often stand unseen among us. The residents of the life after this life describe attending celebrations, such as weddings, birthday gatherings, and their own funerals. Our thoughts come to them in the life after this life and they respond by coming to be with us on special occasions, either by being in the Earth School environment or being with us Mind to Mind from wherever they are.

If our loved one was an infant or a child, that little one is happy and being cared for and playing in a special area with other children and teachers. We will be reunited when we transition to the next realm of our lives.

Do People Who Have Graduated from Earth School Miss Me?

Answer: People who have graduated haven't left us, so they don't miss us, but they miss doing the things we did together.

People living in the next stage of life know how we're doing and know we'll have a reunion soon, so they aren't concerned about us and don't miss us in the same way we miss them. They are able to visit us at any time, and they receive our thoughts so they know how we're doing. But they do say they miss the things they did in Earth School with us.

Are My Pets in the Life after This Life?

Answer: The pets we love are alive and well in the life after this life.

Pets are kept by family members until the owners transition to the next life, at which time the pet returns to the owner without question. Our love creates a bond with our pets in the earth realm, so the pets live on after their bodies die. There are many descriptions of all a person's pets greeting the owner when he or she transitions to the next realm of life.

Pets communicate telepathically with people in the next life and can communicate with us telepathically now.

Will My Loved One Come to Me When I Need Them or Want to Talk with Them?

Your loved ones will return to be with you when you have thoughts that involve them. They don't observe birthdays and anniversaries because there is no time, as we know it, in the life after this life. But when you are thinking about an anniversary or birthday or when the family is coming together, they often stand with you, even though you can't see them. Your thoughts come to them in the life after this life and they respond by being with you on special occasions.

Some people think their loved ones have abandoned them because they aren't receiving the strong physical signs they expect. No one is abandoned. If someone isn't receiving communication it's because they're not responding to the communication when it comes.

Do My Loved Ones in the Life after This Life Communicate with Me?

Answer: Our loved ones communicate with us often, especially in the weeks and months after their transition.

Our loved ones who have transitioned desperately want to tell us not to grieve, that they are alive and well. It saddens them that they can't get messages through to us.

After the period soon after the transition, they are still sensitive to our thoughts and feelings. They come to us when we ask them to, are feeling disturbed, or are in need. They are always available to communicate.

Why Don't I Get Communication from My Loved One in the Next Life Now?

Answer: You do get communication; you just haven't learned how to let it bubble up into your awareness.

Your loved ones want to communicate with you. The primary reason we have the impression our loved ones are not communicating is that we in Earth School haven't learned to receive the communication that comes to us. We are so overwhelmed by the constant din of the earth environment that the communication we're receiving doesn't rise into awareness from the subconscious, where every communication is being registered. When a message does come as subtle feeling, knowledge, or understanding, people often dismiss it as imagination.

Happily, we can learn to communicate by learning how to accept their Mind-to-Mind messaging. For example, the Repair & Reattachment Grief Therapy method used by psychotherapists is 98 percent successful in connecting clients with their loved ones.[271] The reason it is so successful is the love connection between the person on this side of life and the person living in the next life.

You can read more about the procedure and see videos of people who have used it in afterlife communication experiences at www.earthschoolanswers.com/rochelle/.

Anyone can learn to receive the communication on their own. People just have to learn how to be open to it. You can learn about the free online training provided by the Afterlife Research and Education Institute at www.earthschoolanswers.com/selfguided. It will teach you how to be open to your loved ones' communication.

Why Can't People Living in the Next Life Just Come to Me and Communicate?

Answer: Nearly all of them don't know how to get messages through to us. They try, but it's difficult for them because our Minds are so preoccupied. We can receive their weak messages, but we must learn how to relax our Minds to receive them.

Those in the next life generally don't know how to get through to us. The ability to communicate with the earth realm is not prevalent. But people in the life after this life do try to communicate.

To understand what it's like for them, try this little experiment. We know from the research of Rupert Sheldrake and others that people can sense being stared at.[272] People subtly know when someone is looking at them. The next time you're waiting in a line of people, pick someone ahead of you in line who is not engaged in a task, just standing idly. Focus on their neck and imagine tickling them on the neck. After a few seconds, very occasionally people will turn around and look back, and even brush their necks. They don't know why, though. The message came through to their Minds at a subconscious level, but they didn't get the clear message that another person was imagining tickling their necks. They won't turn around and say, "Why are you imagining tickling my neck?" We know the message is there, because they respond to it, but it doesn't rise to the level of their conscious awareness.

Our loved ones try to communicate through thoughts, Mind to Mind. They focus on our Minds to try to get a message through. The messages always come to us at a subconscious level, but the subtle messages don't rise to the level at which we can become conscious of them. We're too preoccupied with life to quiet ourselves and let the thought messages bubble up from the subconscious into our aware Mind.

We can learn how to let those subtle messages come into our conscious awareness. The Afterlife Research and Development Institute has created a free training program you can learn about at www.earthschoolanswers.com/selfguided/ that will teach you how to relax your Mind and let the messages come through.

How Do I Know When They're with Me?

Answer: There are clear indications when a loved one in spirit is with us. We just have to learn to be sensitive to them, not brush them off, and respond to their presence.

Sometimes you suddenly have a memory, perhaps of something you haven't thought of for years. That's your Mind connecting with their Mind. They're thinking of that memory, or they're focusing on you and sending that memory to you. Thank them for it and let the love pour over you.

The sense of presence is a real sense, like seeing or hearing. When you have the sense a loved one is close by, it's because they are there. At that moment you can stop and say "Hello." You can tell the person how you're feeling and how happy you are that they're with you. Then you can go on, or you can stop and have a brief dialogue. You will receive their responses. The responses are the first thoughts that come into your Mind after you say something. If you are attentive to the sense of presence, you will more easily feel it over time.

The sense of presence can trigger sudden grief. The reason is that the sense brings the person to mind, resulting in the sadness that they are not in the body you are familiar with. One person came to the realization that the periods of spontaneous grief weren't just random moments of sadness: "I realized I was not missing her; I was FEELING her."

If you feel a wave of grief, ask if your loved one is nearby. The first thought that comes into your Mind is their response.

You must not worry whether it's them sending it to you. For one thing, if you are receptive they may send many messages to you, so the odds are good it's them. When you have the impression they're with you, even if they're not they will receive the impression and come to you, either physically or Mind to Mind from wherever they are. You must accept all notions of messages that are warm, loving, and uplifting as communications from them. Dark, negative messages are from our monkey mind, not from them.

Loved ones living in the life after this life send thoughts about what we need to do, watch out for, or take advantage of. They also communicate through bodily sensations, such as our feelings of being touched, cobwebby feelings, tingles, pains, and other such bodily sensations. One medium describes becoming anxious when she is receiving communications. Another feels that males give her sensations on the left side of her body, and females on the right side. Sometimes a guide or a loved one will use the same bodily sensation each time they are present to signal us.

People expect material signs or manifestations. They look for the feathers or coins or numbers that show their loved one is connecting with them. What they must realize is that when the feathers or coins or numbers come to them, it is because their loved one is with them at that moment, inspiring them to look at the floor where the feather is or the sidewalk where the coin is or the license plate that has the numbers. Most of the time they are just directing our attention to what is already there, not creating whatever it is. As a result, when you experience that physical phenomenon, they're most likely with you. Communicate with them. That's what they want. The feathers or coins or numbers are not important. They are just the ringing of the phone. We must pick it up and talk. Some suggest we should speak with the newly transitioned aloud as well as telepathically.[273]

At other times people in the life after this life seem to make electrical devices function strangely or butterflies come around or coins appear, or other manifestations. We don't know how they do that or why they're assisted in doing that from the other side, but the signs are certainly indications of their presence.

Why Don't I Have a Sense My Loved One Is Around Me as Much Now?

Answer: After passing, people may stay close to earth for awhile because they know their loved ones are grieving and they want to do what they can to help them. Later, when things have settled down, they go on with the next stage of their lives, but they are always a thought away and will come to us when we ask them to.

People often describe feeling more of the sense of someone's presence in the first weeks or months after the transition, but they have less of a sense of their presence after that. The person most likely has gone on to the next level of their spiritual development, leaving the earth realm. But even after they have gone on to the next planes of their lives, they are still available to communicate. They are only a thought away. When we think of our loved one, they receive the thought, wherever they are, send warm thoughts to us, and are available to communicate. If we are having a problem, are depressed, are ill, or are otherwise in distress, they will return to the earth realm to be with us at that time. They also will come to the earth realm just to look in on us. They will do that more often if we have regular times when we communicate with them and we maintain active communication.

Speakers in the life after this life also explain that they endeavor to help their loved ones still in the earth realm by inspiring them and giving them guidance. However, if the loved ones don't believe the guidance is real or ignore it, those in spirit go on with their life activities without trying to communicate. The communication becomes easier and more frequent as we establish the new relationship by communicating.

Are My Loved Ones Available to Communicate with Me When I Want to Reach Them?

Answer: Your loved ones are always available to communicate. They receive your thoughts and words wherever they are and they respond. You just have to learn to let their responses come into your conscious awareness.

Even though they will have gone on to the life after this life, it's important for you to realize that your loved one is available to communicate. They may not be around as much in the earth realm now, but wherever they are, your loved ones will come to you when you want to communicate. They are only a thought away. They don't ignore you or feel anything negative about you. If you're not getting a connection, it isn't because they've found someone else they like better or they're miffed at you or anything else that results in a separation. It's just that connecting is as difficult for them as it is for us. You must keep up the dialogue even if it seems you aren't getting the response you want or you feel they may not have come to you when you want to communicate. They will come to you and will work at communicating. You just have to find methods that will enable you to receive the communication and respond.

If a medium isn't able to make the connection, it isn't because your loved one isn't available. Good mediums have times when they're able to connect and times when connections just don't come through. That has nothing to do with your loved ones. They always come to you when you ask them to. It's that the medium is tired or mentally preoccupied or incapable.

No one reincarnates and becomes unavailable. Reincarnation is misunderstood. The messages we're getting consistently from people living in the next stage of life say that after transition the Higher Self incarnates a new individual to learn lessons in Earth School. We are linked to that new individual. That is why we can have past-life regressions and people talk about living other lives with each other. Read more about reincarnation on pages 200-201.

Do Mental Mediums Really Communicate with People Living in the Life after This Life?

Answer: Yes. The messages from people in the life after this life come into the medium's conscious awareness. We all receive messages, but most people haven't learned to allow the messages to come into awareness.

Mental mediums can communicate Mind to Mind with people in spirit because their Minds allow the impressions and messages to bubble up from their subconscious to their conscious Minds more easily than the average person. Although everyone's Mind receives the same impressions and messages from Our Universal Intelligence, most people are so focused on the earth environment that the impressions and messages cannot enter their conscious Minds and are lost.

Those speaking from the life after this life must impress their messages upon the medium. Words and names are difficult to get through. The medium's Mind is most receptive to images, such as concepts. The person in spirit may be communicating that an anniversary is coming up, so the medium's subconscious creates an image like a bouquet of white flowers, signaling a special event. The medium may receive a sign like a bell or flashing light to show a message is correct, or a gold ring to show someone was just married. Each medium has their own unique set of symbols. The medium will say things like "I'm seeing a single red rose. That's my symbol for 'I'm sorry.'" The words "Jim says he's sorry" might come to the medium, but it's easier and more likely the person in spirit can communicate the concept to the medium through an image. The image comes from the medium's subconscious to allow it to rise into awareness.

How Do I Pick a Qualified Medium?

Answer: Insist on evidence from the medium that they are connecting. Choose a medium from one of the lists of mediums people have determined are qualified, not from the yellow pages.

You must be careful to visit a medium who is qualified. Many call themselves mediums who are not. Most of the unqualified mediums don't realize anyone can actually communicate with people living in the life after this life, so they figure when they're faking their readings, that's what everyone does. This is unethical.

Insist on evidence. In evidential mediumship, the medium will give many facts that are indisputably true. In a reading during the Canyon Ranch experiments done by Gary Schwartz, John Edwards described facts that were so unique and detailed that they were evidence the person's grandmother was coming through. The grandmother had one black and one white poodle that tore up a reception prepared for a wedding. John Edwards was given that highly evidential information—facts the person being read would say "yes" to.

Both the person living in the next life and the medium want us to know the person is coming through to communicate with us. Both will endeavor to give evidence to validate the person's identity. It isn't disrespectful to the person living in the next life when we ask for evidence. If we are genuinely connecting with them, they will be anxious to prove it. In the early moments of the reading expect real details no one could know.

If the medium "fishes" for information, leave. When the person claiming to be a medium is "fishing" or doing a "cold reading," the medium makes general statements and asks for validation, such as "You have an older person who has passed." Haven't we all? Then the medium will ask, "Is that right?" The person being read says, "Yes, my Aunt Gertie." The medium says, "It's a woman and her first name is 'Gertie.' I'm getting a very uncomfortable feeling in my chest." The person being read says, "She passed from a stroke." The medium says, "That's it. Yes, when the stroke hit she couldn't breathe. And there's someone close to her who passed." "That would be Uncle Don," the person being read would say. The medium would say, "I got the D in the name as a male but got 'Donald' or something like that." The person being read would say, "That's his name. Boy, you're good!"

Be suspicious if the medium gives you only generalized halo statements, such as "Your loved one is well and wishes you the best. She looks in on you." A true reading will have the person the medium is connecting with give details about themselves and their life: what she looked like, how she transitioned, what she used to do with you on earth, or special actions or unique characteristics that are definite evidence the person is coming through. To ensure you don't sign on with a false or mediocre medium, use only a certified medium. For lists of certified mediums, go to www.earthschoolanswers.com/connect/.

Do Physical and Materialization Mediums Enable People to Appear in Séances?

Answer: Physical mediums are born with a special energy that allows people in spirit to materialize in the séance room. The medium doesn't make it happen. A group of spirit experts in materialization use the medium's energy, the sitters' energy, and their spirit energy to materialize people living in the next life in the room with the medium.

Physical mediumship differs from mental mediumship. In physical mediumship people called "sitters" sit in a room with the medium and phenomena happen in the room, experienced by all present. The sitters may experience movement of objects and furniture, raps, taps, lights, voices, and a great variety of other occurrences. The room may be entirely dark or there may be a red or blue light. A small number of mediums have phenomena in white light. Mediums usually sit in a confined space, such as a cabinet.

Some physical mediums exude ectoplasm from any orifice in their bodies. It is said to originate in the pancreas and be a semi-fluid, light-colored bodily substance with epithelial cells that has the consistency of mucous.[274] Ectoplasm in photographs appears on the medium's body or around it, forms into long rods that lift objects, hands, faces, and other things during the séance. The substance is light sensitive, so most séances are held in low light or total darkness to allow ectoplasmic manifestations.

Some mediums exude no ectoplasm. Their inborn talent is an energy force that causes things to happen in the room. Energy is still taken from the sitters and augmented by the spirit team.

A materialization medium is a physical medium with the additional capability of having people from the life after this life materialize in the room. The materialization medium exudes ectoplasm, which drapes around the person in spirit's ethereal body so it can be seen and touched. The resulting materialized form has all the qualities of a body living on earth, including the feel of bones, warmth, the softness of tissue, and even the deformities the individual had when on earth. The materialized entities hold conversations, sing, walk around the room, touch sitters, kiss them, and may allow themselves to be video recorded or photographed using infrared light. Some mediums, such as the Brazilian Carlos Mirabelli, have had the unusual ability to have materializations occur in red, blue, or green light or even in full white light or sunlight.

There have been very few physical and materialization mediums. They are born with the ability; it cannot be learned by someone without the inborn talent.

You can listen to the recording of one séance in which a loved one materializes with materialization medium David Thompson and has a conversation with his loved one who was among the sitters: www.earthschoolanswers.com/dt/.

Are There Methods Psychotherapists Can Use to Help Me Have an Afterlife Communication?

Answer: Yes. Psychotherapists have developed three methods to help grieving clients have their own afterlife communication experiences while sitting in their offices: Induced After-Death Communication, Repair & Reattachment Grief Therapy, and Loving Heart Connections.

We would expect that if people can communicate with their loved ones living in the next life, psychologists and psychotherapists working with grieving people would have developed ways of helping people enter a state of mind in which they are able to communicate with these loved ones for whom they are grieving. In fact, three successful methods have been developed and are used by psychotherapists today.

Induced After-Death Communications Demonstrate That Consciousness Survives Bodily Death

In 1995, Dr. Allan Botkin, a psychotherapist at a Chicago VA hospital, was startled when one of his patients described having an after-death communication in his office. The procedure Dr. Botkin was using to help reduce the vet's grief was eye movement desensitization and reprocessing (EMDR). In EMDR the psychotherapist has patients move their eyes back and forth rapidly as they would in REM (rapid eye movement) sleep. The patients then close their eyes and usually experience profound breakthroughs in understanding. No one is quite sure how it works, but it has proved to be one of the most powerful therapeutic tools the discipline of psychology has ever discovered. To date over 10,000 psychotherapists have been trained to use it and it has been endorsed by many psychological and health organizations, including the American Psychological Association and United States Veterans Administration.

The Vietnam combat veteran Dr. Botkin was working with had been experiencing devastating grief for decades from intrusive memories of a young Vietnamese orphaned girl he had come to love as a daughter, but who died in his arms from a bullet wound. During an EMDR session, the vet said that while his eyes were closed he saw the girl as a beautiful young woman, not the child he had known. That matches what mediums describe as happening when children die—they grow up in the life after this life. The vet's experience healed his grief instantly, and he was certain the girl was alive in the life after this life.[275]

Over the next few weeks 15 percent of Dr. Botkin's patients experienced similar after-death communications with people for whom they were grieving. He named the experience an induced after-death communication (IADC).[276]

In the ensuing months Dr. Botkin learned how to use the therapy method intentionally and had a high success rate with grieving patients at the VA hospital. Over the next several years he trained hundreds of psychotherapists to administer the therapy. Thousands of people have now had induced after-death communications. In virtually every case they alleviate the experiencer's grief almost immediately. Most patients emphatically state that they have had a real communication with their deceased loved ones, and they view the life after this life differently, even those who started the therapy as atheists.

The therapy method and 84 cases are described in our book *Induced After-Death Communication: A New Therapy for Grief and Trauma*.[277] The website describing the method and listing contact information for therapists who use it is www.induced-adc.com. You can read more about the method and view video of people who have had the procedure at www.earthschoolanswers.com/iadc/.

Remarkably, in many of the sessions the patients learned things they weren't expecting to learn and couldn't have known. In other words, the source must have been the deceased. Five such cases from among the 84 in the book follow. In each case, the person experiencing the IADC was given EMDR eye movements and then sat quietly with eyes closed. The IADC unfolded naturally without prompting from Dr. Botkin. He didn't learn about it until the experiencer opened their eyes and described it to him.

In the first case, a reporter had a session with Dr. Botkin as part of her interview of him. She reported having an IADC with a deceased friend in which she saw him playing with a dog. The friend told the reporter that the dog was his sister's, although the reporter didn't know her friend's sister had a dog. After the session she called her friend's sister and asked whether she had a dog. She said, "Yes, I had a dog, but he died." She then described the dog and it was the same breed and color as the one the reporter had seen in the after-death communication.

The reporter also received a message for Dr. Botkin. The reporter looked exactly like an old friend the doctor had known years before. As he was talking to the reporter, he kept having flashbacks of this old friend. During the reporter's IADC she told Dr. Botkin that her deceased friend said, "That was a long time ago, Dr. Lil." She didn't understand what that meant. But Dr. Botkin knew immediately. His patients called him "Dr. Al," which was what the reporter was actually hearing. The deceased friend knew what Dr. Botkin was thinking about the reporter's resemblance to his old friend a long time ago.[278]

In another therapy session in Dr. Botkin's office, a patient's deceased father said to him, "Forgive me for being so cold when we adopted you." That made no sense to the man because he remembered his father as always warm and close to him. That evening he asked his mother, "Was Dad cold to me when I was young?" His mother gasped and said, "Yes. How could you have remembered that? You were only a tiny baby." She explained that his father had been cold to him when he was an infant and wouldn't hold him, but after a few months everything was fine and the patient grew up to have a very close relationship with his father. He had learned something in the IADC he couldn't have learned from any source other than his deceased father.[279]

In a third case, a blue-eyed Swedish Vietnam combat vet asked Dr. Botkin to help him have an IADC with a black soldier in his platoon who had died in a firefight. There had been racial tension in his platoon, but in spite of that he said he was experiencing some grief over the black soldier's death. Dr. Botkin induced an after-death communication. The patient closed his eyes and sat for a couple of minutes. Then he opened his eyes, shaking his head and looking perplexed. "The guy saw right through me," he said. He then explained to Dr. Botkin that he just wanted to find out the black soldier's name so he could put the name on paperwork that would get him additional money for the grief he was suffering. The VA gave money monthly to vets who could prove they had some trauma that was causing them grief. But when he asked the black soldier for his name while in the after-death communication, the soldier said, "Why do you want my name now? You didn't want it then." The vet muttered again "The guy saw right through me" and never brought the issue up again in the therapy sessions.[280]

The deceased black soldier said what Dr. Botkin's patient was not expecting, a statement that could only have come from another living person who was not willing to cooperate with the subterfuge.

In a fourth case involved a normal EMDR session, not an IADC session. A combat vet wanted therapy to reduce his consuming anger with his commanding officer over sending him into combat without a rifle. Since he believed the commanding officer was alive after Vietnam, Dr. Botkin couldn't do an IADC to communicate with him. So he did a normal EMDR session to work on reducing the anger.

But when the vet closed his eyes after the EMDR eye movements, he was surprised to see the commanding officer standing before him in his Mind. The officer said he was very sorry for what he had done, and he realized the problems it caused for the vet in later life. "He looked like he really meant it," the vet said. "I believe him." With that forgiveness, the anger resolved itself for the first time in 31 years. But Dr. Botkin was surprised to see that a living person came through in an IADC session. But the next day the vet checked the lists of everyone who died in Vietnam. He discovered that his commanding officer had died soon after the vet left Vietnam.[281]

The final example is a touching story of a man named Jim who had an IADC with Dr. Botkin to resolve the grief over the death of his friend, Simon. He had been very close to Simon and his wife, Darlene. In the IADC Jim saw Simon and talked with him. After he opened his eyes and told Dr. Botkin what had happened, he said, "I feel he's OK. But you know, I was really hoping to have a message for Darlene. She's not doing well at all." Dr. Botkin induced another after-death communication so Jim could ask Simon for a message for Darlene, but this time Jim only saw two hands: a broad, masculine hand over a feminine hand. He felt they were Simon's and Darlene's hands, but there was no message. Jim was disappointed that he didn't have a message for Darlene but elated at the contact with his friend.

After the session Jim went to Darlene's home. He told her he had had a communication with Simon but was disappointed that he didn't have a message to give her from him, that he had only seen Simon's hand on top of her hand. She began to cry, smiling and nodding her head. She said to Jim, "Last night I had a dream. It was so clear it didn't seem like a dream. I felt, really felt, Simon holding my hand. Jim, he did give you a message from him to me. He was saying that it really was him holding my hand last night."[282]

These experiences are connections with the living person who has never gone far and is just not using a body anymore. The IADCs occur when the psychotherapist helps the patient set aside anger, guilt, shame, and other negative emotions using the powerful EMDR therapy method. That leaves only the deep, underlying sadness. The psychotherapist then takes the person into that sadness, plumbing its depths without flinching from it, until the person has experienced the most painful reaches of it. The person, most often in tears, then closes their eyes and remains open to whatever will happen.

When all negative emotions and the deep sadness are out of the way, what is left is the compassion and love that created the sadness. That compassion and love drops the veil between the Earth plane and the life after this life; the IADC occurs. Then the loved one, who has always been alive, well, loving, and caring, is able to communicate. The results are rich, inspiring, loving reunions that heal grief. Those we love and feel compassion for are never far from us. We just can't quiet the noise of the Earth plane to communicate with them. The IADC psychotherapy method does that.

Repair & Reattachment Grief Therapy Has a 98 Percent Success Rate in Helping People Have Afterlife Communication

The Repair & Reattachment Grief Therapy, developed by Rochelle Wright, a Washington state-licensed psychotherapist, reduces or virtually eliminates the deep grief in which the grieving person is immersed. In a Repair & Reattachment Grief Therapy session, the therapist helps a client whose loved one is now living in the life after this life personally connect with the loved one. No medium is involved. The messages come directly to the person while they sit with their eyes closed.

Rochelle developed the method based on Dr. Botkin's procedure, improving on it by adapting the EMDR protocol to the unique requirements of communicating with someone living in the next life. The communication unfolds naturally when a facilitator helps the person enter a state in which the connection occurs, guided by those on the next plane of life. The facilitator does not lead or prompt the person. The procedure is 98 percent successful and reduces the person's estimate of their grief from a rating of 10 or higher on a 10-point scale of disturbance to scores of 0 to 3 in one session.[283]

The procedure reorients the beliefs, images, feelings of guilt and anger, trauma, and perspectives on the loved one's passing so they are replaced by reassurance, joy, a renewed feeling of love and connection, and peace. The sadness at this separation through the passing is usually desensitized so the person doesn't remember it in the same way, so the sadness dissipates.

Thousands of sessions have now been performed. Many have validations that the connections are with people living in the next life. One example follows.

Carole, whose daughter, Kate, had been killed in a car accident, connected with her daughter in a Repair & Reattachment Therapy session. During the session she received a validation of the experience through the actions of her friend Linda's son, Martine, who also was in spirit. You can hear Carole describing her afterlife connection at www.earthschoolanswers.com/carole/.

This is the account from the book *Guided Afterlife Connections*:

> After another set of eye movements, Carole closed her eyes again. "Now I see Martine, Linda's son. He passed away eight months ago. He's sitting on his couch looking at me, with one leg up and his arms dangling in a funny pose, smiling. But I can still see Kate. Martine's flashing in and out. Now there are two things going on. Kate's outside and Martine's inside. He has his leg up with his arms in that funny position. I can see Kate's dress, but not the bottom. It keeps going to Martine sitting on the couch being silly. I don't understand this."
>
> After the session, Carole wrote [Rochelle] an email describing a remarkable validation of her afterlife connection. She wrote that as she and Linda, Martine's mother, were riding home, she told Linda that she had seen Martine in her Guided Afterlife Connection. Carole showed Linda the comical pose he was in, with his leg up and arms dangling. Linda's eyes opened wide. She said when Martine was clowning around, he would make what they called his "monkey pose," with his leg up and arms dangling. It was exactly what Carole saw, without knowing that Martine did that.
>
> The pose was a distinctive message from Martine to let his mom, Linda, know that he was fine, happy, and clowning as he always did.[284]

I co-authored the book *Repair & Reattachment Grief Counseling* with Rochelle. You can read more about the procedure and see videos of people who have had afterlife communication experiences using the procedure at www.earthschoolanswers.com/rochelle/.

Loving Heart Connections Have Been Shown to Help People Communicate with Loved ones

Ohio state-licensed psychotherapist Jane Bissler has developed a procedure called Loving Heart Connections that people can experience online with a psychotherapist to successfully have an afterlife connection.[285] The procedure is based on scientific research and known psychotherapeutic methods that provide a channel through which afterlife communication is directly experienced.

The sessions are private, using free online video-conferencing, and last for approximately 90 minutes. The two other procedures used by psychotherapists explained in the previous pages are based on the same principles as Loving Heart Connections.

The first test on the protocol showed that 17 of 18 participants had successful personal connections that they testified were very real and heartfelt to them. You can learn more about the procedure at www.clearingyoursoul.com/loving-heart-connections/.

Are There Methods to Help Me Learn to Have My Own Afterlife Connections at Any Time?

Answer: I developed the Self-Guided Afterlife Connections Procedure to allow people to have their own afterlife connections without the aid of a facilitator, medium, or psychotherapist. It is free and available online. Read about it at www.earthschoolanswers.com/selfguided/.

In the Self-Guided Afterlife Connections Procedure, the individual goes through eight stages of training in how to self-hypnotize. The first two stages explain to the participants the need for confidence that the afterlife is a reality and their loved ones are available to communicate. The third takes them into a light hypnotic state through a guided meditation. During this stage, participants learn to allow unfoldments to occur in their Minds without inhibiting them or trying to manipulate what happens. The next four stages contain inductions that guide the participant into having increasingly independent self-inductions. After the last stage the participant is able to perform self-hypnosis and have a connection with a loved one in the life after this life at any time, without aids such as a narration or music.

The result is that 86 percent of participants who complete the training report having a successful connection. The connections contain many validations that participants are communicating with loved ones. One example follows.

A woman described in an email one of her afterlife connections. She had already connected successfully with her mother. Then the scene changed:

> Then, I saw a young girl/teenager. She had familiar features. The name Brenda came to me and I realized it's a friend of mine's daughter. She died in a rollover crash where she was pinned and asphyxiated. The kids with her were allegedly responsible for her being abandoned at the wreck. The feelings I got from her had nothing to do with that wreck or the people around her then. She hovered with me, morphing a bit so I saw her in different stages, ages. I saw her exploring. I saw her as a student, studying. I don't know that she did that on Earth but she is now that she's passed. I heard her say, "I love mom. I miss mom." I asked in my mind, "How can you miss her, you are always with her?" It was more like a misunderstanding. I saw some food item, rolled. It looked like a lobster roll but with jalapeños. I was focused on it too much and it disappeared. I looked to the side and saw her as a little girl, rolling out dough, working on a red checked tablecloth, working so hard. She was darling! Then, I realized, Oh, she misses doing this stuff with her mom. At least that's what I got from it. I saw her enjoying the weather, the fall, the leaves, colors. I saw her and felt her loving the ocean and tide. I could feel her sort of drinking it in. She showed me some other things she was liking about where she was and her condition.

AN EMAIL SHE SENT LATER:

Well, how Dee doo? I wrote Lauren [mother of Brenda in the afterlife connection] and told her the first part of it and how confused I was with the roll ups that had jalapeño in them. I kept thinking, "What on earth!?" So, I wrote Lauren unsure of how much to tell her. I can never remember who is a believer and who isn't. Guess what? She writes back and says it makes sense to her. Yes, they made jalapeño roll ups. WHAT.... I've NEVER heard of such a thing. Look, if I ever thought I was making this stuff up, well, I completely believe now. Where the hell did jalapeño rollups come from?

Why Do I Have Trouble Seeing the Scenes Described in Guided Afterlife Connection Meditations?

Answer: Being able to visualize images in the Mind's eye is a common ability, but not common to all people. You may not have the ability to visualize images clearly or at all. Guided meditations to have afterlife communications may be difficult for you.

People have a cognitive style of mental processing on a continuum from being a visualizer to being a verbalizer. A visualizer spends more time visualizing and is able to bring visual images into Awareness easily. A strong visualizer can experience colored, detailed images. A verbalizer processes verbal information more commonly and experiences indistinct images in the Mind. Most people are somewhere on a continuum between the two extremes of the styles.

People with aphantasia have no experiences of mental images at all. For more about aphantasia, view this video: www.earthschoolanswers.com/aphantasia/. That page has the link to a network for people with aphantasia. It also has a test of your ability to visualize mentally.

You will be somewhere on the continuum of visualizer to verbalizer style and may have aphantasia. When the explanations refer to images, if you can imagine only vague images or have aphantasia, interpret the explanation to refer to the impressions you have about an experience. Don't worry about trying to follow the guided meditation instructions precisely.

When I'm Supposed to Imagine a Dialogue to Have Afterlife Communication, Why Don't I Get Words in My Mind the Way Other People Seem to Get Them?

Answer: You may be a person without an inner monologue. You will have lists and impressions that don't involve a dialogue of words. We don't know how much that affects getting mental afterlife communication, but you may just have to adjust what you get in your communications to be more impressions than the sense of words.

Dr. Russell Hurlburt, psychology professor at the University of Nevada, Las Vegas, suggests that inner speech is not as common as people believe it to be, and having no inner monologue is common.[286]

If you have little inner monologue, when the instructions tell you to imagine you're having a conversation with your loved one in spirit, you won't be able to do so. Instead of trying to imagine words in your Mind, carry on a dialogue by speaking aloud to a chair where you imagine your loved one is sitting. The first notions of a response that come to you are your loved one. The dialogue will come very fast. Keep up the pace without stopping.

You can view a video about not having an inner monologue: www.earthschoolanswers.com/monologue/. Read about not having an inner monologue in a *Psychology Today* blog at the link on the same page.

You can also see an informal talk by someone who has both aphantasia and no inner monologue at www.earthschoolanswers.com/neither/.

Is There Any Way I Can Hear and Record Voices or See and Record Images of People in the Next Life?

Answer: Yes. In instrumental transcommunication (ITC), researchers record voices of people living in the life after this life that contain personal messages. The methods are available for anyone to use.

ITC uses electronic equipment to record voices and images of people living in the life after this life. A variety of methods have been used since the early part of the twentieth century, when technology became available. Some methods have had remarkable results, demonstrating that people living in the life after this life are able to communicate if we can create the right conditions.

In Italy in 1949 Marcello Bacci began receiving voices through his tube radio. Thousands of people came to Bacci's home to have conversations with their loved ones through his radio. The participants all attested to the fact that their loved ones spoke to them this way.

In 1959 Friedrich Juergenson accidentally recorded voices of his mother and father while recording bird calls. Eight years later Dr. Konstantin Raudive used Jurgenson's methods to record tens of thousands of voices in a laboratory. In 1979 George Meek and Bill O'Neill created a device called Spiricom that recorded over 20 hours of the voice of a deceased NASA scientist, Dr. Mueller, who helped Meek and O'Neill refine their instrument.

Hans Otto König and Maria Wauters have developed devices that allow people to have voice contact with their loved ones living in the next life. The listeners validate that the recordings are of their loved ones. You can hear recordings made by König and Wauters at www.earthschoolanswers.com/hok/.

Anabela Cardoso, a career Portuguese diplomat, has been recording voices directly from radios since 1997. She authored *Electronic Voices: Contact with Another Dimension* and *Electronic Contact with the Dead: What Do the Voices Tell Us?* In two videos Cardoso explains how to use ITC to record voices: www.earthschoolanswers.com/cardoso.

The most successful and groundbreaking research is being done in Brazil by Sonia Rinaldi. Each month Sonia records for parents as many as 163 sessions of children in the life after this life, with as many as 200 messages per session. The parents have validated that the voices in the recordings are their children. You can listen to some of these recordings at www.earthschoolanswers.com/sonia/.

Sheri Perl learned Sonia's method and is successfully recording the voices of children living in the life after this life for their parents. Sheri's Prayer Registry allows parents whose children have passed to be part of a large group of other parents. The parents all agree the voices they hear are their children. You can listen to recordings Sheri has made at www.earthschoolanswers.com/sheri/.

Can I Communicate with My Loved Ones in the Next Life in Dreams?

Answer: Yes. Being able to communicate in dreams requires that both the person in spirit and the person having the dream are capable of communicating in the dream state. Asking for a connection each night before going to sleep enhances the possibility that conditions will be right for a dream communication.

Our loved ones in the life after this life communicate with us Mind to Mind, telepathically. But our Minds are so preoccupied with sensory experiences and activities in Earth School that we most often are not able to have the messages they send bubble up from the subconscious into consciousness to understand and interpret them.

We are often able to receive their messages when our conscious Minds are preoccupied—by self-hypnosis, psychotherapy, mindless activities like cleaning or driving, or dreams.

You can enhance your likelihood of receiving and remembering messages from loved ones by asking them to communicate with you in a dream before you go to sleep. Keep a notebook by your bed and, when you arise, immediately write your recollection of any dream activities during the night. Don't be discouraged if you must do this every night for some time. It often takes a while for the communication to be possible.

Can I Get Help from My Loved Ones Living in the Next Life?

Answer: Yes, your loved ones and guides will help with guidance and intuitions and will inspire other people to help you. But you must not expect the help in a specific way, and you must not be upset when you ask for help and it doesn't seem to come.

We are often given help from our loved ones living in the next life. When we are in distress or need, our loved ones come to us from wherever they are. They are always in contact with us. They will give us urgings and intuitions that sometimes come into Conscious Awareness, but most often we dismiss them. If we remain open to their communication, we will receive marvelous counsel about our lives. They will also inspire others to help us, perhaps inspiring someone we wish to hear from to talk to us.

To get help, you just have to ask for it. The activity of giving words to our request is very important. It humbles your frame of mind and leaves it open to the response. Your loved ones come to you when you have expressed your question or need.

Their response will be the first thing that comes into your Mind, before you have a chance to think. If you think about it, you will taint the response with your own answers. If you don't get the answer immediately you must leave it alone, without trying to puzzle out some unusual feeling or words you seem to get. You may get the answer later or in some other way. You must be open to whatever comes, without analyzing or second guessing. The answer will be obvious.

You may not receive the help you want or may receive it in a manner different from what you expect. You must not be disappointed or miffed when you don't receive the help you want. Our loved ones know we must go through our own challenges and make our own decisions. They will not always interfere with guidance.

Can My Loved One in Spirit Predict My Future?

Answer: Our loved ones living in the life after this life are not omniscient and are not normally able to describe the future. At times, however, they may receive and convey to us information about the future when it is in our best interest.

It is a common misperception that people in spirit know everything, including the future. They don't. They are still the normal, everyday people they were when they transitioned away from the body. At times, however, they are given insights like knowledge of future events, especially events happening soon. But the knowledge is conveyed through the loved one from higher-level entities. When we communicate with someone in spirit, we are most often communicating with a group of people who have roles in helping the communication occur. When it is appropriate and good for us to know about future events, our guides, angels, or loved ones will agree to reveal the future to us as given by higher-level entities who also agree it is in our best interest to have the knowledge.

Will I Hold Them Back by Connecting?

Answer: No. They want to communicate with you. They have an eternity to grow in wisdom and love.

I've been asked often whether connecting with our loved ones often will hold them back from going on to the next levels of life. Absolutely not! They have an eternity to grow. This idea that they have to get on with their progress is a peculiarly modern idea that comes out of our goal-driven, fast-paced lives. There's no hurry.

What about the Teachings of My Church That It Is a Sin to Communicate with People in the Afterlife?

Answer: The positions of the writers of sacred texts and of the church leaders are misunderstood. The Christian sacred texts don't have injunctions against communicating with loved ones and in fact have examples of Yeshua (Jesus) communicating with people who have transitioned and promising the disciples they will receive communication from him.

For anyone concerned about communicating with those who have left the earth, you must know that the Old Testament injunctions against mediums and speaking with the people who have transitioned referred to the religions that were popular at the time that were based on seeking advice about how to live using mediums. Yahweh, the God of the Old Testament, was a jealous god who would have no other gods before him. The writers were saying Yahweh didn't like people getting advice from anyone but him. That was the reason for the injunctions.

At the same time, the New Testament contains nothing about not connecting with loved ones. In fact, there is ample evidence of afterlife communications made by the Early Christians. For more go to www.earthschoolanswers.com/christians/.

Are There Negative Beings Who Will Interfere When I'm Communicating?

Answer: There are negative beings and mischievous earthbound people who will communicate when the person on this side of life is not spiritually grounded and is attempting to communicate as a game. But for people who are connecting with loved ones out of love, the negative entities will not have an effect.

"Earthbounds" are people who have transitioned from the body but have not left the earth environment. They have no bodies, so they wander around us unseen. Because they are still attuned to the earth environment, they can sit on chairs, travel in buses, attend gatherings, and do the things people using bodies do. They almost never can actually disturb things by moving objects. Their primary mischief is in influencing people through thought.

Earthbounds will speak to people who are attempting to communicate with any unseen entity as a game. Most recordings by the ghost-hunter groups are from earthbounds.

When we connect with loved ones, on the other hand, there are minimal dangers from earthbounds or negative entities. We are acting out of love, so they can't influence us and find us incredibly boring.

You may do a simple prayer of protection before making a connection with someone unseen, including your loved ones, if that would make you feel more comfortable. This is an example prayer.

> During this time of communication, surround and fill me, the room I am in, and all in this house with a white light of love and divine protection.

In normal activity to communicate with loved ones, there are no problems with earthbounds or entities.

Will My Deep Grief Make It More Difficult to Have an Afterlife Communication?

Answer: Yes. If you fall into grief every time you think about the person, communicating will be more difficult. The grief will drag you down into your Mind so your loved one can't get messages through.

Grief is a heavy, dense emotion. It creates a cocoon around the grieving person that loved ones in spirit trying to communicate cannot easily penetrate. The general rule for people having an Induced After-Death Communication therapy session is that the sadness and periods of grief stabilize after a period of a year. There is still great sadness, but the grief, guilt, anger, and other tapestry of emotions are not so great that they dominate the person's Mind. If you have difficulty receiving the messages, it could very well because your grief is keeping you from being open to having the messages bubble up from your subconscious.

However, you don't have to wait for a year. Communicate now. Your loved ones want you to speak to them, even if you can't receive responses easily.

Is It Possible My Loved One Is Angry with Me and Will Be Harsh in My Connections?

Answer: No. All of the experiences we have with loved ones are positive.

Communications with our loved ones are always filled with love and a concern for the person living in the earth realm. If you ever have a negative experience or feeling, such as feeling the person on the other side shunned you or told you something disturbing or anything else negative, **the communication wasn't from them**. That feeling or message has come from fears and negative emotions we all have while in the earth realm that have risen in our Mind. Push them aside and say, "That's not from (your loved one). I put that in the trash." Think of putting that in a trash can. Then go back to your communication. Receiving negative feelings or messages is very unlikely to happen. Your communications will always be positive.

Our loved ones have the same personality, loves, fears, intolerances, sentiments, humor, and all the rest of what makes them an individual, just as they had on earth. We might see them come to us crying over something or frustrated or even angry over a situation, but the negative emotions will be from situations, not individuals. Their approach to us is full of love and concern. They have grown out of much of the pettiness they may have felt while in the body. The transition from the earth realm is a life-changing event! It results in changed sentiments.

What Are the Experiences I Might Have with Someone Living in the Life after This Life?

Answer: You might have a sense of their presence, telepathic conversations, images and scenes, and the sense of being touched, kissed, or hugged. Everything in this world happens in the Mind, so you might have any of the same experiences in your Mind you have while in a body when you communicate Mind to Mind, including the sensations of being touched, kissed, or hugged. But they will be like the memory of an experience you feel, not like a touch on the arm.

In your communications with people living in the life after this life, you may have the following experiences.

A Sense of Presence

You may have a sense of presence. You will simply know that the person you want to connect with is there. It's as real as the senses of seeing and hearing. You won't see anything and won't "hear" with your ears. But the knowledge or sense that they're with you is a very reliable validation you're connected.

Some people report having chills or tingling or other such physical sensation when a loved one is near. You can get to know those sensations as the signal your loved one is present and anxious to communicate.

Conversations

You will have conversations with your loved one. The more you become accustomed to Mind-to-Mind communication, the more easily the conversations will flow. They are very fast because they are telepathic. The messages don't come in long strings of words. You receive the entire message at one time, without words. You have no time to doubt or wonder or judge what is coming. There is no hesitation.

Images and Scenes

Your loved ones may project images and scenes to you. They may seem irrelevant at the time, as though they were just passing fantasies. When you allow free unfoldment, you may access a variety of images and scenes. They come Mind to Mind, bypassing the eyes, ears, skin, and brain. The result is the same sights in the Mind you might have with your eyes, but since the body limitations aren't there, what comes is fluid, easily changed, and not limited to mundane physical realities. They may seem to jump around or be in fragments. That's because in our Minds loved ones, guides, Higher Selves, and Souls can take us from scene to scene easily and immediately to get messages to us, so they take advantage of that unrestricted ability.

They often give experiences instead of words. Instead of telling you something, they guide you into experiencing it. In one example, the loved one in spirit wanted to convey a message to someone having a Self-Guided Afterlife Connection experience. The person could have received a Mind-to-Mind message such as "Well, you're trying too hard and thinking too much. Just relax and my communication will come to you." Instead this person was given the experience that allowed her to discover the truth that she was trying too hard to make the communication happen. As she sat with her eyes closed, she was guided by her husband in spirit to see a mountain with people working hard to climb to the top. Her husband took her to an elevator at the base of the mountain that quickly took them to the top. He was conveying the message that she didn't have to work so hard at communicating. She should just relax and he would take her into the communication. She understood the message immediately.

The teaching often happens in experiences and senses of messages, not in words. The person in spirit is in charge of the images, scenes, and messages. Our role is to allow them to unfold naturally, even if they seem irrelevant.

The explanation of the message comes with the image. You won't have to puzzle it out. You'll know. You may have the sense of your loved one telling you the message telepathically, or may just know the meaning. If you have to work at figuring it out, you probably didn't get the interpretation.

When they send an image of themselves or appear in a dream, they give you their projection. You are thinking together and they are bringing to mind an image. If you see an image of them, you aren't seeing them as they are now unless they decide to project that image to you. To show that it is them, some have had to project the image of what they looked like in a picture because they can't recall what they looked like when in Earth School. As a result the image may appear as the young, vibrant person they are now, or you may see an image as they were when you last saw them when they were healthy. You may see one, then the other. They probably will be wearing what they wore in Earth School so they look familiar to you, not the robes most wear now in the life after this life. They control the image by projecting it to you Mind.

Sensations of Being Touched, Hugged, and Kissed

Our body experiences include sensations of being touched, but the sensations are entirely in our Minds, just as pain and pleasure are in the Mind, not in a body that is apart from the Mind. As a result people describe being touched, caressed, hugged, and even kissed during afterlife communications, especially during dreams; Induced After-Death Communications; Repair & Reattachment Grief Therapy; and Self-Guided Afterlife Connections. The experiences are as real as being touched physically because all the sensations are happening in the Mind both in a telepathic connection or in daily life. The physical sensations will be like your memory of the feeling of being kissed or hugged or otherwise touched.

Can I Hasten along the Connections by Thinking Up Scenes in My Mind with My Loved One in Them?

Answer: No. Using your imagination will cause your Mind to be filled with what you are creating, blocking the connection and experiences your loved one wants to bring to you. Relax and empty your mind. Allow them to fill it with their messages.

Successful connections require patience and time. You must not go into your first experiences expecting a connection. If you anticipate a connection, that will block the flow of free unfoldment that eventually will result in the connection. You must be willing for the entire session to contain impressions, images, and experiences that seem to have no meaning and are not connected to your loved one. You must allow the communications to come in their own time, in their own way. When you're getting images or impressions that aren't meaningful, you should not think "But where is she? I want to connect and she's not here!" That will shut down the free unfolding and block the connection. The meaningless experiences are part of the process.

You also must not "project" or "imagine" things in an effort to stimulate them. Imagining them running to you or in some scene blocks them from being able to bring to you what they have in Mind. It is very important for you to realize that your loved one has experiences or a message to give you. They are waiting for you to relax and give up control so they can give you what they have planned. If you keep control or intend to have something happen or expect to have a connection as you envision it, you block the image or message they have waiting for you. You can't *make* it come. You must *allow* it to come. You must give up control, no matter how much you want a connection.

What Is It Like to Communicate with Someone Living in the Life after This Life?

Answer: You must learn a new way of communicating. Mind-to-Mind communication comes in whole messages, very quickly. You rarely will hear words in your Mind, although you may translate what you're getting into words naturally. Don't expect to hear a voice in the room.

You must learn a new way of communicating when you communicate Mind to Mind with someone living in the next life. We're not accustomed to having someone communicate within our Minds. We've been thinking, remembering, daydreaming, and talking to ourselves in the privacy of our Minds since we were children. Now, having someone else come in and start thinking and talking in that space in our Minds is a very different experience. To be able to connect and communicate, you must learn new ways of speaking and listening. That takes time and patience.

It's like learning a new language. You can't learn a new language by flying into a country, stepping off a plane, and spending a half hour with native speakers. You'll just be bewildered by what you hear. In the same way, you mustn't expect that you'll learn this new language of Mind-to-Mind communication in one session. You must give it time. You're about to step off the plane into a new realm, and there you'll receive thinking, images, sentiments, memories, and messages that are coming from deep inside you where you are one with the person with whom you're communicating. You will be thinking, reminiscing, and viewing together. That's going to feel like your accustomed thinking, remembering, and talking to yourself, but it's not coming from you.

When you get the communications from your loved ones, guides, Higher Selves, and Souls, they come Mind to Mind, so there are no sounds and there are *usually* no words (although sometimes words come to mind). You just receive the messages. These messages have the qualities of memories or daydreaming. The thoughts from them will come to you as your thoughts do. You may then create words from the messages using your inner voice. That makes it difficult at first to realize the difference between your thinking or imagination and their messages—it's the same inner voice you've thought with since you were a child. You must get past feeling like their messages should come in the voices they used in the earth realm. They usually don't. They usually come without words at all. They come in fully formed messages in the Mind.

You should actively and often speak to them. Don't stop communicating because you don't feel you're getting a response. The response is there. You just have to learn how to allow it to come up from your subconscious. Their response to your thought or voiced comment or question will come immediately after you speak, while you are speaking, or before you speak. It comes in an instant because you are communicating telepathically without words. The whole message comes at once. If you have to stop to think, you've missed it. You must keep up the dialogue.

It's a very normal part of learning how to communicate to go through having to get over the mistaken notion that what's coming into your Mind is "just my imagination." That will happen when you experience having images, thoughts, feelings, bodily sensations, and messages come to you that you just couldn't originate. The more you experience that, the more confident you will become that the messages are coming from them, and the messages will flow more smoothly. You must be patient. Learning Mind-to-Mind communication is like learning to speak a new language. But you will learn it if you just trust and allow the unfoldment to teach you.

Having said that, experiencers occasionally report that they hear clear words spoken in their Minds, with the sound of the voice the person in the life after this life used in the earth realm. Be open to anything.

What Is the Procedure I Should Follow to Have an Afterlife Communication?

Answer: Anyone can have an afterlife communication with a loved one in spirit. Most of us can't become mediums, but we can be our own medium with the people we love. The love bond makes that possible. There are procedures you can follow to connect with your loved ones.

There are things you can do to make conditions better for an afterlife communication. In none of these are you making things happen. The person in spirit is entirely in charge. Your job is to set the conditions in your life so the communication is more likely to occur. The procedure I have developed for AREI is available free online. You can learn more at www.afterlifeinstitute.org/self-guided-afterlife-connections/. A summary of the procedure follows.

You Must Learn to Acknowledge and Process the Natural Unfoldment

Some of what comes into the Mind comes without our intention. Unintended images, thoughts, feelings, bodily sensations, and messages come in deep-sleep dreams, hypnogogic dreaming when half awake, inspirations or flashes of insight, notions, and inspirations. They unfold without our intention to have them come. This entry into our Minds is called "free unfoldment." We don't control free unfoldment. Our language has a number of words or phrases to describe free unfoldments coming to us because they're so common. We might describe them by saying "It just came to me," "I suddenly realized," "I had a flash of inspiration," or "a light bulb went on."

The sources of these unusual images, thoughts, or messages are our loved ones, guides, Souls, Higher Selves, Soul, and people interested in helping us. They all communicate with us regularly, throughout the day.

We are taught by our society not to regard the messages as real or valid, so we don't listen to them. We thus miss many messages from our loved ones, guides, Souls, and Higher Selves.

You Must Be Open and Positive

Open yourself to whatever comes. That will help you become more attuned to the natural unfoldment that comes from your guides, helpers, Soul, and loved ones in the life after this life. Something may come to you: a sense of presence, a feeling of warmth and love, a memory, or a song. Allow whatever comes to come. Don't try to make something happen or change what comes to you. The experiences are like soap bubbles floating past you. If you reach out to draw one closer, as soon as you touch it, the bubble will pop. That is what will happen to your naturally unfolding experiences if you try to make them become something you want or expect.

Our loved ones, guides, helpers, and Souls are in charge of the experiences. Don't reject anything that comes. If you're communicating and suddenly think of the seashore, don't reject that because you saw a picture of a seashore just before trying to make the connection. Stay with whatever comes. If you have the image of Mom or message from Mom and you really wanted to connect with Dad, don't stop the connection. Allow it to unfold. Often the person we want to communicate with intentionally steps aside to allow someone else to come through. The person you want may be next.

Let the Doubt Flow Past

It's natural and normal to have occasional doubts about whether the unfoldment is from your loved one. Our culture is so spiritually backward that we were reared to doubt the reality of our eternal lives, even though the religions teach about eternal life. We all continue to second guess what we're getting from someone living in the life after this life. Just remember that unfoldment isn't coming from you. The unfoldments flow just like a conversation because they are a real conversation. You'll learn that the messages couldn't be coming from you. That will become more obvious to you over time. But don't feel you're not doing well because of the doubts. They're natural and normal.

Follow This Procedure to Have an Afterlife Communication

Anyone can experience afterlife communication with a loved one. It takes relaxing into the state of mind to allow the connection to happen and being hyper attentive to what comes, accepting everything without judgment. Follow this procedure.

Set aside 15 to 30 minutes of time when you are in a quiet area without interruptions. Bring no cellphones to the area. Tell your family or others living with you that you are not to be disturbed. Wear comfortable clothing, preferably without belts or other restrictions. A jogging suit is ideal. Sit in a comfortable chair or recliner. Lying down is not good for most people because there's a good chance you will fall asleep.

Have in mind the person or pet who lives in the life after this life. The person or pet must be significant for you. It shouldn't be someone you know of but don't have a relationship with, such as an actor or historical figure. You may be grieving for this person or pet, or you may have someone in mind you aren't grieving for but had a close relationship with.

If you never see images in your mind, you may have aphantasia. (See www.earthschoolanswers.com/aphantasia/.) If so, instead of the sight of your loved one, you will have the sense they are present. If you don't think words to yourself, you may have no inner monologue. (See www.earthschoolanswers.com/monologue/.) If so, follow this procedure with your eyes open and speak words rather than try to think them in your Mind. You might sit at a table with an empty chair and have a dialogue with your loved one sitting in the chair.

Follow this procedure.

1. Begin with a prayer of protection such as "During this time of communication, surround and fill me, the room I am in, and all in this house with a white light of love and divine protection."

2. Close your eyes and relax. Be aware of your breathing for a few minutes.

3. Then start from your head and think about relaxing your muscles in groups going down to your feet. Pause between each area to perform the relaxation. Relax your head . . . jaw . . . neck . . . shoulders . . . arms . . . torso . . . thighs . . . calves . . . feet. Follow that order, taking time with each. Stay aware of your breathing.

4. After you feel you are totally relaxed, invite your loved one to come to communicate with you. Be hyper-aware of everything that happens. Assume your loved one is there. Don't create your own picture of your loved one. You must be patient and allow whatever unfolds to happen by itself.

5. If you just see blackness and you don't have aphantasia, you're not being attentive enough. Within what seems to be blackness, notice anything you might see. It will be there.

6. When you have a sense of presence, speak in your Mind or audibly about your love for that person.

7. The first notion or thought that comes into your Mind is the response. Don't judge it or analyze it. Your communication will be very fast. Keep the dialogue going without pauses and with only the content of the communication.

8. Carry on the communication as long as you want. We normally suggest you allow the person in spirit to decide when to stop. As you stay in the communication, you'll find it becoming more natural and you'll lose track of where you are.

Try Using Automatic or Inspired Writing

One very good way of learning to keep the flow of the dialogue going is through automatic writing, also called inspired writing. Have a sheaf of a dozen blank pieces of paper on a table or clipboard and a pen that writes easily. Relax your Mind to shut out the physical world following the procedure explained in "How to Have Afterlife Connections" above. Then invite your loved one to communicate with you. Ask a question. As you ask the question, scribble it on the top sheet of paper.

Don't worry about legibility. Don't look at the writing. You might do this with your eyes closed. After you've scribbled the statement or question, keep scribbling the first words that come to mind immediately, without a break. You may receive a thought instead of words. Scribble the thought in words. Then scribble your response. Don't worry about penmanship. And don't stop scribbling. If you stop to wait for a response, you've already missed it. The response came either immediately after you scribbled your question or statement, while you were scribbling it, or even before you scribbled it. Your loved one is responding to the question in your Mind, not what you scribble, so they know and respond to the question before you write it.

Do this regularly and you will find you have less and less need to write all the words coming to you. You'll get the words in whole blocks of thought so quickly you can't write down words. Be patient and allow the weeks and months it may take for this fluency to happen.

13

What Will Happen When My Body Dies?

Answer: When your body dies, you will just have a change of focus. You were focused on the room or bed or highway where you transitioned from the body; then suddenly you have a change of focus to being outside of your body looking down or you awaken in a room with your family or you awaken in a recovery area. Whatever happens, you just were experiencing *there* and suddenly now you're experiencing *here*—it is just a change of focus.

It may seem that something has ceased to exist at the transition, but the person simply is changing attunement to another reality in the Mind of Our Universal Intelligence. It is much like our change of focus from computing our taxes to being interrupted by the phone ringing and talking with a close friend. When we're doing our taxes, we don't have our friend in mind at all. When we're talking to our friend, we don't have the taxes in mind at all. It's as though we are in two different awarenesses. We have just changed focus.

During our lifetimes we focus on having experiences with everyone else in our Earth School lives. It has only been a focus, however, not a location in space or time within a world that exists apart from Our Universal Intelligence. At the transition, we simply change focus to another set of experiences with the people we love and others.

What Will Happen in the Hours and Days Leading Up to the Time My Body Stops Functioning?

Answer: You are cared for at every minute of your life, including just before your transition. But your transition is a special event, so the care is much more obvious. If you are transitioning over time, such as from an illness, you will see loved ones in spirit coming for you and have other experiences showing you are being gently guided into your next life.

Every person has unique experiences in the transition from Earth School that suit the individual. However, there are general occurrences leading up to the transition and during the transition that are similar.

The "Call" to Loved Ones

When the transition is expected, as at the end of protracted illness, there is a "call" to loved ones to come in the period leading up to the transition and at the time of the transition. Those in the life after this life answer the call and are with the person in the days before the transition and are there to help at the moment of transition.

In the case of a sudden transition, there is no time for the call, so loved ones are not immediately with the person. Nonetheless, there are always "deliverers" who come to help the person make the adjustment.

Healers from the Other Side Revitalize the Spirit Energy to Help During the Lead-Up to the Transition

When the end of the Earth School experience is near, Our Universal Intelligence facilitates movement into the next realm to aid us in the transition and revitalizes our spirit energy while the body is failing. During this period, "counselors" from the next life and the spirits or Souls of people still on earth help the person make the adjustment.

Pre-death and Deathbed Visions Are Common

Everything we know about the life after this life tells us that Our Universal Intelligence has set up life so the transition into the next plane of eternal life is as easy as possible; the universe is filled with love and compassion. Pre-death visions are an example of that preparation for a gentle transition.

Pre-death visions are visions of deceased loved ones that patients commonly have in the weeks before they transition. *Deathbed visions* are the visions dying patients have in the days or hours immediately preceding the transition. Both help the person prepare for the transition. One estimate is that they occur in 25 percent of transitions.[287]

Dr. Diane Komp, a Yale pediatric oncologist, described a 7-year-old girl who sat up in bed just before her death from leukemia and told her parents that beautiful angels were singing to her. A boy dying of leukemia said that God spoke to him and that he asked God to live another year so he could explain his death to his 3-year-old brother. Amazingly, against medical odds, the boy lived one more year.[288]

In 1959 Karlis Osis, PhD, psychology professor at the University of Freiburg, and Erlendur Haraldsson, PhD, psychology professor at the University of Munich, studied deathbed visions in the U.S. and India. They found that some transitioning people reported seeing angels and other religious figures, but most reported seeing familiar deceased people who often communicate that they have come to help take them away. The transitioning person's mood and health often change when they have such a vision. During these visions, a once depressed or pain-riddled person is elated and relieved of pain.[289]

The deathbed visions were not due to any medical or psychological influences. They could be explained only as visions of loved ones in spirit helping the transitioning person through the transition process.

Deathbed visions are consistently of people the person knows, are clear and rational, contain reasonable and uplifting messages, and are always calm and never disturbing. Studies of the visions have shown that the visions are not related to the hallucinations that drugs, fever, and certain illnesses can produce; drugs and fever may even inhibit rather than generate them.[290]

These experiences are evidence that people whose bodies had died come to greet the person about to make their own transition away from the body. The gesture is another demonstration that the transition from the body is a life event planned carefully by all involved. It is the birth into the next stage of the person's life.

Watch videos of hospice nurses describing incidents they witnessed with transitioning patients at www.earthschoolanswers.com/visions/.

View a video of Martha Atkins, death and dying educator and executive director at Contemplative Care for the Dying and founder of the Children's Bereavement Center of South Texas, speaking about deathbed and near-death visions at www.earthschoolanswers.com/atkins/.

View a video of Dr. Christopher Kerr, CEO of the Center for Hospice & Palliative Care, speaking about deathbed and near-death visions at www.earthschoolanswers.com/kerr/.

People May Recover Briefly and Talk Lucidly before Passing

Patients with severe psychiatric or neurological disorders who have not been lucid, perhaps for months, may suddenly regain their normal conscious self just before their transition and have lucid conversations with loved ones. The phenomenon is called "terminal lucidity." Their moods are elevated and they speak with vitality. In many cases the brain has deteriorated so much that such an event is impossible. But the Mind is not in the brain, so they are able to have periods with free, clear, lucid conversations even when their brains have deteriorated.

What Will Happen in the Moments of My Transition from This Life to the Next?

Answer: When you go through the transition, you merely stop having experiences using the Earth School body. You do continue to have experiences—because your Mind never was in the body. A variety of experiences happen at the time of the transition, depending on the person. The transition is always easy and painless.

At the moment the earth body stops functioning, the person ceases to have body experiences. The person has not changed. The person's experiences are different. Those who have made the transition all remark how easy the transition is. The transition is always painless. For those who experience a catastrophic death, there may be a brief coma or period of unconsciousness during which the event takes place, or the person may suddenly be standing next to the lifeless body with no experience or recollection of the separation itself.[291] There are accounts of people being taken away from an impending disaster and watching it happen from the safety of a lofty position. For those who have made the transition after a period of declining health, the individual is greeted by people in spirit as the transition occurs. All fear or anxiety dissolves and a profound peace comes over the person.

There are many accounts of floating out of the body in the moments after the body is abandoned. Some of the descriptions note a snapping of what seem to be strings attaching the person's spirit to the body.

People near the body often describe phenomena in the room: a sudden light, at times blinding; a white, grey, or blue-white "soul mist" coming up from the body; a vaporous body shape with the features of the transitioning person; a silver or grey cord or many threads from the body connecting to the vaporous body shape that dissolve or snap; the vaporous body rising and disappearing into a corner of the room; and the vision of loved ones who have come to escort the person from the earth realm. Some report seeing a transfer of energy from the physical body to the new, separate body, called an etheric body, life-body, subtle body, vital body, astral body, or spirit body that is a duplicate of the physical body. The spirit seems to move toward the head and exit from the top of the head, although some have described witnessing some vaporous form exiting from the solar plexus.

The Transitioning Person May See Long-Dead Loved Ones Coming to Take Them on a Trip

The deathbed visions described in the previous section continue during the transition itself. Transitioning people who have been bedridden often talk of going on a trip at the moment of their transition. Then, as they are in the transition experience, they say they see long-dead loved ones who have come to take them away. They may hold conversations with them or reach for them.

Will I Feel Pain at the Transition?

Answer: All speakers from the life after this life say there is no pain during the transition.

People who transition because of illness have no experience of the body's pain at the end, even though the people gathered around the deathbed see struggles or signs of pain.

People who transition because of a horrendous accident are spared the pain of the trauma that results in their transition, although they may experience the fear and trauma leading up to the accident. But they describe being taken out just before the actual trauma.

A man communicating through South African trance medium Nina Merrington explained that he was spared the pain of a fatal auto accident and actually observed the event from outside of it.

> Mike Swain, who died in an auto accident, told his father Jasper Swain, a Pietermaritzburg, South Africa lawyer, that he left his body an instant before the cars actually impacted. Heather, his fiancée's young sister, was also killed in the accident. Mike told of being blinded by the glare of the sun reflecting off of the windscreen of the

oncoming car. "All of a sudden, the radiance changes from silver to gold. I am being lifted up in the air, out through the top of the car. I grabbed little Heather's hand. She too is being lifted up out of the car." When they were about 30 feet above the car, they witnessed the collision below them and heard a noise like the snapping of steel banjo strings. They had suffered no pain.[292]

The talented medium Suzanne Giesemann tells of receiving messages from the Soul of a man named Jim who was currently in hospice dying of cancer. He explained that although his body was in hospice apparently struggling and in pain, his Soul was already at peace. He said to Suzanne, "The body may appear to be suffering, but my soul is fine." When the transition is inevitable and the person seems to not be present, the Soul has gone on and is being spared the pain. You can hear Suzanne telling the story at www.earthschoolanswers.com/suzanne/.

We have no accounts from people living in the next life of suffering the pain of a sudden, accidental transition. The person goes on to the next life before the body dies.

When Might I Experience Glimpses of the Life after This Life as I Gradually Transition?

Answer: It is very common for people making the transition to describe seeing wonderful scenes that are enthralling and uplifting for them just before they make the transition.

People making the transition often describe having glimpses of beautiful landscapes and hearing music and choruses singing, as though a curtain were gradually opening. In her eulogy for Steve Jobs, his sister described his last words:

Before embarking, he'd looked at his sister Patty, then for a long time at his children, then at his life's partner, Laurene, and then over their shoulders past them. Steve's final words were:

OH WOW. OH WOW. OH WOW.[293]

Thomas Alva Edison, the inventor and businessman famous for his work on electricity, sound recording, and motion pictures, opened his eyes shortly before his transition and said "It is very beautiful over there."[294]

Is It Possible People in the Room Could Share Mentally the Experiences as I Make the Transition?

Answer: Yes. There are many accounts of people sharing the experience of transitioning with the person moving on to the life after this life.

Raymond Moody, who coined the term "near-death experience" in his book *Life After Life*[295] in 1975, introduced the concept of shared-death experiences in his 2009 book *Glimpses of Eternity: An Investigation into Shared Death Experiences*.[296]

Dr. Moody described being at the bed of his transitioning mother with other family members waiting for his mother's transition. Dr. Moody said he saw their deceased father in the room, and all reported seeing an unusual light, "like looking at light in a swimming pool at night," he wrote. "It was as though the fabric of the universe had torn and for just a moment we felt the energy of that place called heaven."[297]

View a video of Dr. Moody talking about shared-death experiences at www.earthschoolanswers.com/shared/.

Peter Fenwick, MD, and Elizabeth Fenwick, RN, who research end-of-life phenomena, have collected hundreds of shared-death experiences in the United Kingdom and Northern Europe.[298] They describe one account by a wife at her transitioning husband's bedside.

> Suddenly there was the most brilliant light shining from my husband's chest and as the light lifted upward there was the most beautiful music and singing voices, my own chest seemed filled with infinite joy and my heart felt as if it was lifting to join the light and music. Suddenly there was a hand on my shoulder

and a nurse said, "I'm sorry love. He has just gone." I lost sight of the light and music. I felt so bereft at being left behind.[299]

Dr. Pim van Lommel, who has written extensively about near-death experiences, refers to the shared-death experience as an "empathetic NDE."[300] Dr. van Lommel describes a shared-death experience of a man whose loving partner, Anne, had been killed in a traffic accident. Her seven-year-old son was severely injured in the accident and was not expected to live. As the boy's transition neared, Anne's family gathered at the hospital to console each other. The man stood at the back of the room by a window. This is Dr. van Lommel's account of what happened.

> The moment he died, when his EEG flatlined, I "saw" that his mother came to collect him. You must bear in mind that she'd died five days earlier. There was this incredibly beautiful reunion. And at one point they reached out for me and included me in their embrace. This was an indescribable, ecstatic reunion. Part of me left my body and accompanied them to the light. I know this must sound very strange indeed, but I was fully conscious with Anne and her son as they went to the light, just as I was fully conscious and in the room where all the relatives were incredibly sad because their nephew and grandson had just died. And I joined them. We were heading toward the light, but at a certain point it was clear that I had to return, so I fell back.[301]

Is It Possible That after the Transition I Might Appear to People Who Are a Distance Away?

Answer: Yes. Accounts of people appearing at the moments their bodies die to people hundreds or thousands of miles away are very common.

In one example a man was alone, reading, when he looked up from his book and clearly saw a school friend. The friend then disappeared. A day later he learned his friend's body had died at the same moment when she appeared to him.[302]

In some cases the person transitioning is seen by more than one person. As a woman attending a family party climbed a set of stairs, a lady acquaintance passed her quickly. She wore black silk with a muslin covering over her head and shoulders. Her silk rustled. In a moment, she was gone. The woman was surprised because she did not know this acquaintance was at the party. The next morning a nursery girl who worked at the house was startled to see the same lady, in black silk, in a room. She refused to go into that room again. Shortly thereafter the woman learned that her acquaintance had passed away at the precise time she had seen her at the family party.[303]

An acquaintance, Mike Thomson, described the unexpected appearance of his ex-wife's Uncle Neely. Mike hadn't seen his ex-wife's family since their divorce seven years before. One day, driving alone down a highway, he felt someone next to him. There in the passenger seat sat Uncle Neely. Mike was shaken because he had thought he was alone in the car. Uncle Neely said, "Mike, the Mass is over. Thanks be to God." That was an old joke Mike had had with him. Mike had converted to Catholicism for his wife but hated going to Mass. When the family attended mass together, Uncle Neely would smile at Mike as they walked out after mass and say, "Well, Mike, the Mass is over. Thanks be to God."

Mike looked at the road and then again at the passenger seat. Uncle Neely was gone. When Mike arrived home he was upset and worried; he thought he might be losing his mind, so he didn't tell anyone about the strange event. About an hour later his son came into the room and said, "Dad, Mom called. She said she had some bad news. Uncle Neely died today." As Mike found out later, Uncle Neely had transitioned from his body at the moment he had appeared in Mike's car.

Examples of such appearances by people who have passed away are common. They further demonstrate that the people whose bodies have died continue to live without the brain or body.

Second Lieutenant Leslie Poynter was killed in action during World War I. At 9:00 one evening he appeared to his sister in England, walked into her bedroom, bent over, and kissed her. Smiling happily, he faded from view. Two weeks later, the family received a telegram informing them of his death on the date he had appeared to his sister.[304]

A woman named Mrs. Pacquet experienced her brother Edmund appearing to her mysteriously, although she knew he was at sea serving on a ship. He seemed to be acting out something. She later received word that, six hours before the appearance, he had drowned at sea. He was acting out how he had been caught around the legs by a rope and dragged overboard.[305]

A woman named Gladys Watson was awakened from a deep sleep by someone calling her name. As she awoke, she saw her paternal grandfather. He said to her, "Don't be frightened. It's only me. I've just died." When she awoke she described what she saw to her husband. He refused to believe that her grandfather had visited her and telephoned the family home. He was surprised to learn that her grandfather had died unexpectedly that very evening.[306]

Lord Brougham, an English peer, was traveling in Sweden. He suddenly saw an apparition of a university friend he had not seen or thought about for years. Later he received a letter saying that the friend had died in India at the exact time he saw the apparition. The two had made a pact that whoever passed away first would appear to the other.[307]

Mrs. Arthur Bellamy made a similar agreement with a school friend she had not seen for years. A night after the friend's death Mrs. Bellamy's husband was startled to see a lady sitting on the bed beside his sleeping wife. He later saw a photograph of the school friend and said it was she whom he had seen.[308]

Dr. Minot J. Savage, a Unitarian clergyman, described an incident in which a young boy received a visit from a loving friend who had just passed away. After the boy was put to bed one night, his parents heard him crying. They rushed to him and asked him what was wrong. Sobbing, he said, "Judge says he's dead! He has been here and told me that he is dead!" The next morning the parents learned that the Judge had died at about that time the night before.[309]

At My Passing, Might I Feel What It Is Like to Be Out of the Body?

Answer: Yes. Very often the person in spirit speaking through a medium describes sitting or lying at one moment and standing next to their lifeless body or above it the next.

At the moment of the transition, people commonly realize their physical body is lying motionless while they are floating above it or standing beside it. One example is from the archives of direct-voice medium Leslie Flint. During one of Flint's direct-voice sessions, a man in spirit known as Mr. Biggs described what happened at his transition. He was sitting in his easy chair, felt odd, and found himself standing over his body, which was still slumped in the chair.[310] You can hear Mr. Biggs describing his transition at www.earthschoolanswers.com/biggs/.

Monsignor Robert Hugh Benson, who passed into the life after this life in 1914, spoke clairaudiently through medium Anthony Borgia, describing seeing his body as he made the transition from it. He was lying in bed near the time for his transition when this happened.

> I suddenly felt a great urge to rise up. I had no physical feeling whatever, very much in the same way that physical feeling is absent during a dream, but I was mentally alert, however much my body seemed to contradict such a condition. Immediately I had this distinct prompting to rise, I found that I was actually doing so. I then discovered that those around my bed did not seem to perceive what I was doing, since they made no effort to come to my assistance, nor did they try in any way to hinder me. Turning, I then beheld what had taken place. I saw my physical body lying lifeless upon its bed, but here was I, the real I, alive and well. . . . At no time was I in any mental distress, but I was full of wonder at what was to happen next, for here I was, in full possession of all my faculties, and, indeed feeling "physically" as I had never felt before.[311]

Do I Have Connections to the Body That Must Break?

Answer: There are many accounts of a silver cord connecting the physical body to an etheric or astral body that is the consciousness of the person. It snaps at the time of the transition.

The silver cord is also known as the *Sutratman,* or life thread. It is described as a white or silver elastic umbilical-like cord that must be attached for the body to have vitality. Some describe two silver cords, one coming from the solar plexus (conveying vitality to the body) and one coming from the head (transmitting consciousness).[312] The silver cord makes a notable snap when the body loses its vitality and the person is freed.

The communicators sometimes describe additional glue-like threads that connect the physical body to the etheric or astral body. These threads similarly snap in a chorus as the physical body gives up the spirit.

Is It Possible I Might Have to Make the Transition Alone?

Answer: No one makes the transition alone. In cases of transitioning from an illness, the family is with the person well before, during, and after the transition. After even sudden transitions, there are "deliverers" who counsel the person.

No one makes the transition alone. In gradual transitions, the transition is anticipated, people appear to the person during the period before the transition, and there are people to help the newly transitioned person. When the transition is sudden, as in an explosion, the family already in the life after this life will not be there at the moment of the transition, but there will be someone called a "deliverer" to help the person adjust until loved ones arrive. Many people take on the role of helper or counselor as part of their spiritual growth that continues in the life after this life.

Some people who have ties to earth they do not want to break or who have such a backward view of the life after this life that they refuse to believe it is real may by their unwillingness to understand the change in their status not be open to help. Some become earthbound as a result.

Are Events in a Near-Death Experience the Same as What Happens When the Person Actually Transitions?

Answer: What happens in the moments after the body stops functioning without resuscitation during an NDE is in some ways different from making the transition when the body dies.

In an NDE, the person is still learning lessons and progressing in this life. As a result, the experience prepares the person for a more loving, compassionate life after the experience. At times the NDE contains elements not at all in the experience after transition, such as the negative NDEs. Around 1 to 2 percent of NDEers have negative experiences such as sensing a frightening void or graphic hellish imagery.[313] Everything that happens as long as the person remains in Earth School, including the events in an NDE, happens for reasons relevant to the person's progress in accomplishing the pre-birth plan. The frightening images are intended to teach the experiencer something that will affect their life. No one who has made the transition describes either a frightening void or hellish images.

How Easy Will My Transition Away from My Body Be?

Answer: The transition is quite smooth and painless, without trauma or fear. People who have made the transition describe suddenly feeling calm and comfortable, then being aware they are in a new condition. They don't even notice the transition.

The person may not realize they have transitioned and need help understanding the change. Some are bewildered for a period of time until they make the adjustment. A number of those living in the next life who have spoken about their transitions have described how, in the moments after their bodies died, they felt that they must be dreaming and would wake up.

People who are materialists, with no belief in the survival of consciousness and no understanding of the life they will enter after the transition, may have difficulty accepting the reality of their transition. Their adjustment may be difficult because of the fears they create within themselves about where they are and what will happen to them. It is important for us in Earth School to help people understand who they are in eternity and what happens after the transition to make their transition smoother.

What Will Be My Reaction to My Condition After My Transition?

Answer: You will be happy and surprised at how easy the transition was. After a while, you will be concerned about loved ones on earth and will probably want to visit them.

All people who have made the transition have the same joyous reaction to finding that they continue to live after the body dies. People who have made the transition describe a feeling of being light and free. Any maladies they might have had in Earth School are gone. They experience no pain, even if their bodies were wracked with pain in the last moments of Earth School.

The first perspective of the newly transitioned is that it's very strange to suddenly leave Earth School and be in this new world that is so much more wonderful.

Will I Be a Changed Person after My Transition?

Answer: You will be the same after the transition as before, with all the same personality traits, attitudes, likes, dislikes, and knowledge about life and the life after this life. The transition is the same as boarding a plane in one country and getting off in another. You will be the same person, just in a new environment.

Your Mind will not change after the transition. You will have the same feelings as before. If someone was angry and hostile in this life, the anger and hostility remain. If the person was humble and loving, the humility and loving nature are still be there. All your skills, memories, attitudes, preferences, and desires remain the same. You will not become all-knowing. You will still be the same person, just in a different environment.

In the days and weeks after the transition, your perspective will change. After all, you will be sure of the reality that life continues after the body stops functioning, and the importance of everything on earth will diminish.

You will have changes in perceptive abilities. You will communicate telepathically with other people, animals, and even plants in what the ITC pioneer Friedrich Jürgenson described as "direct perception."[314]

Do People Go into "Soul Sleep" as Some Christians Believe?

Answer: No. There is no soul sleep, in which people go to sleep waiting for the resurrection. Some people do have a short period of "coma" during which the transition occurs. Others may sleep for three to four earth days and awaken to their new life.

The belief among some Christians that people who have left Earth School are sleeping is based on Paul's statements in 1 Corinthians and 1 Thessalonians that Christians who had transitioned have just fallen asleep and are "sleeping in Jesus" (1 Thessalonians 4:13-18). This belief that people who have left Earth School sleep until the resurrection is commonly referred to as "soul sleep." The term for this belief given by John Calvin is "psychopannychia."[315]

There are reports of Christians living in the next stage of life who have not given up this belief. They are banded together feeling they are sleeping until the resurrection. They eventually grow out of the delusion.

After the Transition Will I Enter a Period of Sleep without Realizing What Happened Until I Awaken?

Answer: Although there is no "soul sleep," often the person will have a period of sleep that begins immediately at the transition or shortly after being aware of leaving the body.

The second prominent occurrence is a period of sleep without the person being conscious of what has happened. Sometimes that is a short coma. Others may go through a longer period of sleep for two to four earth days that helps them make the transition into the next life.[316] The length of time may depend on the person's spiritual development that prepares them for the transition. Someone who understands the transition and anticipates it may experience a shorter sleep.[317] They may awaken in a recovery area appearing much like a hospital to them, with attendants who greet them upon their awakening and help them adjust to their new condition.

If I Go to Sleep at the Transition, Where Will I Find Myself When I Wake Up?

Answer: When people go into a period of sleep after the transition, they may awaken in a number of circumstances; for example, in a reception area, in a comfortable home, or in a natural environment, such as under a tree.

For those who enter a period of sleep after the transition, a range of events may occur. No single event occurs for everyone.

Awakening in a Reception Area or Hospital Setting

Some people awaken in a hospital-like setting called a "reception area" or "rest house," where people help them make the adjustment to being dead and their loved ones come to visit. It is most often described as having many beds and no walls.

> It was a home of rest for those who had come into spirit after long illness, or who had had a violent passing, and who were inconsequence, suffering from shock. ... It was built in the classical style, two or three stories high, and it was entirely open upon all sides. That is to say, it contained no windows as we know them on earth.[318]

Monsignor Robert Hugh Benson speaking through Anthony Borgia described an entire floor of a building, with people he called "recumbent forms" sleeping on couches. He explained that the people had had lingering illnesses or sudden and violent transitions and needed this period because of the debilitating effects of their illnesses or a violent event on their Minds.[319]

Rupert Brooke, the celebrated British poet, transitioned in military action in Greece in 1915. He came through in a Leslie Flint session on September 15, 1957, explaining that he didn't awaken in a reception area, but when it was clear he was wandering around perplexed, he was taken to what he called a "cleansing station." The many who were watching over him decided he was confused enough that he needed a period of rest in a relaxed setting.[320] You can hear him describe the place at www.earthschoolanswers.com/rupert/.

Awakening in a Comfortable Home Setting

Some who have transitioned describe awakening in a comfortable room with beautiful furniture and light streaming through windows. Others describe awakening in familiar surroundings, such as in a room where they grew up. Their family now in the life after this life is there when they awaken.

You can hear Princess Alexandra of Denmark, Queen Consort of Edward VII of England, describe in a Leslie Flint session where she found herself upon awakening: www.earthschoolanswers.com/alexandra/. A transcript follows.

> I remember very vividly awakening in a room which was very reminiscent of a room that I've been very fond of, many years previously in my earthly existence. In every way it seemed to be an exact replica: the colourings, the materials, the furnishings. In fact everything about it was a perfect reproduction; in fact, so much so, that I did not realise at first that I passed on at all. And I remember only too well the very beautiful view from the window, with the beautiful green grass, lawn and terrace and at the bottom, far in the distance, the river.
>
> It was a spot which I had been most fond. And in this room on my awakening were many of my relations and friends that I had known. It was almost like a kind of reception, which of course it was. And I must admit it was a great joy to me, to meet all these friends and all these souls that had meant so much to me in my Earthly life, and to have the feeling of peace and the realization that it was an environment in the very room in which I was most happy. It was a room that had given me great joy and pleasure many, many years previously.[321]

Awakening in a Natural Setting

In other accounts given by people who have made the transition, the person awakens in a natural setting and is greeted by a loved one. In one example from Leslie Flint's session recordings, a man named George Wilmot, who had been a "rag and bone" merchant in the earth realm, described waking after his transition in a field under a tree. He said he was greeted by his horse, Jenny, who had transitioned several years previously.[322] You can listen to his account at www.earthschoolanswers.com/jenny/.

Will I Be Given Help after My Transition?

Answer: Yes, all people are given help after the transition. They are met by loved ones, acquaintances, counselors, or "deliverers."

In the period after the transition, some people are bewildered and must become accustomed to the new reality. Loved ones provide perspectives for the newly arrived person and help that person understand the realities of the life after this life.

In most cases the person is greeted by a loved one or acquaintance. Such was the case with a priest named Edwin who transitioned. He explained that when he arrived in the next realm he was joined by a former colleague—another priest—whose body had died some years before. The colleague greeted him as an old friend, saying he was happy to see Edwin there. He said they were both "too jolly, too happy, too carefree, and too natural."[323]

What Will My Experiences Be If My Body Dies Suddenly?

Answer: The experiences when a person's body dies suddenly are different from those of someone who has been ill for a while. The person may go on with activities, unaware they are not in their body. They may be bewildered at the change in conditions, not realizing what has happened. It may be awhile before loved ones come because the transition was not expected.

People who transition suddenly and unexpectedly in the prime of life typically describe transitions that are markedly different from those who transition after a period of illness. Robert Crookall summarizes the events in these transitions that differ from occurrences experienced by people who transition over time. He calls the sudden transition an "enforced death," as contrasted with a "natural death" from an extended period of illness.

(1) The natural death of average man is typically followed by a "sleep" but in enforced death the person concerned tended to be awake and alert at once or almost at once; (2) in natural death consciousness was characterized by such words as "peace," "security," "happiness," "freedom," etc; in enforced death it was at first "confused," "bewildered," etc.; (3) whereas in natural transition the environment was described as "beautiful," "clear," "light," and "brilliant," in enforced death it was often (at first) "misty," "foggy," even "watery"; (4) whereas many who died naturally are conscious of having seen (or felt the presence of) the "silver cord," that feature is very seldom mentioned by those whose death was enforced; (5) whereas men who died naturally were often aware that they were met by discarnate friends (and death-bed visions are common in natural transitions), there was some delay on the part of men whose death was enforced in seeing those who met them (friends and undescribed pre-death visions of discarnate friends).[324]

Often, people who transition suddenly continue with their activities in the moments after transitioning. They may watch events unfold around their lifeless bodies. Finally someone comes to help them understand that they have transitioned out of the body. It could be a loved one, an acquaintance whom they knew had passed, or a helper who has accepted the role of helping people who are confused when they cross into the next stage of life.

A World War I soldier named Alf Pritchett, speaking in a Leslie Flint session, described himself running toward the enemy on the battlefield but noticing that the enemy was running past him, as though they couldn't see him. It wasn't until some time later that he realized he had been killed suddenly, most likely in an explosion, but was still running on the battlefield as the spirit person. His physical body was lying dead on the battlefield somewhere, but everything else—his Mind, personality, and memories—was exactly the same.[325]

Listen to the recording of Alf Pritchett describing his experience in a 1960 Leslie Flint session, 43 years after his body's demise in World War I: www.earthschoolanswers.com/alf/.

Will I Be Aware of What Happens to My Body after the Body Dies and I Go On?

Answer: You will not care about your body, but in any event you will not know what happens to your body. Nearly all people simply are away or asleep when the body is disposed of.

The body is just a body experience, not a physical object in a material universe. Consciousness does not "enter" the body. Consciousness gives rise to the body experience; consciousness creates the body. For the sake of causes and effects in the Earth School realm, the cessation of the body and transition away from the body experience has physical phenomena: snapping of the silver cord, snapping of the threads holding the physical body to the spirit body or etheric body. At times "spirit doctors" called "deliverers," who have come to help the person make the transition, may sever the silver cord.[326]

Those living in the life after this life testify that when the person no longer uses the body it can be buried, cremated, or left to the elements; the person has no need for it or interest in it. Never once in all that I have read from people who have lived through the transition did someone remain attached to their body in any way after the transition, although someone may attend their funeral unaffected by and uninterested in the body lying in the casket.

What Will My Condition Be Immediately After My Transition?

Answer: After the transition people describe a feeling of expansiveness, having vast knowledge, having a highly developed memory, and being unified with the universe. Many remark that their senses are more acute than ever before. Many describe their astonishment at how wonderful they feel and how glorious their surroundings are.

After they have transitioned, people are the same as they were before the transition, with all the senses they had and with body experiences, so they have no indications they are no longer in the body. Many people believe themselves to be in a dream from which they will soon awaken.

Will I Have Reunions with My Loved Ones Already in the Afterlife?

Answer: Yes. There are always wonderful reunions, although no one is forced to see someone from their life they do not want to see.

There are always reunions with the people and pets the person loved while in Earth School, although the reunion may be delayed when the transition is sudden or when the person goes through a period of rest or sleep. Family, friends, and even acquaintances have a joyous coming-home experience with the new arrival. Most are joyful reunions with family members. However, Michael Newton writes about the description he received of a reunion organized by a soul group.[327]

Our Universal Intelligence knows our preferences and sentiments, so anyone a person doesn't want to meet is not part of the reunion.

What Happens to People Who Have No Family to Greet Them or Help Them?

Answer: People who have no family to greet them are met and cared for by people dedicated to helping others.

A sailor named Terry Smith came through in a Leslie Flint session describing a woman who had been assigned to take care of him. Terry found himself first in the life after this life walking down an avenue. He came to a house and a woman greeted him. She told him she was expecting him, and she would be taking care of him. She explained that he drowned when his ship was sunk, along with a great number of other men.[328] An excerpt of Terry Smith's description of the incident is at www.earthschoolanswers.com/terry-2/. A transcript follows.

> So she says, "Yes and everyone of those lads has got someone, somewhere to look after them. Some have got their own people; relations or friends. Some have got other souls and I'm one [who's] in charge of you." She says, "You didn't realize," she says, "but you were directed. You thought you were walking on your own up the road," she says. "But you wasn't." She says, "You were being helped by inspiration from a soul whose job it is to help people when they come over suddenly, like you did."
>
> So I says, "Oh yeah?" You know, sort of listening, like, not quite taking it all in, you know. So I says, "Well I don't understand this at all."
>
> So she says, "Well don't you worry," she says. "You stay with me. I'll look after you. I'll be like your Mum."[329]

Will I Be Required to Meet People I Do Not Want to Meet?

Answer: There is no requirement that we meet people we do not want to meet and we will not meet them even though they want to connect.[330]

As with all of our activities forever in our lives, we choose the people we want to meet and those we want to live with. We don't have to voice our reservations about seeing someone. Our Universal Intelligence knows who we don't want to see.

After My Transition, Can I Visit My Loved Ones Still on Earth?

Answer: Yes, we have the free will ability to visit loved ones still on earth at any time, including soon after the transition.

The first thoughts of many who make the transition is of their loved ones still on earth. They wonder how they are or wish to see them and are either guided to them or immediately are in their presence in Earth School. However, most are very disappointed when their loved ones cannot see or her them. Their loved ones make no response to their presence.

Can I Go to My Funeral If I Want To?

Answer: Yes. People generally are no longer interested in their bodies after the transition, but those speaking from the life after this life often describe going to their own funerals.

Will My Loved Ones' Grief Hold Me on Earth?

Answer: Yes, especially for children, the grief of those still on earth holds them to earth rather than allowing them to go on with their lives.

Those in the next life receive our thoughts and emotions. People, especially children, who have left the earth quite often comment that their greatest disturbance after transition is experiencing the grief of loved ones still on earth.

Dr. Alice Gilbert's son, speaking to her from spirit, said "Great grief, persistent and self-centered, keeps the departed 'tied up,' yet frustrated and helpless."[331]

On the other hand, Frances Banks, communicating from the life after this life through medium Helen Greaves, reported that loving thoughts and prayers "could be likened to a draft of healing water for the newly transmitted soul."[332]

Where Will I Go Upon Entering the Afterlife?

Answer: Most people enter a realm called "Summerland." It is a beautiful world that is very much like earth, but without the negatives. However, this realm and the next are conditions of Mind. They are not in locations.

Everyone goes to "heaven." But the commonly understood meaning of "heaven" is incorrect.

The other realms, including the next stage of life, are in different focuses for the Mind. They are not in a location. Everything is one, but we change focus when we attune from one realm to another. It is much like our Minds when we are sitting and thinking. We remember a concert we attended last week, and for that time the concert is our focus. We hear the instruments and remember the grandiose hall. Then we think of what to have for dinner so our focus changes to be on food. When we are focused on the concert, the images and thoughts of food are still part of us, but we are focused on the concert with no thought of food. And when we are focused on dinner, the memories of the concert are still part of us, but our focus is on dinner. They coexist in us, but we focus on one at a time.

In the same way, while in Earth School, we are focused on the Earth School accessible to us through Our Universal Intelligence. Matter and energy are Our Universal Intelligence giving substance to the focus called "Earth School" so we can love, learn, and be happy. Our Minds are focused on Earth School in the twenty-first century. But we could be focusing on Earth School during Elizabeth I's reign or focusing on another realm entirely different from Earth School. They are not in locations. They are different focuses our individual Minds take on in Our Universal Intelligence.

When we have the experience of the body failing, the Mind just changes focus from Earth School to the life after this life. The Earth

School body experiences are no longer available or desirable. Instead, we have a vital, healthy, young body in the life that is the new focus of our lives. The life after this life is just like Earth School, with its own matter and energy as we know them created by Our Universal Intelligence. Earth School is a spiritual plane. The next plane is another spiritual plane, but much better and without the negatives.

We are experiencing Earth School together because we have the same focus. Our Universal Intelligence gives us each the same experiences so we can participate in Earth School together.

The answer to "Where does the person go after the transition?" is "nowhere"; there is only here, and there is only now. The person has a new focus with new experiences in realms with experiences, matter, and energy created by Our Universal Intelligence that has people, animals, rivers, roads, flowers, and all the rest of the solid substance we have on the Earth School spiritual plane.

What Is the Second Death?

Answer: When the Mind stops having body experiences by leaving the body behind, the person may continue on earth for a variety of reasons. Eventually the person will realize the need to go on to the next realm of life and will leave earth. That is referred to as a "second death."

Most people find themselves in the next stage of life naturally after the body dies. They wake from a sleep in a recovery location many describe as being like a hospital, or they wake in a familiar setting with loved ones around, or they awake in some other circumstances. A few, however, transition from the body and are as much a part of the earth environment as they were before the body ceased to function. They may wander around in the earth environment, riding in cars, walking, going to favorite places, and otherwise acting as though still in a body. If they don't realize fully that they have transitioned from the body, it may be a frustrating time of unsuccessfully trying to communicate with people.

At some time, the person who has been wandering the earth environment realizes they have transitioned away from the body and moves on to the next realm of life away from Earth School. This has been called the "second death. "Counselors and loved ones who have previously made the transition work at trying to help the person move on. The first transition stopped the body experiences. The second transition for some is when they finally leave the Earth School environment. It is a change of state of mind resulting in a change in focus on the new life in what has been called "Summerland" or "Level 3." Activities such as the life review and living in a new home with loved ones do not begin until this second transition has occurred.

Will I Have a Life Review?

Answer: Yes. Evidence from near-death experiences and mediums, who have reported what people living in the life after this life have described to them, corroborate the understanding that all people experience one or two life reviews after making the transition.

In the life review, an individual reviews all the significant actions and events during their life, feeling the sentiments from their point of view as well as from the points of view of others who are involved. No judgment or punishment results. People judge themselves. The purpose is to learn from the Earth School experience.

The life review may take place at any time after the full transition from the earth. A man named Bill Wooton in the life after this life, speaking through direct-voice medium Lilian Bailey, explained that some people put off the life review for many years of earth time, not wanting to face what happened and the reactions of people involved.[333] One source reports that people may put off the life review for hundreds or thousands of years.[334]

Two kinds of life reviews have been described. The first is a review of life events without examining them emotionally. The second is termed "the judgment," in which the person goes through a life review feeling all the feelings and realizing all the thoughts of all people involved in the most salient events. The first, non-emotional review happens quickly and is experienced by earthbounds as well as people who have gone on to Level 3, or Summerland. The emotional life review occurs after the person has left the earth environment and has gone on to Level 3.[335]

It may seem that reviewing an entire life would take a long time, but outside of Earth School time does not have the same meaning. The life review happens in great detail. All events are reviewed as they happened, in normal time. The whole process takes little of what we refer to as time in Earth School.

Will I Be Judged for How I Lived My Life?

Answer: There is no judgment. There is no condemnation.

We evaluate our lives in the life review and come to our own sentiments about the life we led. The life review helps the person learn from the results of their actions and perhaps the person feels regretful, sad, and dismayed, but those emotions are not inflicted upon the person. They are signs we understand the impact our actions had on people so we learn about loving through reviewing our actions.

Is There a Chance I Will Go to Hell?

Answer: No one speaking through mediums from the next life describes a hell or place of torment.

The concept of hell is a myth invented by the church in the second century CE. It is simply inconceivable that Our Universal Intelligence, embodying pure love, would torture people for a moment, let alone an eternity.

There is so much evidence that hell is a myth that I have devoted an entire webpage to it at www.earthschoolanswers.com/hell/.

There is no being called a "devil," "Satan," "Lucifer," or "Beelzebub." That creature is from Zoroastrian mythology.

14

What Will My Life in the Next Life Be Like?

Answer: It will be wonderful, glorious, and exciting. This chapter presents a small sampling of what we now know about life in the next life. We know much more that now fills hundreds of books.

      Just as the seventeenth through the nineteenth centuries saw the rise to prominence of the Newtonian universe and the twentieth century saw the revelation of the quantum universe, the twenty-first century is seeing the ascendence of the spiritual universe.

  We are continually expanding our knowledge of this life and the life after this life as humankind could never do during its 200,000-year history. Mental mediums, physical mediums, trance mediums, channelers, and others are receiving clear communications from people very much alive whose bodies have died. They are excitedly describing their lives in the realm we have called the "afterlife" and humankind's place in eternity. Ordinary people are learning to have their own inspiring contacts with loved ones living in the life after this life. What they are learning is being disseminated to masses of people over the Internet and in publications. Amazon lists over 10,000 books fitting the key term "afterlife." Our accumulated knowledge is revealing to humankind the true nature of this life and the life after this life. Humankind is undergoing a spiritual revolution.

For the clearest, most enlightening description of life in the afterlife, read medium Anthony Borgia's books, especially the trilogy of books in *Life in the World Unseen*.[336] In his books he conveys descriptions of life in the next life from Monsignor Robert Hugh Benson, a priest now living in the life after this life.

What Is the World in the Life after This Life Like?

Answer: The world we are living in now is a spiritual realm, with matter, energy, and forces woven by Our Universal Intelligence. The next spiritual realm of life is the same, but with a different set of matter, energy, and forces we will experience together. On arriving in the next life, people are astonished at its similarity to life on earth.

When I've Been in the Afterlife for a While, Will I Change?

Answer: Yes. We grow continually in our eternal lives. Our change of perspective causes changes relatively soon. Then we continue to develop for eons into celestial spheres. We do not spend eternity as we are now.

We transition to the life after this life by changing our focus, rather like our watching a sunset for a few minutes and then turning around to see a waterfall. When we enter the next stage of life we are the same person we were before we left Earth School. We've just changed the focus of our attention. It is as though we had exited a movie and were returning to the real world where our loved ones are. It is just a change of experiential realms.

The change in focus, however, results in changes in our perspectives. We realize we are eternal beings who just graduated from a temporary Earth School experience. We also have some changes in mental faculties. We are able to communicate telepathically with people and animals. We can travel to a location by intending to be there.

People in the life after this life gather with like-minded people and carry on with the customs of their belief systems, especially religious belief systems. In that way they choose not to change some belief systems, even those that are archaic and unreal.

People who were atheists on earth have an especially difficult time after the transition reconciling their experiences with their belief systems. Some materialist scientists are still materialists in the afterlife. They congregate in the life after this life, sure that there's some physical explanation for what has happened to them, endeavoring to understand it. They work in teams, as they did in Earth School, to study what has happened. They still won't allow themselves to believe in the life after this life and spiritual existence.

Are There Diseases, Accidents, or Deformities I Might Experience in the Life after This Life?

Answer: There are no defects from disease, accidents, or deformities.

Some people who had deformities on earth may not easily lose their sense that they still have the deformity. As a result, they may act as though they had the deformity they had on earth until they grow out of it.

Will I Be a Male or Female in the Next Life?

Answer: Upon entering the next realm, people identify themselves as male and female according to their identities in Earth School. This is not because of anatomy but because the familiarity of these roles cause them to believe and act as though they are one gender or another.

Even though people believe they are male or female, they don't regard each other in quite the same way as on earth: "... they seem to have the same feeling to each other, with a different expression of it."[337] They assume the identity of one gender or the other, but no biology assigns them one or the other.

Can I See, Hear, Taste, Touch, and Smell in the Next Life as I Do on Earth?

Answer: Yes, but with much heightened, richer sensitivity and a range of sensory experiences far beyond those on earth.

People's senses in the life after this life are much more alert. The residents of the next life refer to this life as a dream, with impeded sensory experiences. They refer to their new stage of life as the real life. They realize they just allowed their real senses and capabilities to be diminished for the Earth School experience. When they shed their Earth School bodies, their sensory experiences are richer and fuller than when they were in Earth School.

Do We Remember Things in Earth School?

Answer: Yes, we remember in greater detail and with greater ease than when in Earth School.

Residents of the life after this life say they remember many more details of their time in Earth School. They are able to relive incidents they experienced during their Earth School tenure.

When they apply themselves to learning in the next stage of life, they have what amounts to a photographic memory. They recall everything they set about learning.

What Happens to People with Mental Conditions Such as Down Syndrome and Mental Retardation?

Answer: People with mental conditions during their life on earth enter the life after this life at the mental age they were on earth. They then grow from there to normal adulthood because the physical restrictions are gone.

People who had mental conditions on earth don't suddenly change when they leave the body behind. When a person has suffered from Down syndrome, fetal alcohol syndrome, brain injury, hydrocephalus, or other condition that limits mental development to that of an infant or young child, upon transition to the life after this life the person loses their physical limitations and disabilities and begins to develop, unimpeded, as a child does. The person develops from the level of maturity they had in Earth School into adulthood by the same process and at the same pace as they would in Earth School.

What Will Determine My Living Conditions in the Life after This Life?

Answer: We find ourselves in circumstances that fit the moral character we developed in Earth School.

Dr. Robert Hare conveyed from spirit that one's immediate place in the afterlife is determined by a sort of "moral specific gravity." The moral specific gravity is evident in the person's good works or lack of good works. The afterlife is made up of many planes, spheres, or realms. Someone with a low moral specific gravity will gravitate to a lower plane but can still gradually evolve to a higher plane with the help of more enlightened spirits.[338]

Summerland

Most people find themselves in the realm for people with a higher specific gravity that the Theosophists called "Summerland."

People who are loving and compassionate live in pleasant circumstances with others who are loving and compassionate. Their world is full of love and devoid of discord and loneliness.

The Lower Realms

When people leave Earth School, they enter an environment that suits their mental condition, attitudes, and spiritual level of growth. Those who have been selfish and cruel in Earth School are on a sphere or plane with others who are also selfish and cruel. It happens automatically, without deliberation. That isn't a punishment and it certainly isn't a hell. It's a condition they create by their own expectations for the way life is and ought to be. These realms are created by the negative thoughts and attitudes of the inhabitants. They expect life to be dog-eat-dog, full of greed and selfishness, so that is the way it is for them. They fought and bickered on earth and simply carry that on in the next life. And they are with others who have the same inclinations.

These lower areas are described as being dark, dank, and unpleasant. There are unpleasant sounds, such as mad, raucous laughter and shrieks. The beauties of the higher realm are not present there. The residents remain on that lower plane of life until they grow out of it. No one put them there; no one demands they change; no one punishes them.

The region exists only because there are people with a mental condition that creates the experiences. People remain there until they choose to grow into a higher spiritual level. Then they simply evolve into a higher level naturally. When any person chooses to mature out of the condition, they rise from it immediately.

Will I Have a Body in the Next Life?

Answer: Earth School is a spiritual realm. In this spiritual realm, we have body experiences. In the next, we also have body experiences. The body experiences will be of the body we had in Earth School at its prime, or what we wish we had had at its prime, in our twenties or thirties in Earth School.

All who transition to the next realm describe having a tangible body just as they had when in a physical body. They have no aches and pains, however, and they feel healthy and light. When they see themselves in a reflection, they look as they did in their twenties or thirties if they transitioned at an older age. If they transitioned as children, they grow up on the other side of life to have bodies that correspond to bodies in their twenties or thirties in Earth School. There are no diseases, deformities, or mental difficulties. People have bodies that are whole, healthy, vibrant, and young. There are no "old people" and no old-people ailments.

Will I Be Wearing a Special Type of Clothing?

Answer: You many wear any type of clothing you desire.

When people first enter the next realm of life, they may wear the type of clothing they wore in Earth School. After a while they lose their interest in retaining the habits of Earth School and don a spirit robe. The spirit robes are a variety of colors. The residents of the life after this life don't change clothing one sleeve at a time. When the person wants the spirit robe, it is simply on their body, without effort. If the person wants to put on clothes from Earth School for an occasion, the clothes appear on the person's body.

A. D. Mattson, speaking from spirit through medium Margaret Flavell Tweddell, explains that people think up their clothes, they materialize, and the person puts them on. To change what they're wearing, they can thought-power off the clothes and create something else.[339]

The process of creating by thought is something that must be learned. The architects and builders who create large buildings must work together in a concerted effort of creativity and will.

Most prefer a light sandal for footwear, although some prefer to go barefoot. Most also eventually wear spirit robes rather than the clothing they wore on earth.

Who Will I Live With?

Answer: You will live with people you love, whom you have chosen to live with. No one is required to live with someone they don't want to live with.

We live with people who love us and whom we love. They live with us because they choose to live with us and we choose to live with them. We are not required to live with someone we don't want to be with. We never have to even see them. Hopefully, as the person matures, old animosities fall away, but we always have the free will to be with people we want to be with.

If I Have Had Two Spouses, Which Will I Live With?

Answer: When two or more partners with one spouse come into the life after this life, they will choose to live with each other or not, without concerns about who is whose mate.

The feeling of possessiveness is created in the earth realm only. Concerns about whether I can spend eternity with my soul mate are only held by people still in the earth realm. Those issues resolve themselves in the next realm of life. Consistently, those in the life after this life tell spouses still in Earth School to have a full life, including feeling free to have another partner. There is no possessiveness, jealousy, or covetousness in spirit. Jane Sherwood, communicating with her husband in spirit, writes, "There is no sense of possession in even the most intimate relationships."[340]

No one is forced to live with anyone. We still have free will in the life after this life. If one person wants to live with another but the interest is not reciprocated, the two will not live together.

A commentator from the life after this life explains about living arrangements in the life after this life when people have more than one spouse.

> If someone has more than one spouse or more than one close relationship on earth, the person may live with any one or none of them. Relationships continue to be based on mutual interest and love. We live with whomever we want to live with, and no one can compel someone to live with another.[341]

Where Will I Live?

Answer: We will live in houses as we do in Earth School.

We will live in houses just as we do in Earth School, with yards, flowers, trees, streets, and towns. Houses are described as being elegant and clean. The houses have gardens around them, with natural soil just as on earth. People who enjoyed gardening on earth or wished they had been able to garden tend the gardens. Beautiful flowers grow continually and profusely. No one picks the flowers, however. They are left to grow naturally.

The environment and homes are what the person was accustomed to on earth. A man in spirit speaking through medium William W. Aber explains that people live in circumstances that are similar to those they experienced on earth.

> I have traveled a great deal in spirit life, and I find spirits live as they did on earth. The Hollander does not change his dress or his quaint ways for something that would appear more modern to the Anglo-Saxon visitor. I have often seen the picturesque Swiss homes in spirit life. The Indian villages are here just as on earth, and Red Feather has even treated me to a ride on his pony, and I, in return, took him to a Chinese home. So I find that different nations have different ideas of what constitutes

the beautiful in their spirit homes, the same as they had in earth life.[342]

Each person lives in a home, possibly with loved ones, and otherwise with people who have been given the task to take care of the person. If one person has advanced to a higher level than a friend or relative, the two will see each other only occasionally, but they may meet when they choose to.[343]

The homes are often duplicates of the homes the people loved in Earth School. Sometimes people who were wealthy in Earth School are in smaller houses to help them learn that wealth isn't important. The construction can be changed at any time by an act of the will.[344]

People wander in and out of people's houses without being announced or invited. Everyone is welcomed and loved.

There are no fences or hedges because boundaries are not needed. The homes have no heating or air conditioning because the temperature is always pleasant. The air is comfortably warm, with "gentle perfume-laden breezes."[345]

The homes don't need to be cleaned; nothing becomes dirty. There is no dust or dirt.

Can I Have Any Social Activities in the Next Life?

Answer: People have full, rich social lives that include activities people engage in together.

The activities in the life after this life are much the same as activities in Earth School. In our lives today we often gather to socialize. Gatherings of people in the life after this life are identical. We attend concerts, sitting in rows of seats with other music lovers listening to performances that excite us. The same scene with equally keen music lovers is played out regularly in the next realm. They also have family gatherings where they meet with great joy and affection. People gather in groups for pastimes such as sports or social activities.

What Will My World Be Like in the Next Life?

Answer: In the next life, called by some Summerland, there are a great many environments, but all are pleasant, with surroundings reminiscent of the environment of Earth School, only more beautiful than the residents are able to describe.

The environment depends on the person's state of being and expectations. If someone is still tied to the earth and its environment, they will experience a very earthlike existence for as long as they remain at that level of thought. The communications we receive about the Summerland environment are filled with ecstatic descriptions of a realm just like the earth realm, but much more glorious. Everything that is lovely on earth is exceedingly lovely in the life after this life, and the environment contains additional features undreamt of on earth.

Summerland environments have all the attributes of Earth School. There are mountains, rivers, lakes, forests, meadows, and vast fields of flowers. There are seas and beaches. There are gatherings of all the animals familiar on earth as well as other new species.

Can I Have Flowers in a Garden?

Answer: There are abundant flowers, more beautiful than those we enjoy on earth.

Monsignor Robert Hugh Benson, speaking through Anthony Borgia, hinted at how much more remarkable Summerland is than the earth environment. He noted that the gardens are very orderly, with no wild growths or weeds. A great many flowers are in full bloom, with superb colorings. The flowers pour out great streams of energizing power that uplift the soul spiritually and give it strength. They exude heavenly perfumes. All the flowers are living, breathing, and incorruptible. The sound of music envelops them, making soft harmonies that correspond perfectly with the gorgeous colors of the flowers themselves.[346]

Will I See a Sun, Moon, or Stars?

Answer: There are no celestial objects. There is always pleasant light with no reason for it.

The sky is blue, with no sun, moon, or stars. There is an ambient light of higher quality than the light from the sun. The light is soft, radiant, and brilliant.[347]

There is no night, although some describe a "twilight" period each day in which the ambient light is not so bright. People do "rest," but they don't sleep unless they want to sleep.

Will I Have Uncomfortable Cold and Hot Days?

Answer: The temperature and atmospheric conditions are always comfortable.

The temperature is always pleasant, with no inclement weather, although there is one description of a "mist" that happens every two earth weeks[348] and another of rain that "is good for our bodies."[349]

Will I Attend Things in Buildings and Halls?

Answer: People gather in beautiful, majestic buildings and halls to engage in all manner of activities of interest to them.

Buildings such as halls of learning, schools, art galleries, concert halls, and museums are described as being made of a solid material that has a pearl-like luminescence. The buildings are assembled in vast, beautiful, clean cities. In these halls of learning, people studiously read out of self-motivated interest.

Will I Experience or Participate in Music and Art?

Answer: Music and art are integral, vital components of Summerland life.

The air seems to be full of music. Not everybody has to hear it, though. The people living there can hear the music only if they want to hear it. Anyone can shut it out and be in silence.[350]

There are vast concert halls and orchestras made up of thousands of people playing instruments, some of which are like those in Earth School while others are unique. Music is both heard and seen. As an orchestra plays, beautiful colors appear around the orchestra in keeping with the music, with no devices responsible for the lights. As Monsignor Benson said through Anthony Borgia, "In music, it can be said that the spirit world starts where the earth world leaves off."[351]

The master composers from earth continue writing works that are performed by the vast orchestras. Great painters, sculptors, poets, novelists, dramatists, and others who were talented on earth continue their work in the life after this life.[352]

People who wanted to pursue an art while in the earth realm but were unable to do so may learn the art form and develop into accomplished performers. There are many "amateur" displays of the early artwork.[353]

Will I Be Able to Take Walks as We Do in Earth School?

Answer: You may walk or transport yourself by intending to be somewhere.

People may walk to destinations, although they do have the ability to simply focus on where they would like to be and they are transported there instantly.[354] However, people may not will themselves into another's presence unless the person wants the visitor there. People still have privacy and free will to choose those they want to associate with.

There are automobiles, but they do not burn petroleum products and emit noxious gasses. In some communities, hobby groups of people interested in automobiles have created replicas of particular models of automobiles. They ride in them for sport and pleasure.[355]

Will I Communicate Using My Voice or by Telepathy?

Answer: People may communicate by making vocal sounds or through telepathy.

The longer someone is a resident of the life after this life, the more interested the person is in foregoing the ponderous action of stringing words together and vocalizing them to convey thoughts. Minds are more open to each other so thoughts are accessible by anyone through telepathy.[356]

It is possible to use free will to deliberately keep our thoughts to ourselves. That requires more effort, so if someone is freely, spontaneously speaking, the thoughts will simply pour out into the telepathic discourse.

There is a "universal spirit language" so people who came from various language backgrounds are all able to understand conversations and discourses.[357] People in groups who had similar customs on earth keep their languages as long as they want to, but in communicating with people who speak other languages, the communication is through telepathy so language is not a barrier.[358]

Are There Children in the Life after This Life?

Answer: Yes, there are children who have transitioned from earth at an early age or before their birth on earth. But no new children are conceived in Summerland.

Monsignor Benson, speaking from spirit through medium Anthony Borgia, describes a children's realm that has been called "the nursery of heaven." Children who have transitioned from Earth School live in a special area, called the "children's sphere," where they learn with other children.[359]

Monsignor Benson explains that "there were to be found children of all ages, from the infant, whose separate existence upon the earth-plane had amounted to only a few minutes, or who even had had no separate existence at all, but had been born 'dead,' to the youth of sixteen or seventeen years of earth time."[360]

The child's physical and intellectual advancement is much faster and richer than in Earth School. The children are "given knowledge of a particular subject rather than taught it."[361] They are taught to read, but most other subjects found in Earth School classrooms are not taught to the children. When they reach a suitable age, the children choose their vocation and focus their studies on becoming proficient in its practices.

Can I Relive Things That Happened During My Life?

Answer: Yes. A person may choose to relive experiences they had in Earth School.

All experiences that ever were or ever will be are accessible from Our Universal Intelligence. In the next realm we are able to access events from our own lives from this vast archive. John Thomas, speaking from spirit to his son, Charles Drayton Thomas, explained that it is possible for someone to live over again the happiest scenes of our earth life and enjoy them together with others.[362]

Will My Desires and Expectations Change?

Answer: A person's desires and expectations are the same immediately after the transition as before. The Mind does not change.

People may want to eat, sleep, drink, smoke, and all the other things they did when in the earth realm. Since they expect food, sleep, drinks, and smoking to be available, they are. They don't will them into being. What the person expects to be in their environment is there because of the expectation. However, drinking a beverage with all the properties of wine or stronger drinks does not intoxicate.[363] It isn't necessary to sleep, but if someone wants the experience they lie down and sleep comes naturally.

As the person matures away from earth habits, expectations and desires, the need to eat, drink, sleep, smoke, and other activities carried over from earth extinguish.[364]

One person who came through in a Leslie Flint session loved to smoke a pipe, so he had a pipe. Of course, the smoke was not deleterious to his health and didn't affect the atmosphere. All the pleasurable sensations of smoking a pipe were there, however. Since there is nothing but Mind and experiences, the same experiences will occur. There never was a physical pipe in a world outside of the person in the earth realm—just the experience of smoking. As a result, the same is true in the life after this life.

Raymond Lodge, speaking in the life after this life, said that some of the newly transitioned soldiers smoked cigars. [365]

People new to the next stage of life may prefer to wear the clothes they wore in Earth School, so those clothes are available without their requesting them. What they are given suits their desires and expectations.

Will I Feel Any Emotions?

Answer: Yes, you will experience the full range of emotions. However, there is no trauma or death, so you will not experience the negative emotions associated with the types of disturbing events that happen on earth.

The people living in the life after this life are human beings living in a different country. They still feel the emotions we all feel on earth. They feel joyful, excited, frustrated, sad, and the range of other emotions. Some of their emotions are associated with the situations and emotions of those still living on earth. They receive people's thoughts and feelings, so when someone they love is feeling joy or sadness, they respond by being joyful or sad. They frequently lament that the grief of people on earth is disturbing to them because of their transition.

Will I Have a Job?

Answer: Everyone is occupied with what is of greatest interest to them. That results in the services we associate with being provided by people in jobs. However, you will not be paid. You will perform the services out of love and joy.

People are industrious because being active, accomplishing goals, and serving others brings them bliss. Their work is recreation.[366] People act out of love for one another, without expecting compensation for the work. They give of themselves in ways that make both them and the receiver joyful. Everyone works out of enjoyment and a desire to serve others. No one is compelled to perform any task. People are not required to be anything they don't wish to be.

All occupations known to people on earth are represented in the life after this life, except police, prison guards, undertakers, and other such occupations that fit only the earth environment.[367]

There are gardeners, musicians, architects, counselors of newly transitioned people, teachers of children, craftsmen in all crafts, and all manner of occupations. Builders build houses for people who desire to have a house without expectation of being paid. They use their thoughts to create, but there is still labor involved in the building.

A person may continue an occupation from Earth School. Artists still paint; builders still build houses; scientists still perform their research; and teachers still teach. Shakespeare and Oscar Wilde are still writing plays.

If a person always desired to play the piano while in Earth School but never had the chance, they may learn to play the piano in the life after this life and give recitals or be part of the vast orchestras. Someone who loved to grow flowers on earth but ended up being an auto mechanic can become a gardener in the life after this life.

Medical doctors in the next life help doctors in Earth School to practice medicine and surgery. "Many a spirit doctor has guided the hand of an earthly surgeon when he is performing an operation," Monsignor Benson explains from spirit.[368] There are great "halls of rest" for people who have transitioned suddenly and violently where nurses and doctors tend to them.

Counselors or support people work with individuals who had a difficult time on earth and are still recovering from the experiences.

Since there are no factories, people who engaged in manufacturing occupations on earth find other occupations and preoccupations. Many teach children who have left Earth School and grow up in the afterlife. Some people do "rescue" work, helping people who have made the transition understand where they are and guiding them along as they adjust to their new lives. People engage in the occupations that give them bliss.

People are not required to work, but if someone chooses not to work, that person eventually rises out of the indolence.[369]

If I Am a Scientist or Engineer, Can I Continue My Work There?

Answer: Yes, scientists and engineers are continuing their work in the next life. They then convey their advancements to scientists and engineers on earth by inspiriting them.

People who were scientists on earth do not become all-knowing when they transition to the life after this life. They continue to learn from the point at which they were before the transition, using more advanced technology and equipment they develop using their newly found knowledge. New principles and discoveries are conveyed to them from higher-level Minds. They in turn impart them to scientists in the earth realm working in the same field, although virtually all the scientists on earth are not aware of it. As a result, the scientists working in the next life and scientists on earth advance together, with the scientists in the next life slightly ahead of the scientists on earth.[370]

If I Am an Artist, Dancer, Musician, or Other Master of the Arts, Will I Be Able to Inspire Performers and Artists on Earth?

Answer: Yes. You may continue your art in the next life and inspire people in Earth School whom you want to help develop their talents. You will share in the joy of their accomplishments.

Those on the next planes of existence are greatly interested in inspiring people in Earth School and helping them to create beautiful art works, symphonies, performances, and other artwork. Some explain that they are looking for promising people to inspire. They also continue their own development of their craft far beyond the capabilities they had while in Earth School.

Chopin explained from spirit in a Leslie Flint session that musicians gather and compose and play compositions, make comments to each other, and receive helpful advice. Together they go to other realms to listen to the music composed there, which is unique to that realm and condition.[371]

Chopin was having one of several conversations he had with a musician on earth named Rose Creet, who was sitting with Leslie Flint. He had explained that he was helping Rose perfect her performance. In this conversation, Chopin remarked to her, "I'm going to make of you an excellent pianist."[372]

Can I Enjoy the Recreation I Loved on Earth?

Answer: Yes, all recreation activities except those that involve harming people or animals are freely available in the next life.

When someone wants to engage in a pleasurable activity, the circumstances are available. The desire for the activity among people interested in it makes the equipment or circumstances available, without request. Mary Ann Ross, speaking in a Leslie Flint session, says that she always wanted to play the piano when she was on the earth.

After her transition, when she entered the house in which she was to live, she was amazed to see a piano there. The man accompanying her was a piano teacher. When she sat to play the piano, she received mental guidance from her teacher so she played well very quickly.[373] You can listen to the recording of Mary Ann Ross describing from spirit when she first saw the piano and played it at www.earthschoolanswers.com/ross4/.

Monsignor Robert Hugh Benson, speaking from the life after this life,[374] explains that people do not suffer fatigue of body or Mind. However, if someone becomes restless with one form of work, the person may engage in another form of work for a while or in an endless variety of recreation activities. Whatever people enjoy doing in Earth School they may continue in the next stage of life. There are concerts, halls of art, gardening, beautiful scenic paths, and the whole abundance of pleasurable activities we have in Earth School, plus more.[375]

Historical performances are given by the actual people involved in the original events.[376]

There is no hunting or other activity that would terrorize or injure animals. There is no slaughter allowed, under whatever cloak it masquerades, such as sport. In this realm animals cannot die, but they could be subject to terror. Therefore subjecting an animal to terror constitutes injury and is not allowed. [377]

There are races and other contests, but those engaged in them have only a friendly rivalry. There is no reward involved. The participants enjoy becoming more capable and accomplished, not being better than someone else. People play sports such as baseball and football in areas designed for the sports.[378]

There are beautiful theaters for concerts and plays, and vast libraries that contain every work produced by humankind, both in this stage of life and the next. There are halls devoted to painting, sculpture, literature, fabrics, tapestries, and many other subjects, filled with people practicing their skills and enjoying the camaraderie of people with the same interests. Every art object and discovery is represented there. None is lost.[379]

There are recreational devices such as boats and motorcycles. They are not powered by machinery. The boats sail effortlessly and the motorcycles travel with ease because of the intention of the person controlling the effort to have the boat or motorcycle propel itself forward.[380]

Are There Animals in the Life after This Life?

Answer: The fields and woodlands are populated with all the animal species, but they don't prey on one another and they are not afraid of each other.

The animals are described as living in separate areas, but people can walk up to them and hold them. The animals are at a higher state of being than in Earth School, able to communicate through a telepathy that doesn't require speech. They understand themselves as being one with humankind and are completely comprehended by those with whom they come into contact. No animals are killed. No animal products are used in making things.

There are beautiful birds with gorgeous plumage singing and twittering in a symphony of sound. As with the other animals, the birds communicate telepathically with the people.

Will I Be Able to Keep Learning by Attending Classes or Schools?

Answer: Yes, you will be able to learn any skill or learn about any subject of interest to you. You may attend classes in any of the many schools.

There are schools, but they are not places where students memorize facts. The memory works perfectly, so there is no need to memorize. Students are able to learn quickly, with sharpened understanding. Each student follows their own course of study, independent of others.

There are expansive halls of learning where people are being taught or are practicing their skills. Raymond Lodge, communicating from spirit to his father through the medium Gladys Osborne Leonard, explained that they attend lectures at the halls of learning, where they prepare themselves for the higher spheres while living in lower ones.[381]

Will I Be Able to Read Books and Go to Libraries?

Answer: Yes, there are libraries with vast numbers of books.

While there are libraries, much more knowledge is available from sources other than the books found in them. Jane Sherwood's husband in spirit, communicating through her, explains that people can study in libraries but soon learn how to access information from memory bank reference libraries that contain records of everything that has ever happened.[382]

Every book ever written is in the libraries, but people don't need to check them out. They can simply have the book read itself to them. People can even understand the original meaning of the author, as though the author were with them explaining it.

People can also converse with the authors rather than read the books.

Will I Continue to Grow in Wisdom, Love, and Compassion?

Answer: Yes. You will continue to advance in your wisdom, love, and compassion by learning and having experiences.

Earth School provides experiences we cannot have while in the comfortable environment we enter in the next stage of life. Earth School contains people of different spiritual levels, some hostile and violent, others kind, loving, and other-centered. As we live with this great variety of people, we face challenges, hostility, conflict, success, joy, and tragedy. We grow in spiritual maturity by facing obstacles and overcoming them.

The conditions in Summerland that most people enter are so pleasant that many choose not to evolve into higher levels of being for a long time. They remark that they are content to stay where they are, although they know there are higher levels. Some people prefer to stay where they are for long periods of time. Higher-level teachers and guides try to help them learn so they can advance, but there is no pressure and no one requires anyone to leave a level and progress to another level.

Most people, however, want to advance spiritually. They want to grow in their sensitivities, love, and compassion. There are courses of study they may choose to go through, and they may be tasked to help people still on earth, including family, so they deepen their empathy and sensitivity.

In the life after this life we know we are one with all people, both those in the next life and those in the earth realm, and one with Our Universal Intelligence. As a result, our spiritual growth is accelerated. People continue learning and growing, but without the struggles of Earth School. There are schools, workshops, teaching by ascended masters, gatherings where people talk about their experiences and learning, and all the other experiences that help people to grow. As a result, people change over time. They become wiser, educated, loving, compassionate, and other-centered.

Alvin D. Mattson, speaking from the life after this life through medium Margaret Flavell, described a group of 20,000 people who had been Lutheran on earth gathering to hear Martin Luther speak.[383]

Is There Time in the Next Life?

Answer: There is a time of sorts, but it is not like time on earth. There are no days, years, or seasons because there is no sun. There are no clocks, or references to time using "o'clock."

Changes occur, and people have the same types of experiences as they had on earth that occur over time, so there is a time of sorts. However, they don't count time, and since they realize their eternal nature there is no hurry to accomplish things. Their sense of time, in other words, is quite different.

They do have celebrations. Some who would have celebrated Christmas and Easter on earth continue to celebrate them. Visitors from higher realms who are perfect beings come to the celebrations.

Is There a Government?

Answer: As with all collections of people, there is a form of government to help with decisions that will affect all people.

People in spirit explain that there is a government, but not one that limits and restricts. It is more in the nature of a place where anyone who needs it can go for advice and guidance.[384]

On higher levels, there is governing by general consent of the individuals. People are not truly self-governing on an individual basis at the higher levels, "for as they reach the higher levels there is more of a communal governing or a governing by general consent, so that it is not an individual thing or an I am my own law."[385]

What Religion Will I Join in the Next Life?

Answer: There are no established churches or religions.

People gather for spiritual discussions, but there are no holy scriptures, rituals, or dogma among those who have released themselves from Earth School's belief systems.

Some people still cling to the old beliefs, staying in pockets with others who have the same worldviews. Everyone enters the life after this life with all the same assumptions and perspectives they had on earth. As a result, there are some Christian groups living together who are sure they're in a holding pattern waiting for the rapture and their return to a physical existence in Earth School. Some who believed that the spirit sleeps until the resurrection are "sleeping," although they're given guidance and inspiration to begin understanding that they're already in the next stage of their eternal life.

Some people continue to hold to their theological teachings for extended periods so they don't progress. All these people with narrow, restricted views eventually grow out of them into freedom and spiritual maturity. No one stays in these conditions forever.

What Are the Attitudes Toward Jesus and God among People in the Next Life?

Answer: Those living in the life after this life agree that Jesus (Yeshua bar Yosef) came to earth to teach humankind but was not a god and could not "save" someone.

Episcopal Bishop James A. Pike learned about the figure of Jesus from his son in spirit speaking through a medium. Pike asked his son who those living in the life after this life believe Jesus was. His son was concerned that the truth would be harmful to his father because of his position in the church, but he conveyed this message.

> People must have an example you know. They talk about him [Jesus]—a mystic, a seer, yes, a seer. Oh, but, Dad, they don't talk about him as a savior. As an example, you see? ... I would like to tell you, Jesus is triumphant, you know ... not a savior, that's the important thing—an example.[386]

The messages from residents of the life after this life also describe God as the life force that is the foundation of all being, not a male figure separated from humankind.

Will I Be Able to Have Sex If My Partner and I Want It?

Answer: Yes, if you want it.

We have been assured that if we want to enjoy the pleasures of sex in Summerland, we are able to do so. J. M. Peebles, considered a father of the Spiritualist movement, describes sexual activity and full pleasures in the life after this life: "Men and women, continuing as they do their individuality, sex necessarily exists in the world of spirits, but in heaven there are no perversions of these functions."[387]

Will My Gender Identity or Sexual Orientation on Earth Have Any Effect on Me in the Next Life?

Answer: There is no discrimination according to a person's sentiments about their gender identity or sexual orientation. The person carries on with the attitudes and interests they had on earth. These are not assigned to a gender or sexual orientation.

How Long Can I Stay on the Next Plane of Life?

Answer: We are able to stay in the next life for as long as we want to.

One man named Omar in Monsignor Robert Hugh Benson's messages from spirit through Anthony Borgia said he had been in the Summerland stage of life for 2,000 earth years.[388] At another time Monsignor Benson said that the rulers of realms spend many thousands of earthly years in the spirit world before they are placed in charge of people.[389] Leslie Flint had people come through in his séances from the Roman Empire.[390]

A person may stay in the plane called Summerland as long as they want to.[391] Progression to the higher spheres depends on the desire of each person and the effort to acquire knowledge. But staying forever in one place would be a miserably dull eternal existence. People advance beyond the Summerland level eventually. As we advance in our wisdom and spiritual stature, we are able to ascend to higher levels of consciousness. The higher someone goes the more elevated they are in knowledge and goodness. People advance to higher levels gradually, not by graduating from one sphere to another.

How Big Is the World We Enter after This Life?

Answer: The next world, this world, and the millions of other realms constitute a vastness we cannot comprehend.

The people communicating to us from the life after this life explain that it is vaster than we can imagine. There are millions of realms of existence, occupied by vast numbers of people at various levels of spiritual maturity and interest. It is incorrect to view the next life as a few discrete planes. Instead, there is level after level of continuously different planes where people are together based on their interests and attitudes.

People remain individuals who continue to grow spiritually until they have developed into celestial beings inhabiting the highest realms. These higher-order beings do come to work with people on the lower levels. They also teach in a chain of being, providing guidance and instruction to people on lower levels who then administer it to the general public in the life after this life or to people living in Earth School.

People are able to visit lower levels, but may not visit higher levels unless accompanied by a guide; even then can only venture to the outer fringes of the higher level.

What Are the Divisions, Areas, or Levels of Life?

Answer: There are a number of descriptions of realms referred to as "planes," "spheres," "vibrations," or "levels." They are not spatial locations; they are states of mind.

Some refer to seven levels.[392] The spheres or levels are only gross descriptions of millions of conditions and environments. For example, there might be millions of environments with untold numbers of people living in circumstances that fit the criteria for being on Level 3.

There are no boundaries, as in geographical divisions. However, each sphere is completely invisible to the inhabitants of the spheres below it, so there is a boundary of awareness.[393] People on lower levels cannot visit higher levels unless brought close to a higher level by one of the higher-level people.

We needn't fear advancing to a higher state of being. We remain individuals; we do not merge into some higher being called the Source.

Descriptions of the Levels

Most people transition from Earth School to Level 3 or Summerland. Those with degenerate personalities gather together naturally in the second sphere. The fourth, fifth, and sixth levels are described as filled with light, love, and happiness. Among the residents of the seventh level are Yeshua bar Yosef (Jesus), John the Beloved, Confucius, Seneca, Plato, Socrates, and Solon.[394] These celestial beings remain individuals, capable of communicating with people in the earth realm. Confucius, described as being in the seventh level, has come through in a Leslie Flint session[395] and in a session Dr. Neville Whymant had with medium George Valiantine.[396]

The movement from Level 3, or Summerland, to the fourth is a change in mentality or spirit. After the gradual transition from Level 3 into the condition of Level 4, consciousness operates at spiritual "levels" in the spiritual or celestial body, with the heavens as the environment. The body undergoes a progressive refinement and purification and consequently an increase in responsiveness.[397]

The higher level is even more exquisite than Level 3, Summerland. The individuals are in shapes unknown to us, exquisite in color and radiant with light. They do not use words. The individual in this plane of consciousness, "must struggle and labor, knows sorrow but not earth sorrow, knows ecstasy but not earth ecstasy. The sorrow is of a spiritual character, the ecstasy is of a spiritual kind."[398]

We receive hints and glimpses into the fifth through the seventh levels. Frederick Myers in spirit, speaking through trance medium Geraldine Cummins, described the levels.[399] The fifth level is called the Plane of Flame.

> Myers tells us that an inhabitant here remains himself, yet is all those other selves [in his group] as well. He no longer dwells in form—as it is conceived by man—but he

> dwells still in what might be described as an "outline" ... an outline of emotional thought: a great fire which stirs and moves this mighty being. Such a being is continuously conscious. ... He tastes of heaven and yet the revelation of the last mystery tarries, still awaits the completion of the design of which he is part.[400]

On the sixth plane, the individuals are formless white lights. The Minds of the inhabitants are dominated by reason. Myers described the sixth plane.

> Emotion and passion, as known to men, are absent. White light represents the perfect equanimity of pure thought. Such equanimity becomes the possession of the souls who entered this last rich kingdom of experience. ... They are capable of living now ... as the pure thought of their Creator. They have joined the immortals.[401]

Myers continued to describe the seventh plane.

> Without a body of any kind, you merge with the Great Source and reign in the great calm of eternity. Yet you still exist as an individual [and] are wholly aware of the imagination of God. So you are aware of the whole history of the earth from Alpha to Omega. Equally all planetary existence is yours. Everything created is contained within that imagination, and you . . . know it and hold it. An eon of spiritual evolution is usually required before taking this final step: only a very few pass out Yonder during the life of the earth. A certain number of souls attain to the sixth state, but remain in it or, in exceptional cases for a lofty purpose, descend again into matter. They are not strong enough to make the great leap into timelessness, they are not yet perfect.[402]

Throughout these ascensions into increasingly higher levels, there is no loss of individuality by merging with a universal consciousness. We remain individuals, even when we have left behind any interest in earth-like environments and bodies. Crookall explains,

"Only the Absolute, Transcendent, Unmanifested, Infinite 'Father' is 'pure spirit,' 'purely subjective.'"[403]

Our attachment now to our bodies, our lives, and our relationships causes us to recoil from the thought of leaving behind all we are familiar with by graduating to higher and higher levels. Yet we will never be forced to advance. And when we decide to advance, we will have matured far beyond where we are now, just as an adult has matured far beyond being an infant. We will not want to stay an infant forever. We will yearn to become more than we have been.

Bibliography

Aber, W. W., and J. H. Nixon. *Beyond the Vail.* Kansas City, MO: Hudson-Kimberly, 1901.

Admin, M. "Hundreds in India Ritually Starve Themselves to Death Each Year." Knowledge Nuts. Accessed April 1, 2014. https://knowledgenuts.com/2014/04/01/hundreds-in-india-ritually-starve-themselves-to-death-each-year.

Afterlife Research and Education Institute, Inc. "Afterlife Communication: David Thompson's Séances Today." https://adcguides.com/davidthompson1.htm.

"The Alfred Pritchett séance." Leslie Flint Educational Trust. November 4, 1960. https://www.leslieflint.com/alfred-pritchett.

Allen, Miles Edward. *The Realities of Heaven.* CreateSpace Publishing, 2015.

"Amazing blind teen uses echolocation to 'SEE.'" Familes.com. October 26, 2006. https://www.families.com/amazing-blind-boy-uses-echolocation-to-see-watch-the-video-clip.

Artigas, Mariano. *The Mind of the Universe: Understanding Science and Religion.* West Conshohocken, PA: Templeton Foundation Press, 2001 (citing Francis Crick, *The Astonishing Hypothesis,* New York: Scribners, 1994).

Austin, A. W., ed. *Teachings of Silver Birch.* London: Psychic Book Club, 1938.

Baird, J. L. *Sermons, Soap and Television—Autobiographical Notes.* London: Royal Television Society, 1988.

Baldwin, Neil. *Edison: Inventing the Century.* Chicago: University of Chicago Press, 2001.

Balfour, Arthur James. *A Defence of Philosophic Doubt; Being an Essay on the Foundations of Belief.* Sydney, Aus.: Wentworth Press, 2019.

Bander, P. *Voices from the Tapes.* New York: Drake Publishers, 1973.

Barker, Elsa. *Letters from a Living Dead Man.* Dallas, TX: Hill-Pehle Publishing, 2012, originally published in 1914.

Beischel, Julie, and Gary Schwartz. "Anomalous information reception by research mediums demonstrated using a novel triple-blind protocol." *Explore* 3, no. 1 (January 2007): 23-27.

Begley, S. "In our messy, reptilian brains." *Newsweek* online. Accessed April 9, 2007. http://www.msnbc.msn.com/id/17888475/site/newsweek.

Bennett, E. *Apparitions and Haunted Houses: A Survey of Evidence*. London: Faber, 1939.

Bering, Jesse. "One Last Goodbye: The Strange Case of Terminal Lucidity." *Scientific American* online. November 25, 2014. https://blogs.scientificamerican.com/bering-in-mind/one-last-goodbye-the-strange-case-of-terminal-lucidity.

Berkovich, S. "A scientific model why memory aka consciousness cannot reside solely in the brain." Near-Death Experience Research Foundation. Accessed October 25, 2007. https://www.nderf.org/NDERF/Research/Berkovich.

Berne, Eric. *Games People Play: The Psychology of Human Relationships*. New York: Penguin Books, 2009.

Besant, Annie, and Charles Webster Leadbeater. *Forms: A Record of Clairvoyant Investigation*. Brooklyn: Sacred Bones Books, 2020; originally published in 1901.

Betty, Stafford. *The Afterlife Unveiled*. Washington, D.C.: O Books, 2011.

Bissler, Jane. "Voices Across the Veil Direct Personal Communication." https://voicesacrosstheveil.afterlifedata.com/direct-personal-communication.

Blackburn, Elizabeth, and Elissa Epel. *The Telomere Effect: A Revolutionary Approach to Living Younger, Healthier, Longer*. New York: Grand Central Publishing, 2017.

"Blind man's 'superpower' lets him bike, skate and navigate the world." The HUMAN Limits. August 8, 2016. https://www.youtube.com/watch?v=EFvH7NF4MSw.

Blum, D. *Ghost Hunters: William James and the Search for Scientific Proof of Life After Death*. London: Penguin Press, 2006.

Borgia, Anthony. *Life in the World Unseen*. London: Psychic Press, 1985.

Botkin, Allan L., and R. Craig Hogan. *Induced After-Death Communication: A Miraculous Therapy for Grief and Loss.* Charlottesville, VA: Hampton Roads Publishing, 2014.
Boulton, Peter, and Jane Boulton. *Psychic Beam to Beyond: Through the Psychic Sensitive Lenora Huett.* Camarillo, CA: DeVorss & Co., 1983.
Bray, S. *A Guide for the Spiritual Traveler.* Queensland, Aus.: Scroll Publishers, 1990.
Brune, P. F. "The rediscovered beyond." World ITC. December 2006. www.worlditc.org/d_07_brune_rediscovered_beyond.htm.
Bryner, Jeanna. "Huge Stores of Oxygen Found Deep Inside Earth." NBC News. October 1, 2007. https://www.nbcnews.com/id/wbna21082196.
Burbidge, Augustus Henry. *The Shadows Lifted from Death.* Stuart, FL: Roundtable Publishing, 2011.
Burt, C. *The Gifted Child.* New York: Wiley, 1975.
Byrne, Brian Patrick, Leon Markovitz, Jody Sieradzki, and Tal Reznik. "All the People God Kills in the Bible." Vocativ. April 20, 2016. https://www.vocativ.com/news/309748/all-the-people-god-kills-in-the-bible/index.html.
Calvin, John. *Psychopannychia.* Warrendale, PA: Ichthus Publications, 2018; originally published in 1542.
Campbell, Thomas. *My Big Toe: A Trilogy Unifying Philosophy, Physics, and Metaphysics: Awakening, Discovery, Inner Workings.* Huntsville, AL: Lightning Strike Books, 2007.
Carnegie Mellon University. "Happy People Are Healthier, Psychologist Says." ScienceDaily. November 8, 2006. https://www.sciencedaily.com/releases/2006/11/061108103655.htm.
Carrington, H. *The World of Psychic Research.* New Jersey: A. S. Barns & Co., Inc., 1973.
Carter, C. Rebuttal to Keith Augustine's Attack of "Does Consciousness Depend on the Brain?" Accessed May 30, 2007. https://www.survivalafterdeath.info/articles/carter/augustine.htm.
Chalmers, D. J. "The Puzzle of Conscious Experience." *Scientific American* special issue, "Mysteries of the Mind," 1997.

"The Chinese Philosopher séance." Leslie Flint Trust. July 30, 1959. https://www.leslieflint.com/confucius-july-1959.

Choi, C. "Strange but True: When Half a Brain Is Better than a Whole One." *Scientific American* online. May 24, 2007. http://www.sciam.com/article.cfm?articleId=BE96F947-E7F2-99DF-3EA94A4C4EE87581&chanId=sa013&modsrc= most popular.

"The Church of England and Spiritualism—the full text of the Majority Report of the Church of England committee appointed by Archbishop Lang and Archbishop Temple to investigate Spiritualism." London: Psychic Press Ltd., 1939. https://www.cfpf.org.uk/articles/religion/cofe_report/cofe_report .html.

Colella, Francesca. "How Many People Are Starving Around the World?" The Borgen Project. January 20, 2018. https://borgenproject.org/how-many-people-are-starving-around-the-world.

Cook, E. W., B. Greyson, and I. Stevenson. "Do any near-death experiences provide evidence for the survival of human personality after death? Relevant features and illustrative case reports." *Journal of Scientific Exploration* 12 (1998): 377-406.

Corey, M. *The God Hypothesis: Discovering Design in Our "Just Right" Goldilocks Universe.* Washington, D.C.: Rowman & Littlefield, 2007.

Crookall, Robert. *The Supreme Adventure, Analyses of Psychic Communications.* Cambridge, UK: James Clarke & Co., Ltd., 1961.

Cummins, Geraldine. *Beyond Human Personality.* London: Ivor Nicholson and Watson, Ltd., 1935.

"Daniel Dunglas Home 1833-1886." SurvivalAfterDeath.info. Accessed July 16, 2007. https://www.survivalafterdeath.info/mediums/home.htm.

Davis, Andrew Jackson. *Death and the After Life.* Boston: Kobe and Rich, 1865.

Desmedt, J. E., and D. Robertson. "Differential enhancement of early and late components of the cerebral somatosensory evoked potentials during forced-paced cognitive tasks in man." *Journal of Physiology* 271 (1977): 761-782.

Dodds, E. R. "Presidential Address." *Proceedings of the Society for Psychical Research.* London: 1962.

"The Dorcas séance." Leslie Flint Trust. 1964. leslieflint.com/dorcas.

Dossey, L. *Recovering the Soul: A Scientific and Spiritual Search.* New York: Bantam Books, 1989.

Doyle, A. C. *The History of Spiritualism, Vols. I and II.* New York: Arno Press, 1926.

"Dr. Bruce Lipton—A New Hope: Epigenetics and the Subconscious Mind." Dr. Ron Ehrlich. https://drronehrlich.com/dr-bruce-lipton-a-new-hope-epigenetics-and-the-subconscious-mind-2.

Duncan, Helen, and C. E. Bechhofer Roberts. *The Trial of Mrs. Duncan.* London: Jarrolds Publishers, 1945.

Easton, J. C. "Survey on physicians' religious beliefs shows majority faithful." *The University of Chicago Chronicle* 24, no. 19 (July 14, 2005).

Edmonds, John Worth, and George T. Dexter. *Spiritualism.* New York: Partridge & Brittan, 1855.

Eisen, William, ed. *The Agashan Discourses.* Camarillo, CA: Devorss & Co., 1978.

Errands, Marjorie. *The Tapestry of Life* (Psychic Press Ltd., London, 1979).

Fenwick, Peter, and Elizabeth Fenwick. *The Art of Dying: A Journey to Elsewhere.* London: Continuum International Publishing, 2008.

Flint, Leslie. *Voices in the Dark.* New York: Macmillan Publishing, 1971.

Fodor, Nandor. *These Mysterious People.* London: Rider & Co. Ltd., 1934.

Fontana, David. *Is There an Afterlife?: A Comprehensive Overview of the Evidence.* Washington, D.C.: O Books, 2005.

"Frédéric Chopin séance." Leslie Flint Trust. July 7, 1955. https://www.leslieflint.com/chopin-july-7th-1955.

Funk, I. *The Psychic Riddle.* New York: Funk & Wagnalls Company, 1907.

Geley, Gustave. *Clairvoyance and Materialization: A Record of Experiments.* London: T. Fisher Unwin Limited, 1927.

"The George Wilmot séance." Leslie Flint Trust. www.earthschoolanswers.com/jenny.

Goldsmith, S. K., T. C. Pellmar, A. M. Kleinman, and W. E. Bunney, eds. "Reducing Suicide: A National Imperative." Washington, D.C.: Institute of Medicine, The National Academies Press, 2002.

Gonzalez, Guillermo, and Jay W. Richards. *The Privileged Planet: How Our Place in the Cosmos Is Designed for Discovery.* Washington, D.C.: Regnery Publishing, 2004.

Gorius, Léa. "How Much Does It Cost to End Poverty?" The Borgen Project. December 16, 2017. https://borgenproject.org/how-much-does-it-cost-to-end-poverty/.

Gilbert, Alice. *Philip in the Spheres.* Detroit: The Aquarian Press, 1952.

Goswami, Amit. "Quantum Politics: Part 1." March 31, 2015. https://www.amitgoswami.org/2015/03/31/quantum-politics-part-i.

Goswami, Amit. *The Self-Aware Universe: How Consciousness Creates the Material World.* New York: TarcherPerigee, 1995.

Greaves, Helen. *Testimony of Light.* London: C.W. Daniel, 1969.

Greyson, B. "Near death experiences as evidence for survival of bodily death." Survival of Bodily Death: An Esalen Invitational Conference, February 11-16, 2000.

Gurney, Edmund, F. W. H. Myers, and Frank Podmore. *Phantasms of the Living.* London: Trubner, 1886.

Haig, Scott. "The brain: the power of hope." *Time Magazine* 169 (2007): 118-119.

Hameroff, Stuart. "Overview: Could life and consciousness be related to the fundamental quantum nature of the universe?" Quantum Consciousness. Accessed December 15, 2007. http://www.quantumconsciousness.org.

Hapgood, Charles H. *Voices of Spirit.* New York: Delacorte Press / Seymour Lawrence, 1975.

Hawking, Stephen. *A Brief History of Time.* New York: Random House Publishing Group, 2011.

Heagerty, N. Riley. *The Hereafter.* Lulu.com, 2020.

Heffern, Rich. "Spirituality and the fine-tuned cosmos." *National Catholic Reporter.* December 12, 2003.

Helen Duncan: The Official Pardon Site. Accessed July 29, 2007. http://www.users.zetnet.co.uk/helenduncan.

Herr, Norman. "Television & Health: III Violence." CSUN. Internet Resources to Accompany the Sourcebook for Teaching Science. http://www.csun.edu/science/health/docs/tv&health.html.

Hodgson, R. "A further record of observations of certain phenomena of a trance." *Proceedings of the Society for Psychical Research* 13 (1897-1898): 297.

Hogan, R. Craig. *There Is Nothing but Mind and Experiences.* Normal, IL: Greater Reality Publications, 2020.

Holden, J. "Holden describes the frequency of after-death communication." University of North Texas News Service. November 5, 2005. http://web2.unt.edu/news/story.cfm?story=9441.

Holzer, H. *Ghost Hunter.* New York: Bobbs Merrill Company, 1963.

Honorton, C., and D. C. Ferrari. "Future telling: A meta-analysis of forced-choice precognition experiments, 1935-1987." *Journal of Parapsychology* 53 (1989): 281-308.

Horowitz, Rabbi Ephraim. "Life by Accident." AISH. https://www.aish.com/ci/sam/48970356.html.

"Hypnosis for Pain Relief." Arthritis Foundation. https://www.arthritis.org/health-wellness/treatment/complementary-therapies/natural-therapies/hypnosis-for-pain-relief.

"Hypnosis, No Anesthetic, for Man's Surgery." CBS News. April 22, 2008. https://www.cbsnews.com/news/hypnosis-no-anesthetic-for-mans-surgery.

Inglis, B. *Science and Parascience — A History of the Paranormal 1914-1939.* London: Hodder and Stoughton, 1984.

"An introductory analysis of the NDE (near-death experience)." *Two Worlds* (1996). https://cryskernan.tripod.com/intro_analysis_of_the_%20NDE%20_.htm.

Jeffrey, Grant R. *Creation: Remarkable Evidence of God's Design* (New York: Crown Publishing Group, 2009).

"John Grant séance." Leslie Flint Trust. June 9, 1969. https://www.leslieflint.com/john-grant-june-1969.

Johnson, R. C. *The Imprisoned Splendour.* Wheaton, IL: Quest Books, 1982.

Jung, C. G. *Collected Works of C. G. Jung, Volume 11; Psychology and Religion*. Princeton, NJ: Princeton University Press, 1975.

Jung, C. G. *Letters, Volume 1*. Princeton, NJ: Princeton University Press, 1973.

Jürgenson, Friedrich. *Sprechfunk mit Verstorbenen*. Freiburg im Br.: Hermann Bauer Verlag, 1967.

Kak, S., D. Chopra, and M. Kafatos. "Perceived Reality, Quantum Mechanics, and Consciousness." *Cosmology* 18 (2014): 231-245.

Kalish, R. A., and D. K. Reynolds. "Phenomenological reality and post death contact." *Journal for the Scientific Study of Religion* 12, vol. 2 (1973): 209-21.

Kardec, Allan. *The Spirits' Book*. Miami, FL: FEB Publisher, 2018.

Kean, Leslie. *Surviving Death: A Journalist Investigates Evidence for an Afterlife*. New York: Crown Archetype, 2017 (citing Peter Fenwick, "End-of-Life Experiences").

Keen, M. "Physical phenomena at the David Thompson séance of October 25th 2003." https://www.survivalafterdeath.info/articles/keen/thompson.htm.

Keen, M., and A. Ellison. "Scole: A response to the critics? The Scole Report." *Proceedings of the Society for Psychical Research* 58, part 220 (1999).

Kelway-Bamber, Claude H. *Claude's Book*. London: Methuen & Co. Ltd., 1919.

Klopfer, Bruno. "Psychological Variables in Human Cancer." *Journal of Prospective Techniques* 31 (1957): 331-40.

Komp, Diane M. *A Window to Heaven: When Children See Life in Death* (Grand Rapids, MI: Zondervan Publishing, 1992).

Kounang, Nadia. "What is the science behind fear?" CNN. October 29, 2015. https://www.cnn.com/2015/10/29/health/science-of-fear/indexhtml.

Kruse, Eckhard. "Audio Signal Processing to Investigate Alleged Paranormal Phenomena in Mediumistic Séances." *IEEE Aerospace and Electronic Systems Magazine* 33, no. 2 (February 2018): 52-56.

Kübler-Ross, Elisabeth. *On Death and Dying*. New York: Scribner Classics, 1997.

Kübler-Ross, Elisabeth. *On Life After Death.* Berkeley, CA: Celestial Arts, 1991.
Lazarus, Richard. *The Case Against Death.* London: Warner Books, 1993.
Leslie Flint Educational Trust. https://leslieflint.com.
Lewin, R. "Is your brain really necessary?" *Science* 210, no. 4475 (1980): 1232-1234.
Libet, B. "Subjective antedating of a sensory experience and Mind-brain theories: Reply to Honderich." *Journal of Theoretical Biology* 114, no. 4 (May 31, 1985): 563-570.
"Life After Death: Episode 8, The testimony of science." Hosted by Tom Harpur, based on his book. Phoenix, AZ: Wellspring Media, 1998. TV documentary.
Lipka, M., and C. Gecewicz. "More Americans now say they're spiritual but not religious." Pew Research Center. September 6, 2017. https://www.pewresearch.org/fact-tank/2017/09/06/more-americans-now-say-theyre-spiritual-but-not-religious.
Lipton, Bruce. *The Biology of Belief.* Carlsbad, CA: Hay House, 2016.
Lipton, Bruce. "THINK Beyond Your Genes—March 2018." Bruce H. Lipton, PhD. https://www.brucelipton.com/think-beyond-your-genes-march-2018.
Lodge, Oliver. *Raymond or Life and Death.* New York: George H. Doran, 1916.
Lombroso, Cesare. *Criminal Man.* Durham, NC: Duke University Press Books, 2006.
Lu, Donna, Alison George, Daniel Cossins, and Layal Liverpool. "What you experience may not exist. Inside the strange truth of reality." *New Scientist* online. January 29, 2020. https://www.newscientist.com/article/mg24532670-800-what-you-experience-may-not-exist-inside-the-strange-truth-of-reality.
"The Lucillus séances." Leslie Flint Trust. August 1, 1962. https://www.leslieflint.com/lucillus.
Maraldo, Pamela. *Medicine: In Search of a Soul: The Healing Prescription.* Carlsbad, CA: Balboa Press, 2017.
"The Mary Ann Ross séance." Leslie Flint Trust. January 20, 1969. https://www.leslieflint.com/mary-ann-ross.

Masters of Light. AREI physical mediumship circle. Séance, December 23, 2018.

Mayell, Hillary. "Thousands of Women Killed for Family 'Honor.'" *National Geographic* online. February 12, 2002. https://www.nationalgeographic.com/culture/2002/02/thousands-of-women-killed-for-family-honor.

McKenzie, A. *Apparitions and Ghosts: A Modern Study*. London: Arthur Baker Ltd., 1971.

Meek, G. *After We Die, What Then?* Columbus, OH: Ariel Press, 1987.

Mershimer, Loy. "A Theology of Ghosts." Thoughts of Loy, blogspot. September 19, 2005. http://loymershimer.blogspot.com/2005/09/theology-of-ghosts.html.

"Michael Fearon séance." Leslie Flint Trust. 1954. https://www.leslieflint.com/michael-fearon-1954.

Moeller, Rachael. "Study Suggests Common Knee Surgery's Effect Is Purely Placebo." *Scientific American* online. July 12, 2002. https://www.scientificamerican.com/article/study-suggests-common-kne.

Montgomery, Guy, Katherine DuHamel, and William Redd. "A meta-analysis of hypnotically induced analgesia: How effective is hypnosis?" *International Journal of Clinical and Experimental Hypnosis* 48 (2000): 138-153.

Moody, Raymond. "Family Reunions: Visionary Encounters with the Departed in a Modern-Day Psychomanteum." *Journal of Near-Death Studies* 11, no. 2 (Winter 1992): 112.

Moody, Raymond. *Glimpses of Eternity: An Investigation into Shared Death Experiences*. London: Rider, 2011.

Moody, Raymond. *Life After Life*. New York: HarperOne, 1975.

Moore, C. A. "The unseen realm: Science is making room for near-death experiences beyond this world." *Desert Morning News*. February 18, 2006.

Morin, R. "Do Americans Believe in God?" *Washington Post* online. April 24, 2000. www.washingtonpost.com/wp-srv/politics/polls/wat/archive/wat042400.htm.

Morse, Melvin, with Paul Perry. *Parting Visions*. New York: Villard Books, 1994.
"Mr. Biggs communicates." Leslie Flint Trust. 1966. https://www.leslieflint.com/mr-biggs-1966.
Murphet, H. *Beyond death—The Undiscovered Country*. Wheaton, IL: Quest Books, 1990.
Nahm, Michael, and Bruce Greyson. "Terminal Lucidity in Patients with Chronic Schizophrenia and Dementia: A Survey of the Literature." *The Journal of Nervous and Mental Disease* 197, no.12 (2009): 942-944.
Nahm, Michael, Bruce Greyson, Emily Kelly, and Erlendur Haraldsson. "Terminal lucidity: A review and a case collection." *Archives of Geronology and Geriatrics* 55 (2012): 138-142.
Newton, Michael. *Destiny of Souls: New Case Studies of Life Between Lives*. Woodbury, MN: Llewellyn Publications, 2000.
Oppenheim, J. *The Other World*. Cambridge, UK: Cambridge University Press, 1985.
Osis, Karlis, and Erlendur Haraldsson. *At the Hour of Death*. Norwalk, CT: Hastings House, 1997.
Patt, Stephan. "Brain localization of consciousness? Neurological considerations." Seventh International Interdisciplinary Seminar. "Exploring the human mind: the perspective of natural sciences." Ponte di Legno, Italy. December 28, 2003. http://web.quipo.it/glopresti/pdl/ppt/Patt%20-%20Brain%20localization%20of%20consciousness.pdf.
Patterson, Jill. "How Evil Is a Socially Constructed Concept: Evil Across Societies." *The Manitoban* online. February 9, 2021. http://www.themanitoban.com/2012/10/how-evil-is-a-socially-constructed-concept-evil-across-societies/12309.
Pearson, Ronald. *Intelligence Behind the Universe!* London: Headquarters Publishing Company, 1990.
Peebles, James M. *Immortality and Our Employments Hereafter: With What a Hundred Spirits, Good and Evil, Say of Their Dwelling Places*. London: Forgotten Books, 2015; originally published in 1907.
Penman, Danny. "Could there be proof to the theory that we're ALL psychic?" *Daily Mail* online. January 28, 2008.

http://www.dailymail.co.uk/pages/live/articles/news/news.html?in_article_id=510762&in_page_id=1770.

Penman, Danny. "Many Scientists Are Convinced That Man Can See the Future." RedOrbit. May 5, 2007. https://www.redorbit.com/news/science/925987/many_scientists_are_convinced_that_man_can_see_the_future.

Peters, Adele. "It would cost just $330 billion to end global hunger by 2030." Fast Company. October 15, 2020. https://www.fastcompany.com/90564107/it-would-cost-just-330-billion-to-end-global-hunger-by-2030.

Phillips, J. B. *Ring of Truth*. London: H. Shaw, 1977.

"Physicists Challenge Notion of Electric Nerve Impulses; Say Sound More Likely." Science Blog. University of Copenhagen. March 7, 2007. https://scienceblog.com/12738/physicists-challenge-notion-of-electric-nerve-impulses-say-sound-more-likely/.

Pike, James A., and Diane Kennedy Pike. *The Other Side: An Account of My Experiences with Psychic Phenomena*. Eugene, OR: Wipf and Stock, 1968.

Pobanz, Kerry. "Depossession Healing: A Comparison of William Baldwin's 'Spirit Releasement Therapy' and Dae Mo Nim's Ancestor Liberation." *Journal of Unification Studies* 9 (2008): 143-162.

Presti, David E. Review of Edward F. Kelly et al., *Irreducible Mind: Toward a Psychology for the 21st Century*. Rowman & Littlefield. Accessed October 5, 2007. https://rowman.com/ISBN/9781442202061/Irreducible-Mind-Toward-a-Psychology-for-the-21st-Century.

"Psychic Detectives." Transcript. CNN. "Nancy Grace." December 30, 2005. http://transcripts.cnn.com/TRANSCRIPTS/0512/30/ng.01.html.

"The Queen Alexandra séance." Leslie Flint Educational Trust. 1960. https://www.leslieflint.com/queen-alexandra.

Radin, D. *The Conscious Universe: The Scientific Truth of Psychic Phenomena*. New York: HarperCollins Publishers, 1997.

Randall, E. C. *The Dead Have Never Died*. New York: A. A. Knopf, 1917.

Rees, W. D. "The hallucinations of widowhood." *British Medical Journal* 4 (1971): 37-41.

Ring, K., and S. Cooper. "Mindsight: Near-Death and Out-of-Body Experiences in the Blind." *The Journal of Nervous and Mental Disease* 188, no. 11 (November 2000): 789-790.

Ring, K., and M. Lawrence. "Further evidence for veridical perception during near-death experiences." *Journal of Near-Death Studies* 11, no. 4 (1993): 223-229.

Rogge, Michael. "Direct Voice: Conversation between mother and her deceased son." Man and the Unknown. http://www.xs4all.nl/~wichm/fearon.html.

Rogge, Michael. "Paranormal Voices Assert: Death No End." Man and the Unknown. https://wichm.home.xs4all.nl/deathnoe.html.

Rogge, Michael. "Parapsychology and Personal Survival after Death." Man and the Unknown. 2019. https://wichm.home.xs4all.nl/paraps.html.

Rogo, D. S. *Leaving the Body: A Complete Guide to Astral Projection*. New York: Fireside/Simon & Schuster, 1993.

Rogo, D. S. "Researching the out-of-body experiences." In Michael Schmicker, *Best Evidence*, Lincoln, NE: Writers Club Press, 2002.

Roy, Archie. Letter to Michael Roll. May 19, 1983. Campaign for Philosophical Freedom. https://www.cfpf.org.uk/letters/1983/1983-05-19_ar2mr/1983-05-19_ar2mr.html.

"The Rupert Brooke séance." Leslie Flint Trust. September 15, 1957. https://www.leslieflint.com/rupert-brooke.

Sabom, M. *Recollections of Death: A Medical Investigation*. New York: Harper & Row, 1998.

Schroeder, G. L. *The Hidden Face of God*. New York: Simon & Schuster, 2001.

Schwartz, Gary, and W. L. Simon. *The Afterlife Experiments*. New York: Atria Books, 2003.

Schwartz, Gary, Linda G. S. Russek, Lonnie A. Nelson, and Christopher Barentsen. "Accuracy and Replicability of Anomalous After-Death Communication Across Highly Skilled Mediums." *Journal of the Society for Psychical Research* 65 (2001): 1-25.

Scull, Maggie. "Timeline of 1981 hunger strike." *The Irish Times* online. March 1, 2016. https://www.irishtimes.com/culture/books/timeline-of-1981-hunger-strike-1.2555682.

Sharp, K. C. *After the Light*. Lincoln, NE: Author's Choice Press, 2003.

Sheldrake, Rupert. "The 'sense of being stared at' experiments in schools." *Journal of the Society for Psychical Research* 62 (1998): 311-323.

Sheldrake, Rupert. "Videotaped Experiments on Telephone Telepathy." *Journal of Parapsychology* 67 (2003): 147-166.

Sherwood, Jane. *The Country Beyond*. London: Neville Spearman, 1969.

Simpson, A. Rae. "MIT Young Adult Development Project." MIT. 2018. http://hrweb.mit.edu/worklife/youngadult/index.html.

Simpson, Mona. "A Sister's Eulogy for Steve Jobs." *The New York Times*. October 30, 2011.

"Sir Thomas Beechum [sic]." Produced by Leslie Flint Trust. YouTube video, 34:07. https://www.youtube.com/watch?v=Q_eHJWWwjTg.

Smith, G. *The Unbelievable Truth*. Carlsbad, CA: Hay House, 2004.

Snyder, J. J. "Science confirms survival." The Campaign for Philosophical Freedom. Accessed September 20, 2007. http://www.cfpf.org.uk/articles/background/snyder.html.

Spraggett, A. *The Case for Immortality*. Scarborough, Canada: New American Library of Canada, 1974.

Stringfellow, Alice. *Leslie's letters to his mother*. Fayetteville, AR: Democrat Publishing and Printing Co., 1926.

"Study suggests brain may have 'blindsight.'" NBC News. October 31, 2005. https://www.nbcnews.com/health/health-news/study-suggests-brain-may-have-blindsight-flna1c9437216.

"Suicide in Children and Teens." American Academy of Child & Adolescent Psychiatry, no. 10 (June 2018).

Talbot, Michael. *The Holographic Universe*. New York: Harper Perennial, 2011), 98-100.

Targ, R., and H. Puthoff. "Information transmission under conditions of sensory shielding." *Nature* 251 (1974).

Tart, C. "Psychophysiological study of out-of-the-body experiences in a selected subject." *Journal of the American Society for Psychical Research* 62, no. 1(1968): 3-27.

Taylor, Ruth M. *Witness from Beyond.* Chicago: Chicago Review Press, 1980.

"The Terry Smith séance." Leslie Flint Trust. July 16, 1966. https://www.leslieflint.com/terry-smith.

"Theodicy, God and Suffering – A debate between Dinesh D'Souza and Bart Ehrman." Produced by Gordon College Center for Christian Studies. November 11, 2010. YouTube video, 1:42:27. https://www.youtube.com/watch?v=Isg6Kx-3xdI.

Thomas, Charles Drayton. *Life Beyond Death with Evidence.* Hong Kong: Hesperides Press, 2008; originally published in 1923.

Thomas, Charles Drayton. "Report re Lodge via Leonard." *Journal of the Society for Psychical Research* 33 (1945): 136, 138-160.

"Tiny-brained man's lifestyle wows doctors." NBC News. July 19, 2007. https://www.nbcnews.com/id/wbna19859089.

Tippit, Sarah. "Study: Brain Functions in Clinically Dead." ABC News. June 29, 2001. https://abcnews.go.com/Technology/story?id=98447&page=1.

Touber, Tijn. "Life goes on." *Ode* 3, no. 10 (December 2005).

Tudor-Pole, W. *Private Dowding.* (New York: Dodd, Mead & Company, 1919)

Twenge, Jean M. "The Sad State of Happiness in the United States and the Role of Digital Media." World Happiness Report. March 20, 2019. https://worldhappiness.report/ed/2019/the-sad-state-of-happiness-in-the-united-states-and-the-role-of-digital-media/.

Twenge, Jean M., G. N. Martin, and W. K. Campbell. "Decreases in psychological well-being among American adolescents after 2012 and links to screen time during the rise of smartphone technology." *Emotion* 18, no. 6 (2018): 765-780.

Tymn, Michael. *The Afterlife Revealed.* Guildford, UK: White Crow Books, 2011.

Tymn, Michael. "Distinguished researchers found evidence for survival." After-Death Communication. https://kuriakon00.tripod.com/after_death_communication/research.html.

Tymn, Michael. "Ghost Stories: Ghost loses chess match." All About Paranormal. September 1, 2008. https://www.allaboutparanormal.co/2008/09/ghost-stories-ghost-loses-chess-match.html#axzz6rppHBgXf.

Tymn, Michael. "Try Shock Therapy to Protect Against Vagabond Spirits?" White Crow Books. June 28, 2011. http://whitecrowbooks.com/michaeltymn/entry/try_shock_therapy_to_protect_against_vagabond_spirits.

Tymn, Michael. "A veridical death-bed vision." Paranormal and Life After Death. March 14, 2008. https://paranormalandlifeafterdeath.blogspot.com/2008/03/.

Ullman, Montague. "Herpes Simplex and Second Degree Burn Induced Under Hypnosis." *The American Journal of Psychiatry* 103, no. 6 (May 1947).

Utts, Jessica. "An Assessment of the Evidence for Psychic Functioning." *Journal of Scientific Exploration* 10, no. 1 (1996): 3-30.

Van Lommel, Pim. "6. Neurophysiology in a normal functioning brain." International Association for Near-Death Studies. Accessed November 15, 2007. https://iands.org/research/nde-research/important-research-articles/43-dr-pim-van-lommel-md-continuity-of-consciousness.html?start=5.

Van Lommel, Pim. *Consciousness Beyond Life: The Science of the Near-Death Experience.* New York: HarperCollins, 2010.

Van Lommel, Pim. "Near-death experience in survivors of cardiac arrest; a prospective study in the Netherlands." *Lancet* 358 (December 15, 2001): 39-45.

Vandersande, Jan. *Life After Death: Some of the Best Evidence.* Denver: Outskirts Press, 2008.

Von Schrenk-Notzing, Baron. *Phenomena of Materialization, a contribution to the investigation of mediumistic teleplastics.* New York: E. P. Dutton, 1920.

Walia, Arjun. "'Consciousness Creates Reality'—Physicists Admit the Universe Is Immaterial, Mental, & Spiritual." Collective Evolution. November 11, 2014. https://www.collective-evolution.com/2014/11/11/consciousness-creates-reality-physicists-admit-the-universe-is-immaterial-mental-spiritual (citing Richard Conn Henry, "The Mental Universe," Nature 436, 2005: 29, who is quoting Sir James Jeans).

Ward, Suzanne. *Matthew, Tell Me about Heaven.* Camas, WA: Matthew Books, 2012.

Weiskrantz, L. "Blindsight revisited." *Journal of Cognitive Neuroscience* 6 (1996): 215-220.

White, Mary Blount. *Letters from the Other Side.* Hinesburg, VT: Upper Access, Inc., 1995.

Wickland, Carl. *Thirty Years Among the Dead.* Guildford, UK: White Crow Books, 2011.

Williams, Kevin. "People Have Near-Death Experiences While Brain Dead." Near-Death Experiences and the Afterlife. Accessed April 1, 2007. http://www.near-death.com/experiences/evidence01.html.

Wright, Rochelle, and R. Craig Hogan. *Repair & Reattachment Grief Therapy.* Chicago: Greater Reality Publications, 2015.

"Youth mental health report: Youth Survey 2012-16." Mission Australia, in association with the Black Dog Institute. April 18, 2017.

Zammit, V. *A Lawyer Presents the Case for the Afterlife.* Sydney, Aus.: Ganmell Pty Ltd., 2006.

Endnotes

[1] Allan L. Botkin and R. Craig Hogan, *Induced After Death Communication: A Miraculous Therapy for Grief and Loss* (Charlottesville, VA: Hampton Roads Publishing, 2014).

[2] Rochelle Wright and R. Craig Hogan, *Repair & Reattachment Grief Therapy* (Chicago: Greater Reality Publications, 2015).

[3] "Afterlife Communication: David Thompson's Séances Today," Afterlife Research and Education Institute, Inc., https://adcguides.com/davidthompson1.htm.

[4] Leslie Flint Trust, https://leslieflint.com.

[5] Arjun Walia, "'Consciousness Creates Reality'—Physicists Admit the Universe Is Immaterial, Mental, & Spiritual." *Collective Evolution*, November 11, 2014, https://www.collective-evolution.com/2014/11/11/consciousness-creates-reality-physicists-admit-the-universe-is-immaterial-mental-spiritual (citing Richard Conn Henry, "The Mental Universe," Nature 436, 2005: 29, who is quoting Sir James Jeans).

[6] R. Craig Hogan, *There Is Nothing but Mind and Experiences* (Normal, IL: Greater Reality Publications, 2020), 27-32.

[7] Hogan, *There Is Nothing but Mind*.

[8] Donna Lu et al., "What you experience may not exist. Inside the strange truth of reality," *New Scientist* online, January 29, 2020, https://www.newscientist.com/article/mg24532670-800-what-you-experience-may-not-exist-inside-the-strange-truth-of-reality.

[9] Mariano Artigas, *The Mind of the Universe: Understanding Science and Religion* (West Conshohocken, PA: Templeton Foundation Press, 2001), 11 (citing Francis Crick, *The Astonishing Hypothesis*, New York: Scribners, 1994).

[10] Thomas Campbell, *My Big Toe: A Trilogy Unifying Philosophy, Physics, and Metaphysics: Awakening, Discovery, Inner Workings* (Huntsville, AL: Lightning Strike Books, 2007).

[11] Anil Seth, "Anil Seth on a New Science of Consciousness," Closer to Truth Chats, September 3, 2021. https://www.youtube.com/watch?v=BDFB6hf87yk&list=WL&index=2&t=1416s.

[12] Stephan Patt, "Brain localization of consciousness? Neurological considerations," Seventh International Interdisciplinary Seminar, "Exploring the human mind: the perspective of natural sciences," Ponte di Legno, Italy, December 28, 2003, http://web.quipo.it/glopresti/pdl/ppt/Patt%20-%20Brain%20localization%20of%20consciousness.pdf.

[13] G. L. Schroeder, *The Hidden Face of God* (New York: Simon & Schuster, 2001), 158.

[14] Stuart Hameroff, "Overview: Could life and consciousness be related to the fundamental quantum nature of the universe?" Quantum Consciousness, accessed December 15, 2007, http://www.quantumconsciousness.org.

[15] David E. Presti, review of Edward F. Kelly et al., *Irreducible Mind: Toward a Psychology for the 21st Century*, accessed October 5, 2007, https://rowman.com/ISBN/9781442202061/Irreducible-Mind-Toward-a-Psychology-for-the-21st-Century.

[16] D. J. Chalmers, "The Puzzle of Conscious Experience," *Scientific American* special issue "Mysteries of the Mind," 1997.

[17] Sarah Tippit, "Study: Brain Functions in Clinically Dead," ABC News, June 29, 2001, https://abcnews.go.com/Technology/story?id=98447&page=1.

[18] S. Berkovich, "A scientific model why memory aka consciousness cannot reside solely in the brain," Near-Death Experience Research Foundation, accessed October 25, 2007, http://www.nderf.org/Berkovich.htm.

[19] "Life After Death: Episode 8, The testimony of science," hosted by Tom Harpur, based on his book (Phoenix, AZ, Wellspring Media, 1998), TV documentary. Quoting Stanislav Grof.

[20] C. Carter, Rebuttal to Keith Augustine's Attack of "Does Consciousness Depend on the Brain?" Accessed May 30, 2007, http://www.survivalafterdeath.org/articles/carter/augustine.htm.

[21] C. Burt, *The Gifted Child* (New York: Wiley, 1975).

22 Carter, Rebuttal.

23 S. Kak, D. Chopra, and M. Kafatos, "Perceived Reality, Quantum Mechanics, and Consciousness," *Cosmology* 18 (2014): 231-245.

24 Tijn Touber, "Life goes on," *Ode* 3, no. 10 (December 2005).

25 Jesse Bering, "One Last Goodbye: The Strange Case of Terminal Lucidity," *Scientific American* online, November 25, 2014, https://blogs.scientificamerican.com/bering-in-mind/one-last-goodbye-the-strange-case-of-terminal-lucidity.

26 Michael Nahm and Bruce Greyson, "Terminal Lucidity in Patients with Chronic Schizophrenia and Dementia: A Survey of the Literature," *The Journal of Nervous and Mental Disease* 197, no. 12 (2009): 942-944.

27 Scott Haig, "The brain: the power of hope," *Time Magazine* 169 (2007): 118-119.

28 Michael Nahm et al., "Terminal lucidity: A review and a case collection," *Archives of Geronology and Geriatrics* 55 (2012): 138-142.

29 C. Choi, "Strange but True: When Half a Brain Is Better than a Whole One," *Scientific American* online, May 24, 2007, http://www.sciam.com/article.cfm?articleId=BE96F947-E7F2-99DF-3EA94A4C4EE87581&chanId=sa013&modsrc=most_popular.

30 "Tiny-brained man's lifestyle wows doctors," NBC News, July 19, 2007, http://www.msnbc.msn.com/id/19859089/.

31 R. Lewin, "Is your brain really necessary?" *Science* 210, no. 4475 (1980): 1232-1234.

32 Lewin, "Is your brain really necessary?"

33 Lewin, "Is your brain really necessary?"

34 D. Radin, *The Conscious Universe: The Scientific Truth of Psychic Phenomena* (New York: HarperCollins Publishers, 1997).

35 Jessica Utts, "An assessment of the evidence for psychic functioning," *Journal of Scientific Exploration* 10, no. 1 (1996): 3-30.

36 Radin, *The Conscious Universe*, 104.

37 R. Targ and H. Puthoff, "Information transmission under conditions of sensory shielding," *Nature* 251 (1974).

38 Danny Penman, "Could there be proof to the theory that we're ALL psychic?" *Daily Mail* online, January 28, 2008,

http://www.dailymail.co.uk/pages/live/articles/news/news.html?in_article_id=510762&in_page_id=1770.

[39] Penman, "Could there be proof"

[40] J. E. Desmedt and D. Robertson, "Differential enhancement of early and late components of the cerebral somatosensory evoked potentials during forced-paced cognitive tasks in man," *Journal of Physiology* 271 (1977): 761-782. Roland, P. E., & Friberg, L. (1985). Localization in cortical areas activated by thinking. *Journal of Neurophysiology*, 53, 1219-1243. Eccles, J. C. (1988). The effect of silent thinking on the cerebral cortex. *Truth Journal*. Retrieved December 15, 2007 from http://www.leaderu.com/truth/2truth06.html,.

[41] Amit Goswami, "Quantum Politics: Part 1," March 31, 2015, https://www.amitgoswami.org/2015/03/31/quantum-politics-part-i.

[42] "Physicists Challenge Notion of Electric Nerve Impulses; Say Sound More Likely," Science Blog, University of Copenhagen, March 7, 2007, https://scienceblog.com/12738/physicists-challenge-notion-of-electric-nerve-impulses-say-sound-more-likely.

[43] Carter, Rebuttal.

[44] "Study suggests brain may have 'blindsight,'" NBC News, October 31, 2005, https://www.nbcnews.com/health/health-news/study-suggests-brain-may-have-blindsight-flna1c9437216.

[45] S. Begley, "In our messy, reptilian brains," *Newsweek* online, accessed April 9, 2007, http://www.msnbc.msn.com/id/17888475/site/newsweek.

[46] L. Weiskrantz, "Blindsight revisited," *Journal of Cognitive Neuroscience* 6 (1996): 215-220.

[47] "Amazing blind teen uses echolocation to 'SEE,'" Familes.com, October 26, 2006, http://special-needs.families.com/blog/ amazing-blind-boy-uses-echolocation-to-see-watch-the-video-clip.

[48] "Blind man's 'superpower' lets him bike, skate and navigate the world," The Human Limits, August 8, 2016, https://www.youtube.com/watch?v=EFvH7NF4MSw.

[49] "Blind man's 'superpower.'"

[50] K. Ring and S. Cooper, "Mindsight: Near-Death and Out-of-Body Experiences in the Blind," *The Journal of Nervous and Mental Disease* 188, no. 11 (November 2000): 789-790.

[51] L. Dossey, *Recovering the Soul: A Scientific and Spiritual Search* (New York: Bantam Books, 1989), 18.

[52] Kevin Williams, "People Have Near-Death Experiences While Brain Dead," *Near-Death Experiences and the Afterlife,* Accessed April 1, 2007, http://www.near-death.com/experiences/evidence01.html.

[53] M. Sabom, *Recollections of Death: A Medical Investigation* (New York: Harper & Row, 1998).

[54] K. C. Sharp, *After the Light* (Lincoln, NE: Author's Choice Press, 2003).

[55] K. Ring and M. Lawrence, "Further evidence for veridical perception during near-death experiences," *Journal of Near-Death Studies* 11, no. 4 (1993): 223-229.

[56] E. W. Cook, B. Greyson, and I. Stevenson, "Do any near-death experiences provide evidence for the survival of human personality after death? Relevant features and illustrative case reports," *Journal of Scientific Exploration* 12 (1998): 377-406.

[57] Pim Van Lommel, "Near-death experience in survivors of cardiac arrest; a prospective study in the Netherlands," *Lancet* 358 (December 15, 2001): 2039-45.

[58] Michael Schmicker, *Best Evidence* (Lincoln, NE: Writers Club Press, 2002), 203.

[59] Melvin Morse with Paul Perry, *Parting Visions* (New York: Villard Books, 1994).

[60] C. Tart, "Psychophysiological study of out-of-the-body experiences in a selected subject," *Journal of the American Society for Psychical Research* 62, no. 1(1968): 3-27.

[61] V. Zammit, *A Lawyer Presents the Case for the Afterlife* (Sydney, Aus.: Ganmell Pty. Ltd., 2006), 69.

[62] Radin, *The Conscious Universe,* 96-97.

[63] "Psychic Detectives," Transcript, CNN, "Nancy Grace," December 30, 2005, http://transcripts.cnn.com/TRANSCRIPTS/0512/30/ng.01.html.

[64] "Psychic Detectives."

[65] Radin, *The Conscious Universe*, 118-124.

[66] C. Honorton and D. C. Ferrari, "Future telling: A meta-analysis of forced-choice precognition experiments, 1935-1987," *Journal of Parapsychology* 53 (1989): 281-308.

[67] Danny Penman, "Many Scientists Are Convinced That Man Can See the Future," RedOrbit, May 5, 2007, https://www.redorbit.com/news/science/925987/many_scientists_are_convinced_that_man_can_see_the_future.

[68] Rupert Sheldrake, "Videotaped Experiments on Telephone Telepathy," *Journal of Parapsychology* 67 (2003): 147-166.

[69] B. Libet, "Subjective antedating of a sensory experience and Mind-brain theories: Reply to Honderich," *Journal of Theoretical Biology* 114, no. 4 (May 31, 1985): 563-570.

[70] Penman, "Many Scientists Are Convinced."

[71] Radin, *The Conscious Universe*, 101.

[72] R. Morin, "Do Americans Believe in God?" *Washington Post* online, April 24, 2000, http://www.washingtonpost.com/wp-srv/politics/polls/wat/archive/wat042400.htm.

[73] W. D. Rees, "The hallucinations of widowhood," *British Medical Journal* 4 (1971): 37-41.

[74] J. Holden, "Holden describes the frequency of after-death communication," University of North Texas News Service, November 5, 2005, http://web2.unt.edu/news/ story.cfm?story=9441.

[75] R. A. Kalish and D. K. Reynolds, "Phenomenological reality and post death contact," *Journal for the Scientific Study of Religion* 12, vol. 2 (1973): 209-21.

[76] Botkin, *Induced After-Death Communication*.

[77] Botkin, *Induced After-Death Communication*.

[78] H. Holzer, *Ghost Hunter* (New York: Bobbs Merrill Company, 1963).

[79] J. C. Easton, "Survey on physicians' religious beliefs shows majority faithful," *The University of Chicago Chronicle* 24, no. 19 (July 14, 2005).

⁸⁰ Ronald Pearson, *Intelligence Behind the Universe!* (London: Headquarters Publishing Company, 1990).

⁸¹ Jan Vandersande, *Life After Death: Some of the Best Evidence* (Denver: Outskirts Press, 2008).

⁸² Michael Tymn, "Distinguished researchers found evidence for survival," After-Death Communication, https://kuriakon00.tripod.com/after_death_communication/research.html.

⁸³ Tymn, "Distinguished researchers."

⁸⁴ J. J. Snyder, "Science confirms survival," The Campaign for Philosophical Freedom, accessed September 20, 2007, http://www.cfpf.org.uk/articles/background/snyder.html.

⁸⁵ Tymn, "Distinguished researchers."

⁸⁶ Tymn, "Distinguished researchers."

⁸⁷ Tymn, "Distinguished researchers."

⁸⁸ Tymn, "Distinguished researchers."

⁸⁹ Tymn, "Distinguished researchers."

⁹⁰ Tymn, "Distinguished researchers."

⁹¹ Tymn, "Distinguished researchers."

⁹² Tymn, "Distinguished researchers."

⁹³ Tymn, "Distinguished researchers."

⁹⁴ Tymn, "Distinguished researchers."

⁹⁵ Tymn, "Distinguished researchers."

⁹⁶ Tymn, "Distinguished researchers."

⁹⁷ Tymn, "Distinguished researchers."

⁹⁸ J. L. Baird, *Sermons, Soap and Television—Autobiographical Notes* (London: Royal Television Society, 1988).

⁹⁹ G. Meek, *After We Die, What Then?* (Columbus, OH: Ariel Press, 1987).

¹⁰⁰ Archie Roy, Letter to Michael Roll, May 19, 1983, *Campaign for Philosophical Freedom*, https://www.cfpf.org.uk/letters/1983/1983-05-19_ar2mr/1983-05-19_ar2mr.html.

¹⁰¹ P. Bander, *Voices from the Tapes* (New York: Drake Publishers, 1973), 132.

¹⁰² Bander, *Voices from the Tapes*, 132.

¹⁰³ Tymn, "Distinguished researchers."

[104] Botkin, *Induced After-Death Communication*, 168.

[105] Cesare Lombroso, *Criminal Man* (Durham, NC: Duke University Press Books, 2006).

[106] Tymn, "Distinguished researchers."

[107] B. Greyson, "Near death experiences as evidence for survival of bodily death," Survival of Bodily Death: An Esalen Invitational Conference, February 11-16, 2000.

[108] Tymn, "Distinguished researchers."

[109] Tymn, "Distinguished researchers."

[110] Tymn, "Distinguished researchers."

[111] Tymn, "Distinguished researchers."

[112] Gary Schwartz and W. L. Simon, *The Afterlife Experiments* (New York: Atria Books, 2003).

[113] Tymn, "Distinguished researchers."

[114] Tymn, "Distinguished researchers."

[115] David Fontana, *Is There an Afterlife? A Comprehensive Overview of the Evidence* (Washington, D.C.: O Books, 2005).

[116] Tymn, "Distinguished researchers."

[117] Bander, *Voices from the Tapes*, 132.

[118] C. G. Jung, *Letters, Volume 1* (Princeton, NJ: Princeton University Press, 1973).

[119] Gustave Geley, *Clairvoyance and Materialization: A Record of Experiments* (London: T. Fisher Unwin Limited, 1927).

[120] Tymn, "Distinguished researchers."

[121] Tymn, "Distinguished researchers."

[122] Tymn, "Distinguished researchers."

[123] Tymn, "Distinguished researchers."

[124] Tymn, "Distinguished researchers."

[125] Tymn, "Distinguished researchers."

[126] Tymn, "Distinguished researchers."

[127] Michael Rogge, "Parapsychology and Personal Survival after Death," Man and the Unknown, 2019, https://wichm.home.xs4all.nl/paraps.html.

[128] H. Murphet, *Beyond death—The Undiscovered Country* (Wheaton, IL: Quest Books, 1990), 64.

[129] Arthur James Balfour, *A Defence of Philosophic Doubt; Being an Essay on the Foundations of Belief* (Sydney, Aus.: Wentworth Press, 2019).

[130] Tymn, "Distinguished researchers."

[131] V. Zammit, *A Lawyer Presents*.

[132] A. C. Doyle, *The History of Spiritualism, Vols. I and II* (New York: Arno Press, 1926).

[133] Zammit, *A Lawyer Presents*.

[134] Zammit, *A Lawyer Presents*.

[135] I. Funk, *The Psychic Riddle* (New York: Funk & Wagnalls Company, 1907).

[136] Tymn, "Distinguished researchers."

[137] Tymn, "Distinguished researchers."

[138] P. F. Brune, "The rediscovered beyond," World ITC, December 2006, www.worlditc.org/d_07_brune_rediscovered_beyond.htm.

[139] Bander, *Voices from the Tapes*.

[140] "The Church of England and Spiritualism—the full text of the Church of England committee appointed by Archbishop Lang and Archbishop Temple to investigate Spiritualism" (London: Psychic Press Ltd., 1939), https://www.cfpf.org.uk/articles/religion/cofe_report/cofe_report.html.

[141] Tymn, "Distinguished researchers."

[142] Tymn, "Distinguished researchers."

[143] Robert Crookall, *The Supreme Adventure: Analyses of Psychic Communications* (Cambridge, UK: James Clarke & Co., Ltd., 1961).

[144] Helen Duncan: The Official Pardon Site, accessed July 29, 2007, http://www.users.zetnet.co.uk/helenduncan.

[145] Michael Tymn, "Ghost stories: Ghost loses chess match," All About Paranormal, September 1, 2008, https://www.allaboutparanormal.co/2008/09/ghost-stories-ghost-loses-chess-match.html#axzz6rppHBgXf.

[146] G. Smith, *The Unbelievable Truth* (Carlsbad, CA: Hay House, 2004).

[147] Michael Rogge, "Direct Voice: Conversation between mother and her deceased son," Man and the Unknown, http://www.xs4all.nl/~wichm/fearon.html.

[148] Schwartz, *The Afterlife Experiments*.

[149] Gary Schwartz et al., "Accuracy and Replicability of Anomalous After-Death Communication Across Highly Skilled Mediums," *Journal of the Society for Psychical Research* 65 (2001): 1-25.

[150] Schwartz, *The Afterlife Experiments*.

[151] Julie Beischel and Gary Schwartz, "Anomalous information reception by research mediums demonstrated using a novel triple-blind protocol," *Explore* 3, no. 1 (January 2007): 23-27.

[152] Michael Tymn, "Proof positive of spirit communication."

[153] D. Blum, *Ghost Hunters: William James and the Search for Scientific Proof of Life After Death* (London: Penguin Press, 2006).

[154] R. Hodgson, "A further record of observations of certain phenomena of a trance," *Proceedings of the Society for Psychical Research* 13 (1897-1898): 297.

[155] Schmicker, *Best Evidence*, 249-250.

[156] Schmicker, *Best Evidence*, 250-251.

[157] Zammit, *A Lawyer Presents*, 116-117.

[158] H. Carrington, *The World of Psychic Research* (London: A. S. Barnes & Co., Inc., 1973), 54.

[159] Carrington, *The World of Psychic Research*, 54.

[160] Schmicker, *Best Evidence*, 252-253.

[161] S. Bray, *A Guide for the Spiritual Traveler* (Queensland, Aus.: Scroll Publishers, 1990), 15.

[162] Charles H. Hapgood, *Voices of Spirit* (New York: Delacorte Press / Seymour Lawrence, 1975).

[163] "Daniel Dunglas Home 1833-1886," SurvivalAfterDeath.info, accessed July 16, 2007, http://www.survivalafterdeath.org/mediums/home.htm.

[164] "Daniel Dunglas Home."

[165] J. Oppenheim, *The Other World* (Cambridge: Cambridge University Press, 1985), 11.

[166] Leslie Flint, *Voices in the Dark* (New York: Macmillan Publishing, 1971), 220.

[167] Michael Rogge, "Paranormal Voices Assert: Death No End," Man and the Unknown, http://www.xs4all.nl/~wichm/ deathnoe.html.

[168] Zammit, *A Lawyer Presents*.

[169] M. Keen, "Physical phenomena at the David Thompson séance of October 25th 2003," https://www.survivalafterdeath.info/articles/keen/thompson.htm.

[170] Eckhard Kruse, "Audio Signal Processing to Investigate Alleged Paranormal Phenomena in Mediumistic Seances," *IEEE Aerospace and Electronic Systems Magazine* 33, no. 2 (February 2018), 52-56.

[171] M. Keen and A. Ellison, "Scole: A response to the critics? The Scole Report," *Proceedings of the Society for Psychical Research* 58, part 220 (1999).

[172] Zammit, *A Lawyer Presents*, 75.

[173] Zammit, *A Lawyer Presents*, 12.

[174] Zammit, *A Lawyer Presents*, 128.

[175] Zammit, *A Lawyer Presents*, 128.

[176] Zammit, *A Lawyer Presents*.

[177] E. R. Dodds, "Presidential Address," *Proceedings of the Society for Psychical Research*, London, 1962.

[178] B. Inglis, *Science and Parascience—A History of the Paranormal 1914-1939* (London: Hodder and Stroughton, 1984), 226.

[179] Helen Duncan and C. E. Bechhofer Roberts, *The Trial of Mrs. Duncan* (London: Jarrolds Publishers, 1945).

[180] Elisabeth Kübler-Ross, *On Death and Dying* (New York: Scribner Classics, 1997).

[181] Elisabeth Kübler-Ross, *On Life After Death* (Berkeley, CA: Celestial Arts, 1991).

[182] Raymond Moody, "Family Reunions: Visionary Encounters with the Departed in a Modern-Day Psychomanteum," *Journal of Near-Death Studies* 11, no. 2 (Winter 1992): 112.

[183] J. B. Phillips, *Ring of Truth* (London: H. Shaw, 1977), 117.

[184] Loy Mershimer, "A Theology of Ghosts," Thoughts of Loy blogspot, September 19, 2005, http://loymershimer.blogspot.com/2005/09/theology-of-ghosts.html.

[185] Nandor Fodor, *These Mysterious People* (London: Rider & Co. Ltd. 1934).

[186] Richard Lazarus, *The Case Against Death* (London: Warner Books (1993): 85

[187] Lazarus, *The Case Against Death*, 19

[188] Sabom, *Recollections of Death*.

[189] "An introductory analysis of the NDE (near-death experience)," *Two Worlds* (1996), https://cryskernan.tripod.com/intro_analysis_of_the%20NDE%20_.htm.

[190] Greyson, "Near death experiences as evidence."

[191] Pim Van Lommel, "6. Neurophysiology in a normal functioning brain," International Association for Near-Death Studies, accessed November 15, 2007, https://iands.org/research/nde-research/important-research-articles/43-dr-pim-van-lommel-md-continuity-of-consciousness.html?start=5.

[192] Rabbi Ephraim Horowitz, "Life by Accident," AISH, https://www.aish.com/ci/sam/48970356.html.

[193] Grant R. Jeffrey, *Creation: Remarkable Evidence of God's Design* (New York: Crown Publishing Group, 2009).

[194] Stephen Hawking, *A Brief History of Time* (New York: Random House Publishing Group, 2011).

[195] Guillermo Gonzalez and Jay W. Richards, *The Privileged Planet: How Our Place in the Cosmos Is Designed for Discovery* (Washington, D.C.: Regnery Publishing, 2004).

[196] Jeanna Bryner, "Huge Stores of Oxygen Found Deep Inside Earth," NBC News, October 1, 2007, https://www.nbcnews.com/id/wbna21082196.

[197] Schroeder, *The Hidden Face of God*.

[198] Gonzalez, *The Privileged Planet*.

[199] Gonzalez, *The Privileged Planet*.

[200] Gonzalez, *The Privileged Planet*.

[201] M. Corey, *The God Hypothesis: Discovering Design in Our "Just Right" Goldilocks Universe* (Washington, D.C.: Rowman & Littlefield, 2007).

[202] Rich Heffern, "Spirituality and the fine-tuned cosmos," *National Catholic Reporter*, December 12, 2003.

[203] Hogan, *There Is Nothing but Mind*, 17-18.

204 Hogan, *There Is Nothing but Mind*, 187-192.

205 Norman Herr, "Television & Health: III Violence," CSUN, Internet Resources to Accompany the Sourcebook for Teaching Science, http://www.csun.edu/science/health/docs/tv&health.html.

206 "Suicide in Children and Teens," *American Academy of Child & Adolescent Psychiatry*, no. 10 (June 2018).

207 S. K. Goldsmith et al., eds., "Reducing Suicide: A National Imperative" (Washington, D.C.: Institute of Medicine, The National Academies Press, 2002).

208 Jean M. Twenge et al., "Decreases in psychological well-being among American adolescents after 2012 and links to screen time during the rise of smartphone technology," *Emotion* 18, no. 6 (2018): 765-780.

209 Jean M. Twenge, "The Sad State of Happiness in the United States and the Role of Digital Media," World Happiness Report, March 20, 2019, https://worldhappiness.report/ed/2019/the-sad-state-of-happiness-in-the-united-states-and-the-role-of-digital-media.

210 "Youth mental health report: Youth Survey 2012-16," Mission Australia, in association with the Black Dog Institute, April 18, 2017.

211 M. Lipka and C. Gecewicz, "More Americans now say they're spiritual but not religious," Pew Research Center, September 6, 2017, https://www.pewresearch.org/fact-tank/2017/09/06/more-americans-now-say-theyre-spiritual-but-not-religious.

212 "The Mahatma Gandhi séance."

213 "Michael Fearon séance," produced by the Leslie Flint Educational Trust, 1954, https://www.leslieflint.com/michael-fearon-1954.

214 "Michael Fearon séance."

215 "Sir Thomas Beechum [sic] séance," produced by the Leslie Flint Educational Trust, YouTube video, 34:07, https://www.youtube.com/watch?v=Q_eHJWWwjTg.

216 "John Grant séance," produced by the Leslie Flint Educational Trust, June 9, 1969.

217 "John Grant séance"

218 W. Tudor-Pole, *Private Dowding* (New York: Dodd, Mead & Company, 1919), 45.

[219] Stafford Betty, *The Afterlife Unveiled* (Washington, D.C.: O Books, 2011), 21.

[220] Betty, *The Afterlife Unveiled*, 21.

[221] Kerry Pobanz, "Depossession Healing: A Comparison of William Baldwin's 'Spirit Releasement Therapy' and Dae Mo Nim's Ancestor Liberation," *Journal of Unification Studies* 9 (2008): 143-162.

[222] A. W. Austin, ed., *Teachings of Silver Birch* (London: Psychic Book Club, 1938), 109.

[223] "The Dorcas séance," produced by the Leslie Flint Educational Trust, 1964, https://leslieflint.com/Dorcas/.

[224] E. C. Randall, *The Dead Have Never Died* (New York: A. A. Knopf, 1917), 165-166.

[225] Betty, *The Afterlife Unveiled*, 20.

[226] M. Tymn, "Try Shock Therapy to Protect Against Vagabond Spirits?" White Crow Books, June 28, 2011, http://whitecrowbooks.com/michaeltymn/entry/try_shock_therapy_to_protect_against_vagabond_spirits.

[227] Bruce Lipton, "THINK Beyond Your Genes—March 2018," Bruce H. Lipton, PhD, https://www.brucelipton.com/think-beyond-your-genes-march-2018.

[228] Annie Besant and Charles Webster Leadbeater, *Thought Forms: A Record of Clairvoyant Investigation* (Brooklyn: Sacred Bones Books, 2020; originally published in 1901).

[229] Hillary Mayell, "Thousands of Women Killed for Family 'Honor,'" *National Geographic* online, February 12, 2002, https://www.nationalgeographic.com/culture/2002/02/thousands-of-women-killed-for-family-honor.

[230] Jill Patterson, "How Evil Is a Socially Constructed Concept: Evil Across Societies," *The Manitoban* online, February 9, 2021, http://www.themanitoban.com/2012/10/how-evil-is-a-socially-constructed-concept-evil-across-societies/12309.

[231] Brian Patrick Byrne et al., "All the People God Kills in the Bible," Vocativ, April 20, 2016, https://www.vocativ.com/news/309748/all-the-people-god-kills-in-the-bible/index.html.

[232] Schwartz, *Your Soul's Plan*, 226-227.

233 "Theodicy, God and Suffering – A debate between Dinesh D'Souza and Bart Ehrman," Produced by Gordon College Center for Christian Studies, November 11, 2010, YouTube video, 1:42:27, https://www.youtube.com/watch?v=Isg6Kx-3xdI.

234 Francesca Colella, "How Many People Are Starving Around the World?" The Borgen Project, January 20, 2018, https://borgenproject.org/how-many-people-are-starving-around-the-world.

235 Léa Gorius, "How Much Does It Cost to End Poverty?" The Borgen Project, December 16, 2017, https://borgenproject.org/how-much-does-it-cost-to-end-poverty/.

236 Adele Peters, "It would cost just $330 billion to end global hunger by 2030," Fast Company, October 15, 2020, https://www.fastcompany.com/90564107/it-would-cost-just-330-billion-to-end-global-hunger-by-2030.

237 Maggie Scull, "Timeline of 1981 hunger strike," *The Irish Times* online, March 1, 2016, https://www.irishtimes.com/culture/books/timeline-of-1981-hunger-strike-1.2555682.

238 M. Admin, "Hundreds in India Ritually Starve Themselves to Death Each Year," Knowledge Nuts, accessed April 1, 2014, https://knowledgenuts.com/2014/04/01/hundreds-in-india-ritually-starve-themselves-to-death-each-year.

239 Lipton, "THINK Beyond Your Genes—March 2018."

240 "Dr. Bruce Lipton—A New Hope: Epigenetics and the Subconscious Mind," Dr. Ron Ehrlich, https://drronehrlich.com/dr-bruce-lipton-a-new-hope-epigenetics-and-the-subconscious-mind-2.

241 Elizabeth Blackburn and Elissa Epel, *The Telomere Effect: A Revolutionary Approach to Living Younger, Healthier, Longer* (New York: Grand Central Publishing, 2017).

242 Carnegie Mellon University, "Happy People Are Healthier, Psychologist Says," ScienceDaily, November 8, 2006, https://www.sciencedaily.com/releases/2006/11/061108103655.htm.

243 Montague Ullman, "Herpes Simplex and Second Degree Burn Induced Under Hypnosis," *The American Journal of Psychiatry* 103, no. 6 (May 1947).

244 Rachael Moeller, "Study Suggests Common Knee Surgery's Effect Is Purely Placebo," *Scientific American* online, July 12, 2002, https://www.scientificamerican.com/article/study-suggests-common-kne/.

245 Bruno Klopfer, "Psychological Variables in Human Cancer," *Journal of Prospective Techniques* 31 (1957): 331-40.

246 Anita Moorjani, *Dying to Be Me: My Journey from Cancer to Near Death, to True Healing*. Hay House, Inc. September 1, 2014.

247 Herb Weiss, "Commentary Conquering Cancer through Living Fearlessly," *Pawtucket Times*, November 9, 2012.

248 Pamela Maraldo, *Medicine: In Search of a Soul: The Healing Prescription* (Carlsbad, CA: Balboa Press, 2017).

249 Maraldo, *Medicine: In Search of a Soul*.

250 Michael Talbot, *The Holographic Universe* (New York: Harper Perennial, 2011), 98-100.

251 Carl Wickland, *Thirty Years Among the Dead* (Guildford, UK: White Crow Books, 2011).

252 Guy Montgomery et al., "A meta-analysis of hypnotically induced analgesia: How effective is hypnosis?" *International Journal of Clinical and Experimental Hypnosis* 48 (2000): 138-153.

253 "Hypnosis for Pain Relief," Arthritis Foundation, https://www.arthritis.org/health-wellness/treatment/complementary-therapies/natural-therapies/hypnosis-for-pain-relief.

254 "Hypnosis, No Anesthetic, for Man's Surgery," CBS News, April 22, 2008, https://www.cbsnews.com/news/hypnosis-no-anesthetic-for-mans-surgery.

255 Schwartz, *Your Soul's Plan*, 103.

256 Schwartz, *Your Soul's Plan*, 119.

257 Amit Goswami, *The Self-Aware Universe: How Consciousness Creates the Material World* (New York: TarcherPerigee, 1995).

258 A. Rae Simpson, "MIT Young Adult Development Project," MIT, 2018, http://hrweb.mit.edu/worklife/youngadult/index.html.

259 Michael Newton, *Destiny of Souls: New Case Studies of Life Between Lives* (Woodbury MN: Llewellyn Publications, 2000), 4.

²⁶⁰ Jane Sherwood, *The Country Beyond* (London: Neville Spearman, 1969), 217.

²⁶¹ "John Grant séance," Leslie Flint Trust, June 9, 1969, https://www.leslieflint.com/john-grant-june-1969.

²⁶² Schwartz, *Your Soul's Plan*, 15.

²⁶³ Schwartz, *Your Soul's Plan*, 228.

²⁶⁴ Schwartz, *Your Soul's Plan*, 229.

²⁶⁵ Masters of Light, AREI physical mediumship circle, Séance, December 23, 2018.

²⁶⁶ Bruce Lipton, *The Biology of Belief* (Carlsbad, CA: Hay House, 2016).

²⁶⁷ Herr, "Television & Health."

²⁶⁸ Nadia Kounang, "What is the science behind fear?" CNN, October 29, 2015, https://www.cnn.com/2015/10/29/health/science-of-fear/index.html.

²⁶⁹ Eric Berne, *Games People Play: The Psychology of Human Relationships* (New York: Penguin Books, 2009).

²⁷⁰ C. G. Jung. *Collected Works of C. G. Jung, Volume 11; Psychology and Religion* (Princeton, NJ: Princeton University Press, 1975), 81.

²⁷¹ Wright, *Repair & Reattachment*.

²⁷² Rupert Sheldrake, "The 'sense of being stared at' experiments in schools," *Journal of the Society for Psychical Research* 62 (1998): 311-323.

²⁷³ Crookall, *The Supreme Adventure*, 158.

²⁷⁴ Baron von Schrenk-Notzing, *Phenomena of Materialization, a contribution to the investigation of mediumistic teleplastics* (New York: E. P. Dutton, 1920).

²⁷⁵ Botkin, *Induced After-Death Communication*, 12.

²⁷⁶ Botkin, *Induced After-Death Communication*.

²⁷⁷ Botkin, *Induced After-Death Communication*.

²⁷⁸ Botkin, *Induced After-Death Communication*, 82-84.

²⁷⁹ Botkin, *Induced After-Death Communication*, 84-85.

²⁸⁰ Botkin, *Induced After-Death Communication*, 86-87.

²⁸¹ Botkin, *Induced After-Death Communication*, 87-88.

²⁸² Botkin, *Induced After-Death Communication*, 88-89.

²⁸³ Wright, *Repair & Reattachment*.

[284] Wright, *Repair & Reattachment*, 17-18.

[285] Jane Bissler, "Voices Across the Veil Direct Personal Communication," https://voicesacrosstheveil.afterlifedata.com/direct-personal-communication.

[286] Russell Hurlburt, "Not Everyone Conducts Inner Speech: Inner speech Is Frequent but Not for Everyone," *Psychology Today* post, October 26, 2011, https://www.psychologytoday.com/us/blog/pristine-inner-experience/201110/not-everyone-conducts-inner-speech.

[287] C. A. Moore, "The unseen realm: Science is making room for near-death experiences beyond this world," *Desert Morning News*, February 18, 2006.

[288] Diane M. Komp, *A Window to Heaven: When Children See Life in Death* (Grand Rapids, MI: Zondervan Publishing, 1992).

[289] Karlis Osis and Erlendur Haraldsson, *At the Hour of Death* (Norwalk, CT: Hastings House, 1997).

[290] Osis, *At the Hour of Death*.

[291] Crookall, *The Supreme Adventure*, 174.

[292] Tymn, *The Afterlife Revealed* (Guildford, UK: White Crow Books, 2011), 68.

[293] Mona Simpson, "A Sister's Eulogy for Steve Jobs," *The New York Times*, October 30, 2011.

[294] Neil Baldwin, *Edison: Inventing the Century* (Chicago: University of Chicago Press, 2001).

[295] Raymond Moody, *Life After Life* (New York: HarperOne, 1975).

[296] Raymond Moody, *Glimpses of Eternity: An Investigation into Shared Death Experiences* (London: Rider, 2011).

[297] Moody, *Glimpses of Eternity*, 49- 50.

[298] Peter Fenwick and Elizabeth Fenwick, *The Art of Dying: A Journey to Elsewhere* (London: Continuum International Publishing, 2008).

[299] Leslie Kean, *Surviving Death: A Journalist Investigates Evidence for an Afterlife* (New York: Crown Archetype, 2017), 140-141 (citing Peter Fenwick, "End-of-Life Experiences").

[300] Pim van Lommel, *Consciousness Beyond Life: The Science of the Near-Death Experience* (New York: HarperCollins, 2010), 41.

[301] Van Lommel, *Consciousness Beyond Life*, 41-42.

[302] Edmund Gurney et al., *Phantasms of the Living* (London: Trubner, 1886).

[303] Gurney, *Phantasms of the Living*.

[304] A. McKenzie, *Apparitions and Ghosts: A Modern Study* (London: Arthur Baker Ltd., 1971), 116-117.

[305] D. S. Rogo, *Leaving the Body: A Complete Guide to Astral Projection* (New York: Fireside/Simon & Schuster, 1993), 16-17.

[306] A. Spraggett, *The Case for Immortality* (Scarborough, Canada: New American Library of Canada, 1974), 45-46.

[307] R. C. Johnson, *The Imprisoned Splendour* (Wheaton, IL: Quest Books, 1982), 198-199.

[308] E. Bennett, *Apparitions and Haunted Houses: A Survey of Evidence* (London: Faber and Faber, 1939), 131-132.

[309] Michael Tymn, "A veridical death-bed vision," Paranormal and Life After Death, March 14, 2008, https://paranormalandlifeafterdeath.blogspot.com/2008/03/.

[310] "Mr. Biggs communicates," Leslie Flint Trust, 1966, https://www.leslieflint.com/mr-biggs-1966.

[311] Anthony Borgia, *Life in the World Unseen* (London: Psychic Press, 1985), 11.

[312] Crookall, *The Supreme Adventure*, 130-131.

[313] Jeffrey Long, "Frightening NDEs," Near Death Experience Research Foundation, n.d., https://www.nderf.org/NDERF/EvidenceAfterlife/evidence/Frightening_NDEs.htm.

[314] Friedrich Jürgenson, *Sprechfunk mit Verstorbenen* (Freiburg im Br.: Hermann Bauer Verlag, 1967).

[315] John Calvin, *Psychopannychia* (Warrendale, PA: Ichthus Publications, 2018; originally published in 1542).

[316] Crookall, *The Supreme Adventure*, 132.

[317] Crookall, *The Supreme Adventure*, 136.

[318] Borgia, *Life in the World Unseen*, 23.

[319] Borgia, *Life in the World Unseen*, 27.

³²⁰ "The Rupert Brooke séance," Leslie Flint Trust, September 15, 1957, https://www.leslieflint.com/rupert-brooke.

³²¹ "The Queen Alexandra séance," Leslie Flint Trust, 1960, https://www.leslieflint.com/queen-alexandra.

³²² "The George Wilmot séance," Leslie Flint Trust, www.earthschoolanswers.com/jenny.

³²³ Borgia, *Life in the World Unseen*, 125.

³²⁴ Crookall, *The Supreme Adventure*, 21-22.

³²⁵ "The Alfred Pritchett séance," Leslie Flint Trust, November 4, 1960, https://www.leslieflint.com/alfred-pritchett.

³²⁶ Crookall, *The Supreme Adventure*, 137.

³²⁷ Newton, *Destiny of Souls*, 4.

³²⁸ "The Terry Smith séance," Leslie Flint Trust, July 16, 1966, https://www.leslieflint.com/terry-smith.

³²⁹ "The Terry Smith séance."

³³⁰ Austen, *The Teachings of Silver Birch*, 124.

³³¹ Alice Gilbert, *Philip in the Spheres* (Detroit: The Aquarian Press, 1952).

³³² Helen Greaves, *Testimony of Light* (London: C.W. Daniel, 1969), 58.

³³³ Tymn, *The Afterlife Revealed*, 98-99 (citing Marjorie Errands, *The Tapestry of Life*, Psychic Press Ltd., London, 1979), 56.

³³⁴ Austen, *The Teachings of Silver Birch*, 202.

³³⁵ Crookall, *The Supreme Adventure*, 164-165.

³³⁶ Borgia, *Life in the World Unseen*.

³³⁷ Oliver Lodge, *Raymond or Life and Death* (New York: George H. Doran, 1916), 197.

³³⁸ Tymn, *The Afterlife Revealed*, 101.

³³⁹ Ruth M. Taylor, *Witness from Beyond* (Chicago: Chicago Review Press, 1980), 8.

³⁴⁰ Sherwood, *The Country Beyond*, 71.

³⁴¹ Claude H. Kelway-Bamber, *Claude's Book* (London: Methuen & Co. Ltd., 1919), 204.

³⁴² W. W. Aber and J. H. Nixon, *Beyond the Vail* (Kansas City, MO: Hudson-Kimberly, 1901), 354.

[300] Pim van Lommel, *Consciousness Beyond Life: The Science of the Near-Death Experience* (New York: HarperCollins, 2010), 41.

[301] Van Lommel, *Consciousness Beyond Life*, 41-42.

[302] Edmund Gurney et al., *Phantasms of the Living* (London: Trubner, 1886).

[303] Gurney, *Phantasms of the Living*.

[304] A. McKenzie, *Apparitions and Ghosts: A Modern Study* (London: Arthur Baker Ltd., 1971), 116-117.

[305] D. S. Rogo, *Leaving the Body: A Complete Guide to Astral Projection* (New York: Fireside/Simon & Schuster, 1993), 16-17.

[306] A. Spraggett, *The Case for Immortality* (Scarborough, Canada: New American Library of Canada, 1974), 45-46.

[307] R. C. Johnson, *The Imprisoned Splendour* (Wheaton, IL: Quest Books, 1982), 198-199.

[308] E. Bennett, *Apparitions and Haunted Houses: A Survey of Evidence* (London: Faber and Faber, 1939), 131-132.

[309] Michael Tymn, "A veridical death-bed vision," Paranormal and Life After Death, March 14, 2008, https://paranormalandlifeafterdeath.blogspot.com/2008/03/.

[310] "Mr. Biggs communicates," Leslie Flint Trust, 1966, https://www.leslieflint.com/mr-biggs-1966.

[311] Anthony Borgia, *Life in the World Unseen* (London: Psychic Press, 1985), 11.

[312] Crookall, *The Supreme Adventure*, 130-131.

[313] Jeffrey Long, "Frightening NDEs," Near Death Experience Research Foundation, n.d., https://www.nderf.org/NDERF/EvidenceAfterlife/evidence/Frightening_NDEs.htm.

[314] Friedrich Jürgenson, *Sprechfunk mit Verstorbenen* (Freiburg im Br.: Hermann Bauer Verlag, 1967).

[315] John Calvin, *Psychopannychia* (Warrendale, PA: Ichthus Publications, 2018; originally published in 1542).

[316] Crookall, *The Supreme Adventure*, 132.

[317] Crookall, *The Supreme Adventure*, 136.

[318] Borgia, *Life in the World Unseen*, 23.

[319] Borgia, *Life in the World Unseen*, 27.

[320] "The Rupert Brooke séance," Leslie Flint Trust, September 15, 1957, https://www.leslieflint.com/rupert-brooke.

[321] "The Queen Alexandra séance," Leslie Flint Trust, 1960, https://www.leslieflint.com/queen-alexandra.

[322] "The George Wilmot séance," Leslie Flint Trust, www.earthschoolanswers.com/jenny.

[323] Borgia, *Life in the World Unseen*, 125.

[324] Crookall, *The Supreme Adventure*, 21-22.

[325] "The Alfred Pritchett séance," Leslie Flint Trust, November 4, 1960, https://www.leslieflint.com/alfred-pritchett.

[326] Crookall, *The Supreme Adventure*, 137.

[327] Newton, *Destiny of Souls*, 4.

[328] "The Terry Smith séance," Leslie Flint Trust, July 16, 1966, https://www.leslieflint.com/terry-smith.

[329] "The Terry Smith séance."

[330] Austen, *The Teachings of Silver Birch*, 124.

[331] Alice Gilbert, *Philip in the Spheres* (Detroit: The Aquarian Press, 1952).

[332] Helen Greaves, *Testimony of Light* (London: C.W. Daniel, 1969), 58.

[333] Tymn, *The Afterlife Revealed*, 98-99 (citing Marjorie Errands, *The Tapestry of Life*, Psychic Press Ltd., London, 1979), 56.

[334] Austen, *The Teachings of Silver Birch*, 202.

[335] Crookall, *The Supreme Adventure*, 164-165.

[336] Borgia, *Life in the World Unseen*.

[337] Oliver Lodge, *Raymond or Life and Death* (New York: George H. Doran, 1916), 197.

[338] Tymn, *The Afterlife Revealed*, 101.

[339] Ruth M. Taylor, *Witness from Beyond* (Chicago: Chicago Review Press, 1980), 8.

[340] Sherwood, *The Country Beyond*, 71.

[341] Claude H. Kelway-Bamber, *Claude's Book* (London: Methuen & Co. Ltd., 1919), 204.

[342] W. W. Aber and J. H. Nixon, *Beyond the Vail* (Kansas City, MO: Hudson-Kimberly, 1901), 354.

[369] Kardec, *The Spirits' Book*, 255.
[370] Allen, *The Realities of Heaven*, 138 (citing Stringfellow, *Leslie's letters to his mother*, 49).
[371] "Frédéric Chopin séance," Leslie Flint Trust, July 7, 1955, https://www.leslieflint.com/chopin-july-7th-1955.
[372] "Frédéric Chopin séance."
[373] "The Mary Ann Ross séance," Leslie Flint Trust, January 20, 1969, https://www.leslieflint.com/mary-ann-ross.
[374] Borgia, *Life in the World Unseen*, 129.
[375] Suzanne Ward, *Matthew, Tell Me about Heaven* (Camas, WA: Matthew Books, 2012), 108.
[376] Borgia, *Life in the World Unseen*, 100.
[377] Burbidge, *The Shadows Lifted from Death*, 134.
[378] Eisen, *The Agashan Discourses*, 99.
[379] Borgia, *Life in the World Unseen*, 182.
[380] Ward, *Matthew, Tell Me about Heaven*, 104.
[381] Lodge, *Raymond or Life and Death*, 263.
[382] Sherwood, *The Country Beyond*, 86.
[383] Betty, *The Afterlife Unveiled*, 96 (citing Taylor, *Witness from Beyond*).
[384] Charles Drayton Thomas, *Life Beyond Death with Evidence* (Hong Kong: Hesperides Press, 2008; originally published in 1923), 124.
[385] Peter Boulton and Jane Boulton, *Psychic Beam to Beyond: Through the Psychic Sensitive Lenora Huett* (Camarillo, CA: DeVorss & Co., 1983), 63.
[386] James A. Pike and Diane Kennedy Pike, *The Other Side: An Account of My Experiences with Psychic Phenomena* (Eugene, OR: Wipf and Stock, 1968), 324.
[387] James M. Peebles, *Immortality and Our Employments Hereafter: With What a Hundred Spirits, Good and Evil, Say of Their Dwelling Places* (London: Forgotten Books, 2015; originally published in 1907), 151.
[388] Borgia, *Life in the World Unseen*, 12.
[389] Borgia, *Life in the World Unseen*, 119.
[390] "The Lucillus séances," Leslie Flint Trust, August 1, 1962, https://www.leslieflint.com/lucillus.

[343] Allan Kardec, *The Spirits' Book* (Miami, FL: FEB Publisher, 2018), 173.

[344] Miles Edward Allen, *The Realities of Heaven* (CreateSpace Publishing, 2015), 125 (citing Alice Stringfellow, *Leslie's letters to his mother,* Fayetteville, AR: Democrat Publishing and Printing Co., 1926*)*.

[345] Borgia, *Life in the World Unseen,* 12.

[346] Borgia, *Life in the World Unseen,* 11-12.

[347] N. Riley Heagerty, *The Hereafter* (Lulu.com, 2020), 89-90 (citing Randall, *Frontiers of the Afterlife,* 2010*)*.

[348] Betty, *The Afterlife Unveiled,* 27.

[349] Augustus Henry Burbidge, *The Shadows Lifted from Death* (Stuart, FL: Roundtable Publishing, 2011), 78.

[350] Taylor, *Witness from Beyond,* 64.

[351] Borgia, *Life in the World Unseen,* 46.

[352] Austen, *The Teachings of Silver Birch,* 117.

[353] Stringfellow, *Leslie's letters to his mother,* 83.

[354] Kelway-Bamber, *Claude's Book,* 17.

[355] William Eisen, ed., *The Agashan Discourses* (Camarillo, CA: Devorss & Co., 1978), 99.

[356] Charles Drayton Thomas, "Report re Lodge via Leonard," *Journal of the Society for Psychical Research* 33 (1945): 137-160.

[357] Betty, *The Afterlife Unveiled,* 29.

[358] Sherwood, *The Country Beyond,* 69.

[359] Borgia, *Life in the World Unseen,* 172.

[360] Borgia, *Life in the World Unseen,* 138.

[361] Borgia, *Life in the World Unseen,* 138.

[362] Thomas, *Life Beyond Death with Evidence.*

[363] Stringfellow, *Leslie's letters to his mother,* 82.

[364] John Worth Edmonds and George T. Dexter, *Spiritualism* (New York: Partridge & Brittan, 1855), 89.

[365] Crookall, *The Supreme Adventure,* 78.

[366] Mary Blount White, *Letters from the Other Side* (Hinesburg, VT: Upper Access, Inc., 1995), 24.

[367] Allen, *The Realities of Heaven,* 152.

[368] Borgia, *Life in the World Unseen,* 143.

[391] Stringfellow, *Leslie's letters to his mother*, 115.

[392] Andrew Jackson Davis, *Death and the After Life* (Boston: Kobe and Rich, 1865), 95.

[393] Borgia, *Life in the World Unseen*, 119.

[394] Tymn, *The Afterlife Revealed*, 113.

[395] "The Chinese Philosopher séance," Leslie Flint Trust, July 30, 1959, https://www.leslieflint.com/confucius-july-1959.

[396] Fodor, *These Mysterious People*, 238.

[397] Crookall, *The Supreme Adventure*, 49.

[398] Betty, *The Afterlife Unveiled*, 2 (citing Elsa Barker, *Letters from a Living Dead Man*, Dallas, TX: Hill-Pehle Publishing, 2012, originally published in 1914).

[399] Betty, *The Afterlife Unveiled*, 56-59 (citing Geraldine Cummins, *Beyond Human Personality*, London: Ivor Nicholson and Watson, Ltd., 1935).

[400] Betty, *The Afterlife Unveiled*, 58 (citing Cummins, *Beyond Human Personality*).

[401] Betty, *The Afterlife Unveiled*, 58 (citing Cummins, *Beyond Human Personality*).

[402] Betty, *The Afterlife Unveiled*, 59 (citing Cummins, *Beyond Human Personality*).

[403] Crookall, *The Supreme Adventure*, 49.

www.ingramcontent.com/pod-product-compliance
Lightning Source LLC
Chambersburg PA
CBHW071853290426
44110CB00013B/1123